BAHĀRISTĀN-I-SHĀHĪ

A CHRONICLE OF MEDIAEVAL KASHMIR

BAHĀRISTĀN-I-SHĀHĪ

A CHRONICLE OF MEDIAEVAL KASHMIR

Kashinath Pandit

AKSHAYA PRAKASHAN
NEW DELHI

First Published : 1991
Reprint : 2022

ISBN 978-81-88643-83-7

Published by Harish Chandra for
AKSHAYA PRAKASHAN
208 M.G. House
2 Community Centre
Wazirpur Industrial Area
Delhi - 110052
Mobile : 9818452269
Phones : 011-47021664, 011-47049292
Email : harish@akshayaprakashan.com
Website : www.akshayaprakashan.com

Printed in India

Contents

Acknowledgements

The first and foremost task in translating a manuscript from its original into another language is to establish the archetypus. That is a laborious and time-consuming task because a genuine researcher and translator has to lay his hand on all extant and available copies of the manuscript, which are usually scattered in numerous official or private repositories, within and outside the country. In other words, it means chalking out a workable plan of travel and establishing contact with the source persons, who could be numerous. Thus besides consulting the manuscripts of *Bahāristān-i-Shahī* in several libraries and archives in the country, I had the good luck of visiting the British Museum in London where I found an excellent copy of the manuscript. On close examination, I concluded that the British Museum MS could justifiably be depended upon as near archetypus. In this pursuit, I met many friendly people who helped me achieve my objective. I am beholden to all of them.

I am indebted to my dear friend and former colleague at the Department of English, University of Kashmir, Prof. Tej N. Dhar for taking pains in examining, revising and improving the draft translation. But for his untiring labour and patience and the long and late sittings he had with me, the work could not have seen the light of day. He was kind enough to write the Afterword for the book which is placed before the bibliography.

Late Professor Sham Lal Pandit, former Head, Department of English, University of Kashmir graciously agreed to read the final draft and offered some valuable suggestions.

I must place on record my sincere thanks to late Professor N.N. Raina, formerly Head of the Department of Physics, University of Kashmir for his encouragement and guidance during the preparation of the translation and for agreeing to write a preface to it.

I am also thankful to my publisher Akshaya Prakashan of New Delhi for bringing out this edition of the book, with excellent printing and an attractive get up.

Kashinath Pandit

Translation Methodology

1. Since the chronicle was one long narrative, it became necessary to distribute it into chapters. There are eight of them, each dealing with a particular period or a particular ruling house. Care has been taken to ensure that minimum dislocation of events or their overlapping takes place.
2. As stated elsewhere in the introduction, translation of verses has been left out. Likewise superfluous titles and appendages to names, a practice very common to Persian historiographical style, have also been left out to make the account readable.
3. Effort has been made to reproduce the place names as correctly as possible; some deficiencies have still remained.
4. Transliteration of Persian/Arabic/Sanskrit words, names, phrases etc. has been done in accordance with the accepted system. (See the key to transliteration.) Diacritical marks have been used wherever necessary.
5. Explanatory comments wherever necessary have been put in round parenthesis, but whatever was felt necessary to clear the textual ambiguities has been put in square brackets.
6. Blanks and erasions in the MS have been shown by the sign … in the English translation. Illegible words have

also been indicated likewise followed by the abbreviation *illeg*.

7. Conversion of Hijra years into Christian years has been done on the basis of the Lunar year system of the Muslim calendar and not the Solar year system of the Iranians.
8. Qur'ānic verses, which figure in the chronicle, have been rendered into English wherever possible.
9. Folio numbers of the MS and their corresponding printed pages have been given on a separate sheet.

Abbreviations

Rājat.	*Rājataraṅginī*, tr. M.A. Stein, 2 vols. London, 1900.
Jonar.	*The Rājataraṅginī of Jonarāja*, ed. Srikanth Koul, Vishveshvaranand Institute, Hoshiarpur, 1967.
TḤK	*Tārikh-i-Ḥasan Khuihāmī*, Pīr Ghulām Ḥasan, Vol. II, RPD,* Srinagar 1954.
TMḤ	*Tārīkh-i-Malik Ḥaidar*, Malik Ḥaidar Chādora, MS. RPD. Acc. No. 39.
TNK	*Tārīkh-i-Nārāyan Koul 'Ājiz*, MS. RPD. Acc. No. 934.
Toḥfat.	*Toḥfatu'l-Aḥbāb*, Anonymous, transcript copy RPD. Acc. No. 1155.
illeg.	Illegible text
MS	Manuscript
St.	Stanza
-·-·-	Omission in the text
...	Sentence incomplete
(tr)	Translation
trans.	Transcript

*Note: RPD stands for Research and Publication Department, J&K State Government, Srinagar.

Key to Transliteration

Arabic/Persian	Latin	Arabic/Persian	Latin
ت	t	ص	ṣ
ث	th	ض	ḍ
چ	ch	ط	ṭ
ح	ḥ	ظ	z
خ	kh	ع	‘
ذ	**z**	غ	gh
س	s	لا	h
ش	sh	ق	q

Foreword

There is considerable evidence available that indicates the onset of stagnation and consequent degeneration of Kashmir society by the beginning of the tenth century (A.D.). It was becoming more and more difficult to throw up and sustain a strong central authority for the whole of Kashmir Valley. This led to a long period of intensive wars among Damras and the contemporary central authority.

Professor D.D. Kosambi, using a scientific methodology for his investigations, has been able to provide us profound insights in the appearance of this phenomenon. We quote: "The need to import trade goods, particularly salt and metal, difficult transport, lowering of grain prices with great increase in village settlements due to extensive water-works, meant concentration of wealth in a few hands *for each small group of villages* (emphasis added). A Kashmiri village could not be as nearly self-sufficient as one in India for the rigours and more varied climate made it impossible to do without wool, which had to be produced for exchange against cereals as a commodity.... In Kashmir the man who bad surplus acquired more wealth by trade, took to arms, and turned into a Damra.... The conflict between King and Damra feudal baron and central power, led ultimately to a Kashmirian Hindu king plundering temple property and melting down the images for profit, without change of religion or theological excuses, simply to maintain the army and a costly state apparatus. Because this could not continue forever, we have the ultimate victory of feudalism, and the weakening of the central power.... To pay for its essential import (salt and metal) Kashmir had an ideal commodity over a mountain to a large market, and without serious competition.... Without the *Crocus* or some equivalent commodity, the internal history of Kashmir would have been far less turbulent." (*The Sardasatabdhi Commemoration Volume,* The Asiatic Society of Bombay, 1957, pp. 108-120)

The above analysis refers to a much earlier period than the one dealt with in detail in *Bahāristān-i-Shahī.* Nevertheless, some useful clues may be found here to the otherwise seemingly senseless quarrels and conflicts of this period, before the Mughal takeover in AD 1587.

The disintegration of Kashmir society gathered momentum from the 10th century onwards, through endless conflicts between Damras and contemporary kings. It was during this period that the new ideas of Islam and some of its adherents slowly began to penetrate the Valley, and later culminated in the deposition of the last Hindu ruler Kota Rani by Shah Mir, a fugitive Khashya Muslim chieftain from *Panchghavara* (present Rajouri-Budhal) region who seized the throne of Kashmir by perfidy. He founded the first Muslim ruling dynasty of Kashmir under the title Sulṭān Shamsu'd-Dīn Shāh Mīr in A.D. 1339 ushering in a new epoch in Kashmir history.

The introduction of a foreign faith in Kashmir meant greater movement and activity on the trade routes to Western and Central Asia. In particular contact with Persian civilization became quite close, and linguistic barriers were crossed on a broad front. Alongside, favourable opportunities were created now for enterprising and ambitious missionaries and other adventurers from this region to thrive in the beautiful Valley by building a strong social base for their power and wealth.

All these vital processes have now to be sorted out and critically examined by our new generation of intelligentsia in the spirit of modern historiography. Meanwhile, all the available documents that have escaped destruction, archaeological remains, linguistic and literary evidence, social customs, need to be critically examined by our new generation of historians. This may be regarded as an essential aspect of the great task of building a New Kashmir of our dreams.

There is no doubt that *Bahāristān-i-Shahī* is a valuable historic document that deserves to be widely known, and studied for the first-hand evidence provided by some influential courtier of Yūsuf Shāh Chak, overthrown and imprisoned by the Mughal Emperor Akbar in AD 1587. The anonymous writer appears to have worked on his theme largely during the first two decades of the seventeenth century.

With the deposition and arrest of Yūsuf Shāh Chak, the ancient Kashmir Kingdom lost its independence. Kashmir had to wait for 360 years to once again breathe the air of freedom. But by a strange quirk of destiny, within four odd decades of freedom, forces of regress began reassembling and ultimately dragged Kashmir polity onto a path of strife.

Dr. Kashinath Pandit has done his labour of love by working on the original Persian manuscripts and has produced a faithful English version of the same, to make the contents available to a wider audience. He is singularly qualified for this major task. Coming from a Baramulla Brahman family with a long tradition of classical learning and scholarship spread over several generations he got a Master's degree in Persian from the Panjab University, with distinction. At the age of twenty-nine, he joined the University of Teheran (Iran) for a doctorate in Iranian and spent nearly four years there. He has also produced a work on the historical background of some of the more famous poems of Hafiz of Shiraz.

Dr. Pandit has travelled widely in Central Asia and is well known to the scholars in the Tajik Academy particularly. The diversity and depth of his knowledge of the region are of timely importance to us in the Valley in the context of recent developments. There is no doubt about his present work being an important contribution towards the understanding of our past.

N.N. Raina

June 25, 1989
125 Narsingh Garh
Srinagar, Kashmir

(Author's Note: A few minor changes have been made in the original text of the Foreword following the wishes of late Dr. N.N. Raina conveyed to me personally by him when we met in New Delhi after our exodus from Kashmir in 1990.)

Introduction

Kashmir may rightfully boast of a long tradition of producing histories and historical works of considerable value. No fewer than a dozen histories are referred to by Kalhaṇa which, besides other materials, served him as sources for his celebrated chronicle *Rājataraṅgiṇī* written in Laukika 4225 corresponding to A.D. 1149/50. Kalhaṇa's impact on the historians and chroniclers who followed him is evident in at least the works of four of them who endeavoured to carry on the tradition of recording the events of the rulers of their time: Jonarāja, Śrivara, Prājyabhaṭṭa and Suka. While the work of Prājyabhaṭṭa is lost to us, the history of Suka takes us to the time of the second tenure of Sulṭān Fatḥ Shāh in A.D. 1538. The historical accounts of these four Sanskrit historians are relatively brief; they make only veiled references to events which deserved to be treated in greater detail. But they wrote under several constraints, and that perhaps explains why their perception and presentation of events did not match that of Kalhaṇa's. It is also likely that what has survived the ravages of time is only a fragment of what they had written. Nevertheless, these accounts are valuable to us; at least we have something to fall back upon.

The tradition solidly established by Kalhaṇa, which was marked by objectivity in approach and treatment, was followed by many later historians of Kashmir. From the time of the advent of Islam in Kashmir (placed by some historians somewhere in the last decade of the thirteenth century, though the presence of the people of Islamic faith in Kashmir had been reported by Kalhaṇa in as early as the eighth century)[1] to the reign of Mahārāja Pratāp Singh the third Dogra ruler (d. A.D. 1925), many histories of Kashmir were produced in Persian. After the expansion of Islam in Iran and Central Asia, the art of recording the events and affairs of rulers and their subjects developed in a manner in conformity with the Islamic traditions. When the conversion process in Kashmir reached its culmination in the fourteenth and fifteenth centuries and the social and political turbulence died down, the resultant peaceful order stimulated hitherto suspended intellectual and artistic activity. For more than a century after the founding of Muslim rule in Kashmir, Sanskrit continued to be used officially alongside Persian, though it was evident that the latter would very soon replace the former both as official language and the language of the elite. No wonder, therefore, that a patron of learning like Sulṭān Zainu'l-'Ābidīn worked for preserving the rich cultural heritage of Kashmir by starting a bureau of translation for translating Sanskrit works into Persian. Kalhaṇa's *Rājataraṅgiṇī* was translated during this very time. Unfortunately, much of the material produced during this time has been lost. Persian historiography had a rich tradition behind it. When Persian language took roots in Kashmir, the science of writing histories also absorbed the tradition which had already been established.

One cannot compute exactly the number of histories of Kashmir which have been written in Persian from early times to the present day. However, a record of extant Persian histories preserved in the Research and Publication Department of Jammu & Kashmir State, Srinagar, lists as many as seventeen works in manuscript form. The earliest among these is *Tārīkh-i-Kashmir* written by Sayyid

1. *Rājataraṅgiṇī*, Bk. iv, St. 397.

'Alī b. Sayyid Muḥammad in A.D. 1579, and the most recent is *Tārīkh-i-Kabīr* written by Ghulām Moḥiu'd-Dīn in A.D. 1900. Apart from these, there are several other works in the form of diaries, travelogues, and stray writings of considerable historical importance which have not been included in the list of histories.

Of the seventeen histories, of Kashmir, already known to scholars, only two have been printed so far: *Wāqa'āt-i-Kashmir* by Muḥammad Azam Dedamari and the two volumes of *Tārīkh-i-Kashmir* by Pīr Ghulām Ḥasan Khuihāmī. The unedited text of *Bahāristān-i-Shāhī* was also published a few years ago by a local scholar as a supplement to a long eulogy of the author's now deceased patron and benefactor. *Gulāb Nāma* by Dīwān Kripā Rām has also been translated from Persian into English, but it is more of a biography of the founder of the Dogra dynasty of the rulers of Jammu & Kashmir, than a work of history.

In the absence of competent and annotated English translations of these Persian histories of Kashmir, the non-Persian knowing scholars are severally handicapped. But the task of editing, translating and publishing these manuscripts is not an easy one; it calls for a high standard of scholarship, dedication and institutional and organizational support. That these valuable histories are languishing in dust is a sad commentary on the state of scholarly research in these areas. Unless government bodies and universities take initiative in providing the right kind of incentives to competent scholars, these manuscripts cannot reach scholars in the field. It needs to be mentioned here that high level scholarship in classical languages is becoming rare in our country.

By and large, the historians of Kashmir writing in Persian language followed the pattern – format, style, theme etc. – of Iranian historians though the canvas of the former is limited. When they accepted the Persian / Tajik model of historiography, they accepted both its good and bad qualities. It appears that many Persian historians of Kashmir had perused the historical works of outstanding Iranian or Central Asian historians and they had familiarised themselves with their technical language, style and method to a considerable extent. They had also acquainted themselves with the variety of themes which the Iranian, Central Asian or Indian historians treated in the course of their recordings.

Histories of Kashmir in Persian language which I had the opportunity of examining during the course of my research, invariably follow the traditional pattern of Persian histories which had been produced in Iran, Transoxiana (*Mā'warā-an-Nahr*), Afghanistan and India. They begin with an elaborate doxology, followed by praises and eulogies for the Holy Prophet, the Imans, and the ruling house or the king or the patron at whose instance the work was undertaken or to whom it was dedicated. However, the Persian histories produced in Kashmir deviate in some respects from the traditional norm. In the East, particularly in Iran, a historian wrote at the behest of a ruler, a minister or a powerful courtier or a feudal lord. In a few cases the historian would himself be a minister or an influential person close to the ruling circles and the corridors of power, and wrote mainly to please his patron than out of his intellectual curiosity. Martin's perceptive comment on Timurid art explains it clearly: "All art, in the Orient is court art, or is dependent on Maecenas. It was so, in the 'Abbasid Court at Baghdad in the ninth century, it was so in Egypt and Spain; it was so everywhere. This fact must be remembered, as it explains much that would otherwise be incomprehensible".[2]

Most of the historians of Kashmir who wrote in Persian had very thin or no connection with the court or the ruling

2. *The Miniature Painting and Painters of Persia, India, and Turkey*, Quartich, 1912, vol. i, pp. 35-6.

house, and never held any important official positions. This accounts for the presence of very few distortions or misrepresentations in their expositions, and gives their work a degree of objective credibility not known before. Whatever bias these may have is because of the angularities of their character or because of circumstances beyond their control. This bias is, therefore, neither pronounced nor offensive. But because they were not associated with the court or royalty, put them to a disadvantage: they had no access to original and living sources of information.

Generally mediaeval Persian historiography in or outside Iran suffered from one particular drawback. To show off his command over the language, a historian would invariably cultivate a highly ornate and turgid style. He would devote more attention to rhetorical embellishment than to objective analysis of facts and events or to drawing of logical conclusions. This probably explains why many historical works were used as textbooks of highly ornate Persian prose rather than as histories. History was not included in the curriculum of *madrasah* (seminaries) in Iran and elsewhere as an independent subject of study. The historians did not realize they needed a different kind of style for producing histories. This lessened the value of many of these works. The historians' tendency to use an ornate style was probably because they wrote only for a small circle of upper class intellectuals, and not for the public at large. Once arts and sciences came out of the close confines of courts and elitist circles and spread to wider sections of society, historians gradually gave up the old ornate style and wrote with a greater degree of objectivity and factual precision.

Keeping this in view, it is gratifying to note that histories produced in Persian language in Kashmir are very readable narratives composed usually in a simple and clear style. This is mostly because they were generally unconnected with courts, rulers and high-ranking personalities. Another reason was that Persian was not their mother tongue. It had been brought here from Iran and Transoxiana by Muslim missionaries for propagating the Islamic faith. When the ruling power passed on to the Muslims, Persian became the court and official language in due course of time. Anybody using it had to be clear and precise. The historians, too, followed the same example. Not having to do anything with the king or his court, the histories produced by Kashmiris were put in the category of non-official and popular histories. The historians did not need to vie with one another to strive for linguistic embellishments. This makes it easier to render them into readable English than the histories produced in Iran or Transoxiana in mediaeval times.

Having noted the general features of Persian histories produced in Kashmir in mediaeval and early modern times, it has to be admitted that these histories do have some limitations which they share with the histories produced in Iran and elsewhere in the Persian / Tajik speaking regions. First, there is a pronounced streak of exaggeration in them; no matter whether they are praising or censuring. Second, they lack systematic distribution of themes into separate parts or through what we now call chapterization. Besides, there are sudden shifts from one theme to another; the reader is not sufficiently prepared for a new course of events. Hence any attempt on the part of an editor or a translator at distributing the narrative into chapters and assigning them headings has to be an arbitrary one. Finally, besides frequent repetitions, their narrative continuity is often disrupted by uncalled-for interpolations.

In the choice of their subject-matter, Persian histories of Kashmir suffer from several other deficiencies. They deal with subjects like court intrigues, political and personal rivalries among nobles and chieftains, tales of extraordinary heroism, hunting expeditions and pleasure trips, harem squabbles and such other trivial matters. The treatment is generally exaggerated. Vital matters of social importance are ignored or underestimated. Common people hardly figure in their account of the affairs of the state. Even after going through long chunks of such histories one cannot frame even a hazy idea of the kind of society that existed at a given point of time. As against this, court intrigues, in-fightings, petty skirmishes, and supernatural powers of the saints receive more than reasonable attention. When not engaged with these things, the historian writes copiously about mystics, spiritualists, mendicants, especially about their seemingly miraculous powers. He has very little or almost nothing to say about the vast agrarian and artisan sections of society; their economic and social activities; their relations with the ruling class; taxes, revenue and fiscal matters; arts and crafts; status of women, folk-lore and local traditions; interaction between various sections and classes of society engaged in productive activity, military and administrative set-up and a multitude of other related themes. He does not identify himself with the social milieu of his times.

But notwithstanding all that is said, it will be unjustified to censure these historians for the deficiencies enumerated above, because socially-oriented history is a recent development, at least in our part of the continent. Though this approach to history gained popularity in the West from the time of the Renaissance, the East lingered on for many more centuries with her ages-old tradition till the era when imperialism and its agencies received a setback in Asia and elsewhere outside Europe. In such a situation, the burden of scanning impartially the material available to them, investigating it and drawing conclusions in a manner that society and its variegated aspects are brought under focus has to fall on the present-day historians. And the task calls for extraordinary care and responsibility.

The most crucial period of the mediaeval history of Kashmir is from the time of the downfall of the Hindu rule up to the beginning of Shāhmīrī rule. Surprisingly, Persian historians have virtually neglected this period of far-reaching consequence. It has led to the exacerbation of controversies based on wild speculations. They have become so firmly entrenched that it seems difficult to rectify them. The process of early Islamization of Kashmir is a complex one because, unlike Iran or Transoxiana, there was no outright invasion of Kashmir by Islamic warriors; no Arab legions marched into Kashmir with their swift horses and slender swords. It was a curious process interspersed with many ugly happenings which are mentioned in the pages of this work. But the initial non-violent character of the event makes it into quite a fascinating development. The story of conversion of hundreds of thousands of people to Islam over a long stretch of time has not been told in a manner in which it should have been. No historian, for example, has tried to go deep into the socio-economic and socio-political causes of the phenomenon. This lacuna in the mediaeval histories of Kashmir is difficult to explain.

Bahāristān-i-Shāhī

Historians have mentioned some historical works which were produced in Kashmir before *Bahāristān-i-Shāhī* was written, but these are lost. Three histories are invariably mentioned in this connection: those of Mullā Nāderī, Qāzi Ibrāhim and Mullā Ḥasan Qāri. In their absence, *Bahāristān-i-Shāhī* enjoys the status of being the first fully detailed history of Kashmir written anonymously in A.D. 1614. (The forty-eight folio MS history written by Sayyid 'Alī is mainly an account of the saints, particularly of Sayyid 'Alī Hamadānī).

Of the two extant manuscript copies of *Bahāristān-i-Shāhī*, one is in the British Museum (Add. 16, 706) and the other is in the India Office (I.O. 509). An abridged MS copy is in Bankipore Library.

When compared with the India Office copy, the one preserved in the British Museum has some omissions, erasions and over-writings. Many place-names are illegible or carelessly written. In a few instances, the corresponding dates in Laukika calendar are missing. On these counts, the India Office copy has been considered more dependable, though, in both the cases, the date of transcription or the name of the copyist has not been recorded. Not ignoring the importance of the manuscript copy in the British Museum, a genuine text was established after careful collation of the two MSS, and the translation is of the collated version. In doing so many ambiguities have been removed and omissions reconstructed. However, a few though minor discrepancies could not be resolved and these have been indicated in the English version.

The India Office manuscript copy carries the date of compilation of the chronicle in its colophon in the shape of a chronogram, viz. *Nāmeh-e-Shāhān-i-Kashmir:* it is A.H. 1023 corresponding to A.D. 1614. The chronogram is actually the concluding verse of a short *mat<u>h</u>navi* (a long poem) appended to the text. This is somewhat curious because such appendages are generally found in collections (*jung*) and not in exclusive works of history. Moreover, the *mat<u>h</u>navi* in question is of a different theme – being didactic in nature – bearing no relation whatsoever to the theme of the chronicle. The MS does not bear either the date of its transcription or the name of its author scribe and the place of writing. It cannot be decisively established as to when the author began writing the name of its author and the place of writing. It cannot be decisively established as to when the author began writing the chronicle; one or two clues however do suggest that the entire work was completed in not less than two decades. It seems that there are big time-gaps in the course of writing the chronicle, for the author refers to Kashmir sometimes as 'this country' and at other times as 'that country'.

This also proves that while writing it the author was sometimes in Kashmir and sometimes outside Kashmir.

The clues suggesting more than two decades as the period over which the chronicle was written are: On folio 12^{b} of the MS, the author writes that 270 years have elapsed since the ravages of Zulchu took place. The incursion of Zulchu, as per the author's statement (fol. 11^{a}/p. 17) took place in A.H. 727 / A.D. 1323. As such he had been writing about this particular event in A.H. 997 corresponding to A.D. 1593. This was the time when Kashmir had passed under the control of the Mughals for over six years. The chronicle was brought to its completion twenty-one years later. In other words, we can say that it took the author no fewer than twenty-one years to complete it, presuming that he had begun it in A.H. 997 / A.D. 1593. The presumption is based on the fact that Zulchu's incursion into Kashmir being an event of early history of Kashmir, the chronicler had to write twelve folios to arrive at the description of this event.

The MS fills 212 folios of $8^{5}/8$" × 5" size written in fairly legible *nasta'līq* hand. A few omissions, errors and erasions which have crept into the text, advertently or inadvertently, have been set right as far as possible after collating with the Br. Museum copy. Whatever discrepancies are left do not seriously obstruct the continuity of the text or impair its readability. Some orthographic peculiarities of the MS are:

(a) letter ش is invariably accompanied by three dots at its bottom.

(b) letter گ invariably carries only one horizontal stroke instead of two.

(c) letter ے (*yā-e-majhūl*) has not been used which contrasts with the Practice followed in many Persian histories produced in India.

(d) letter ی is invariably accompanied by two dots at its bottom.

(e) *hamza* (ئ) is generally represented by two dots at the bottom of *ya*.

(f) when a word ending with letter *alif* is required to be compounded with the following word, its sign of *hamza* is replaced by *ya*.

Such orthographic peculiarities are generally found in Persian-Tajik manuscripts of Transoxiana produced during the mediaeval period. For example, a manuscript history entitled *Mehmān Nāmeh-e-Bukhārā*, of Faḍlu'llah Rozbehān Khunji completed in A.D. 1509 in Herat bears a marked resemblance to the work in question in its orthographic peculiarities. It suggests that the style of writing, calligraphy and also the general pattern of Persian works of history in those days were largely influenced by the Turanian style, rather than the Indian.

In one particular formal aspect, the India Office MS is different from general Persian historical writings. A common pattern of Persian-Tajik and Arabic works is that the author begins with the opening sentence of the Islamic prayer, viz. *bismillah ar-rahmān ar-rahīm*, followed by one or two paragraphs in doxology, praises to the Holy Prophet, the Imams, and lastly to the ruler or the patron as the case may be. But in the case of *Bahāristān-i-Shāhī*, except for the opening sentence of the Islamic prayer, all other doxological features are conspicuously absent. The book begins directly with the mythical story of the origin of Kashmir. If we presume that its author was of the Shia' faith and that he wrote at a time when factional feuds were recurrent, we can understand his doing away with the established practice of writing prefatory material to works of history.

The MS is frequently interspersed with verses which occasionally fill a folio or two. Their theme is generally related to the context. However, it is difficult to ascertain whether these verses have been borrowed from some versified history of Kashmir or not, although there are a few positive clues to suggest such a possibility. If the author really made use of one, it could either be the now lost work of Mullā Nāderī, which is mentioned in several Persian histories of Kashmir, or that of Sayyid Qāsim, which is mentioned cursorily on folio 42^{b}/p. 60 of the text, presuming that the reference is not to Abu'l-Qāsim b. Hindushah Firishta. The rhyme and meter of these verses correspond to the one we find in the *Shahnāma* of Ferdowsi. It is important to bear in mind that the *Shahnāma* had set the trend for future poet-historians in the choice of meter for recording popular events and legends of heroism and valour. *Shahnāma*, the great epic, had been popular with the men of letters in Kashmir as early as the fifteenth century. Jonarāja tells us that "Bhaṭṭāvtara, who had perused *Shahnāma* composed a work named *Jainavilass* as the counterpart of the king's (Zainu'l-'Ābidīn) instructions".[3]

While rendering *Bahāristān-i-Shāhī* into English, the Persian verses which frequently figure in the text have been left out. This is not because the verses do not deserve to be translated, but because it would have proved a source of distraction to the reader.

Sources

There is no specific mention in the text of the chronicle about the sources from which the author drew material for his work. Nevertheless, keeping in view the importance of the subject, an attempt will be made to trace sources that have a direct or indirect bearing on the text.

For the Hindu period of his chronicle, the author probably drew on some Sanskrit work or works, for he has referred to some such source by a phrase *ba qalam-i-Kashmiri*, although the word Sanskrit has not been used

3. *The Rājataraṅgiṇī of Jonarāja*, (tr.) Dutt, J.C., Delhi, 1986, p. 13.

anywhere in the text. Repeated allusions to such histories suggest that Persian translations of some known Sanskrit histories were within the reach of the author. These could have been the chronicles written by Kalhaṇa, Jonarāja, Śrivara or Suka. We know for certain that by that time Kalhaṇa's *Rājataraṅgiṇī* and the chronicle of Jonarāja had been rendered into Persian either in full or in part. Jonarāja tells us that Sulṭān Zainu'l-'Ābidīn was instrumental in getting *Rājataraṅgiṇī* translated into Persian.[4] We also know that 'Abdu'l-Qādir Badāunī had, under Akbar's instructions, prepared an abridged version of the history of Kashmir; this is stated by him in the *muqaddima* to his work *Muntakhabu't-Tawārīkh*.[5]

The four Sanskrit historians who followed Kalhaṇa were a witness to events for the periods detailed below:

Jonarāja	A.D.	1398-1459	61 years
Śrivara		1459-1486	27 years
Prājyabhaṭṭa		1486-1513	27 years
Suka		1613-1638	25 years

Since *Bahāristān-i-Shāhī* was written in A.D. 1614, Suka's history falls outside its time-span. Śrivara's account is much more detailed than those of others. This is clear from the following table:

Kalhaṇa	3698 years in 7830	slokas (verses)
Jonarāja	300 years in 976	slokas
Śrivara	27 years in 2241	slokas
Suka	25 years in 398	slokas

The last time when the author of the work refers to a Sanskrit history (*ba qalam-i-Kashmiri*) is in connection with the

4. *The Rājataraṅgiṇī of Jonarāja*, (tr.) Dutt, J.C., Delhi, 1986, p. 146. Also see *Zaina Rājataraṅgiṇī of Śrivara*, ed. Rughnath Singh, Varanasi, 1977, Pt. I, Stt. 1 : 5 : 85.
5. (Tr.) Sir Wolseley Haig, Patna, 1973, Vol. iii, p. 536. See text vol. ii, p. 374.

dafeat of Kāji Chak at the hands of Mīrzā Ḥaidar Dughlat; the year recorded is 16 which corresponds to A.H. 947 / A.D. 1540.

Apart from the translations of the chronicles of Jonarāja, Śrivara and others, and presuming that these works had been translated into Persian, some more histories in Persian verse or prose had been produced by the time the author of *Bahāristān-i-Shāhī* appeared on the scene. These could also have carried the accounts of Hindu rulers of Kashmir used by the author. But the loss of Persian translation of Sanskrit histories of Kashmir from Kalhaṇa to Suka (presuming the translations had been made) has made any verdict on the sources of the history of Hindu period in *Bahāristān-i-Shāhī* a matter of conjecture. For writing his account, the author seems to have used some distorted and frightfully defective Persian rendering of *Rājataraṅgiṇī*. His casual attitude towards this period is indicated by the fact that only eleven out of a total of 212 folios of the MS are devoted to it. It seems that the author wrote about it as a routine formality.

As far as the account of the Sulṭāns of Kashmir is concerned, the following Persian histories produced until the writing of *Bahāristān-i-Shāhī* in A.D. 1614, come to our notice:

1. *Tārīkh-i-Kashmir*, Sayyid 'Alī, A.D. 1579.
2. *Tārīkh-i-Kashmir*, Mullā Ḥusain Nāderi, A.D. 1580.
3. *Ta<u>d</u>kiratu'l-Ārifin*, Mullā 'Alī Raina, A.D. 1587.
4. *Tārīkh-i-Kashmir*, being the translation of Jonarāja's history, A.D. 1590, Munich MS. Its author is unknown and the work covers 131 years of history given by Jonarāja.
5. *Tabaqāt-i-Akbari*, Niẓāmu'd-Dīn Tarawi, A.D. 1592.
6. *Tārikh-i-Rashīdī*, Mīrzā Ḥaidar Dughlat.
7. *Bābur Nama*, Zahiru'd-Dīn Bābur.
8. *Tārikh-i-Firishta*.

No doubt these historical works were produced either before *Bahāristān-i-Shāhī* was written or were produced simultaneously, but it is difficult to say which of these histories the author used as his sources; he does not make any specific reference to any work or works.

From the concluding portions of the chronicle, one gathers the impression that the author had been an eye-witness to some happenings of those times. It could also be said that he had access to important personalities. That is why he gives some minute details of events in this part of the work. However, in the absence of an authentic biography of the author, who is not even identified, it would not be safe to link him with either the court of the Chaks or the powerful house of the Sayyids of Baihaqī, whom he praises in extravagant terms for their bravery and statecraft. That the author preferred to remain anonymous is also significant. Some scholars have tried to lift the veil of anonymity from his name, but such efforts could be only conjectural and had better be ignored.

We may now try to analyse the clues available in the chronicle to the possible sources used by the author. This will help in evaluating the authenticity of the work in its totality, and also serve as an incentive to further research in the field.

1. Commenting on the ravages of Zulchu (*c.* A.D. 1323), the author writes (fol. 11^a/p. 17) that the chroniclers of the events of Kashmir have not recorded an event more disastrous and catastrophic than that of Zulchu's incursion into Kashmir. This is a very faithful reproduction of Jonarāja's comment on the event.[6] This confirms that the Persian version of Jonarāja's *Rājataraṅgiṇī* was used by the author.

6. *Jonarāja*, ed. Srikanth Koul, Hoshiarpur, 1967, p. 165.

2. Describing the military exploits of Sulṭān Shihābu'd-Dīn, (fol. 21ª/p. 32), the author writes that details pertaining to the Sulṭān's military incursions have been elaborately recorded in the history of … (blank) written in Kashmiri. The author also writes that if the stories and anecdotes of Sulṭān Shihābu'd-Dīn's remarkable bravery are fully described (as had been available to him), people would think them a result of his poetical exaggeration and as such would be taken as false.… This is exactly what Jonarāja has said about the Sulṭān.[7] Furthermore, the expression "chronicles of mighty monarchs and events of kings of Kashmir" with which the text of *Bahāristān-i-Shāhī* begins is perhaps the expanded Persian rendering of the Sanskrit term *'Rājataraṅgiṇī'*. Not mentioning the name of the author or the title of the 'Kashmiri history' (*ba qalam-i-Kashmiri*) in the text (fol. 20ª/p. 31) appears to be a deliberate act, and not an inadvertent omission. Perhaps the author did not want to acknowledge the debt he owed to Jonarāja.
3. On fol. 29ª/p. 40, the author refers to a panegyric composed by Sayyid Maḥmūd Baihaqī in praise of Sulṭān Ghiathu'd-Dīn of Dehli and says that "for fear of its length, historians have recorded only the following verses". Then follow the verses. This indicates that the author knew some Persian historical works of India which dealt with the period he was writing about.
4. On fol. 42ᵇ/p. 60, the author quotes one Sayyid Qāsim describing the numerical strength of Mīr Sayyid Nāṣir Baihaqī's troops in readiness against the

7. See *The Rājataraṅgiṇī of Jonarāja*, (tr.) Dutt, J.C., New Delhi, 1986, p. 40.

troops of the Rājā of Jasrot (or Rājā Jasrath?). The event pertains to the days of Sulṭān Zainu'l-'Ābidīn's accession to the throne in A.D. 1422. Who this Sayyid Qāsim was and what exactly he wrote is not known. One possible guess could be that he is Qāsim b. Hindushāh, commonly known as Firishta.

5. On fol. 62ᵇ / p. 78, the author describes the conspiracy hatched by Kashmiri dissidents to assassinate Sayyid Ḥasan Baihaqī and writes, "It has been written in Kashmiri...." This indicates that a history of Kashmir of that period written in Sanskrit did exist and was made use of by the author either in its Persian translation or through the assistance of an interpreter. If we accept that the Persian version of a Sanskrit history did exist at this point of time, then it has to be that by Śrivara. His chronicle mentions clearly the dream of Mīr Sayyid Ḥasan regarding his impending killing next morning. The dream is described in its entirety by our chronicler on folio 62ᵇ / p. 78.

6. On fol. 75ᵇ / p. 90, there is a description of the fierce fighting which broke out between the troops of Fatḥ Shāh and Muḥammad Shāh and the mishap of Mīr Sayyid Muḥammad's horse falling into a ditch on the battlefield. The chronicler says that the event is well known in Kashmiri history. This too confirms that Śrivara's history served as a source for this portion of the chronicle.

7. On fol. 145ᵃ / p. 193, while describing a confrontation between Yūsuf Shāh Chak and Sayyid Mubārak Khān, the author notes, "... historians have given an account of this battle in prose as well as in verse". This suggests the existence of some history or histories in Persian / Sanskrit written both in verse and in prose. The statement is followed by verses filling one whole folio of the MS. It is likely that these

verses have been borrowed directly from some versified history in Persian / Sanskrit.

8. The first mention of the Islamic calendar in the chronicle has been made to record the year of Laxman Dev's death, viz. A.H. 531 / A.D. 1136 (fol. 8^b / p. 8). Thereafter, the Muslim calendar has been used along with the Laukika calendar of the Kashmiris which has been introduced for the first time to denote the year A.H. 878 / A.D. 1473 (Laukika 46 Vivat 12). This too suggests the existence of Sanskrit / Persian histories of Kashmir during the period under our consideration.
9. On fol. 10^b / p. 16, the author writes that he confirmed the name (of Zulchu) as Zulāji from Mīrzā Ḥaidar. This indicates that Mīrzā Ḥaidar Dughlat's history *Tārīkh-i-Rashīdī* also served him as a source for his chronicle.

Evaluation

Bahāristān-i-Shāhī is essentially an account of the political events of Kashmir in mediaeval times, especially from the time of the incursion of Zulchu into Kashmir in A.H. 727 / A.D. 1323 to A.H. 1023 / A.D. 1614, the year when Sayyid Abu'l-Ma'ālī, the second son of Sayyid Mubārak, and the last of Yūsuf Shāh Chak's closest associates, proceeded to Thatta in Sindh to assume charge of his *jāgīr*, conferred upon him by Jahangir Padishah. The Hindu period with which the chronicle begins is casually treated in the first eleven folios. While dealing with the later period, the narrative acquires breadth and depth, especially from the death of 'Alī Shāh in A.H. 986 / A.D. 1578. Some portions of the history, mostly the latter ones, were probably written by the author at a place outside Kashmir because, while referring to Kashmir, he says 'that country' whereas in the earlier portions he calls it 'this country'.

The narrative does not deal only with the rulers of Shāhmīrī and Chak dynasties, but also treats of the story of the Baihaqī Sayyids whose ancestor, Mīr Sayyid Maḥmūd, had been defeated by Timur and had fled to Delhi along with his followers during the reign of Sulṭān Ghiāthu'd-Dīn. The Sulṭān of Delhi had granted him a *jāgīr* in Jaricha near Delhi. During the reign of Sulṭān Sikandar of Shāhmīrī dynasty (A.D. 1393-1416), Sayyid Maḥmūd came to Kashmir for the first time along with a band of his soldiers and associates. Thereafter the Baihaqī Sayyids gradually rose in power and position and played an active, and often a decisive, role in the affairs of Kashmir. One from their clan, named Sayyid Mubārak, ruled over Kashmir for a short period of two months in A.D. 1578. The account of the Sayyids of Baihaqī is treated at such length in the chronicle that some scholars have said that it is a history of the Sayyids than that of the Sulṭāns of Kashmir. His lavish praise of the Sayyids makes us presume that he was very close to them, perhaps a beneficiary of that house. He does not hesitate to lay bare the contempt which the Sayyids had for the local Kashmiri population. This became the cause of constant friction and acrimony between them and the local chiefs. From contemporary sources we learn that the Sayyids had to make strenuous efforts to become acceptable to the Kashmiris. Śrivara writes that although they claimed their descent from the house of the Prophet, they did not receive adequate veneration from the Kashmiri Hindus who had been converted to Islam. Therefore, in order to make the converted Hindus understand their high status, the Sayyids told them that they were 'Musalmān Brahmans' as against 'Hindu Brahmans'.[8]

8. Śrivara calls them *chhij*, and the rest of the Hindus converted to Islam as mlechhas. See *Zaina Rājataraṅgiṇī*, ed. Raghunath Singh, Varanasi, 1977, Pt. I, Stt. 4 : 77.

As a work of history, *Bahāristān-i-Shāhī* has its weak spots as well. The author often makes sudden shifts from one event to another. For example, while describing Sulṭān Zainu'l-'Ābidīn's works of public utility and of architecture (p. 68), the author brings in the story of the Sulṭān's action against the recalcitrant Pāndav Chak of Kupwara. Such interpolations figure with greater frequency during a period of about a hundred years of political turmoil and administrative chaos following the death of Sulṭān Zainu'l-'Ābidīn in A.D. 1473. This causes confusion in determining the sequence of events in their chronological order.

The tone of the narrative gives the impression that the author had been writing under some constraints of conscience. Except for the fact that Mullā Ḥasamu'd-Dīn was his great-grandfather (fol. 33^{b}/p. 44), we know nothing about his life. That he was an adherent of Shia' faith becomes clear from the loud manner in which he extols the propagation of religion by Shamsu'd-Dīn Araki, Mūsā Raina, and Kāji Chak, all staunch Shias, and the account of their destruction of Hindu temples and forcible conversion of Hindus to the Islamic faith, or the pogroms unleashed against that community. He severely criticises Mīrzā Ḥaidar Dughlat for his hypocritical visit to the shrine of the Shias at Zadibal in Srinagar. But his treatment of the factional feuds between the Shia' and Sunni people of Kashmir and the weakening of the former with the beginning of the Mughal imperialistic designs in Kashmir is very subdued. At crucial moments, he conceals more than what he reveals; at other places, he side-tracks the main issue. For example, he does not tell us the exact reason of Sayyid 'Alī Hamadānī's dissatisfaction with Sulṭān Quṭbu'd-Dīn (fol. 34^{b}/p. 36), although the latter gave the Sayyid full respect, implemented his instructions in matters of religion and faith, and even attended congregational prayers at the hospice which the Sayyid had built on the ruins of a demolished temple in

'Alāu'd-Dīn Pora (p. 36). Another example of ambiguity is about the exit of Sayyid Muḥammad Hamadāni from Kashmir in the reign of Sulṭān Sikandar, A.D. 1393 (p. 47). The author makes no mention of who Sayyid Ḥisārī was and why he was hostile towards the Sayyid. The matter becomes more intriguing when we are told that Sayyid Muḥammad received patronage and protection from the Sulṭān and also the support from his newly-converted general Suh Bhat (renamed Saifu'd-Dīn; meaning, 'Sword of Faith'). This Suh Bhat had also given his daughter in marriage to the Sayyid and, as such, he could not be sent away easily. Likewise, the author writes nothing about the differences which arose between Mīr Shams Araki and Mīr Sayyid Muḥammad Baihaqī (fol. 72ª/p. 86) which forced the former to proceed on his self-imposed travels or exile to Tibet. The closing part of the chronicle which deals with the dramatic circumstances in which Yūsuf Chak first conducted negotiations with the Mughals and then ended up as their prisoner is also somewhat intriguing. Similarly, the author's exposition of Mughal imperialistic designs in Kashmir is also full of inconsistencies and ambiguities.

The author throws a veil of ambiguity over some sensitive matters by referring to the supervening of the Divine Will in human affairs. He gives the impression that he believed that God's Will shapes the destinies of human beings, but when we look carefully at the facts described by him, it seems that the divine interference in human affairs is only a facade to conceal the machinations of persons who wielded power in the name of religion. Thus Shams Araki predicts that the Omnipotent would give to Kājī Chak the command of the government of Kashmir, and elicited from the latter a firm promise of strictly abiding by his dictates to propagate his creed (fol. 81ª/p. 107). It was only after receiving the approval of The Omnipotent that Kājī Chak resorted to the large-scale massacre of Hindus. When the eyes of 'Alī Khān were gouged out by the orders of Yūsuf Shāh, the author calls it a "matter of divine ordination (fol. 89[a]/p. 116). By attributing crucial happenings to powers beyond human control and not subjecting them to the law of cause and effect, the author faithfully follows the tradition of most of the Oriental historians of mediaeval history. There is hardly any attempt in the narrative to logically analyse the events or to see time in a precise and natural frame.

The chronicle deals mostly with rulers, their powerful nobles, ministers and the domineering groups and factions of feudal chiefs. Common folk do not figure in it. We hardly get to know anything about the Kashmiri society of that time. The author does not record the participation of common masses in happenings crucial to their interests and lives. We also do not learn anything about class interests, agriculture, economy, taxes, revenue system, trade and commerce, and a host of other social matters.

In spite of these drawbacks, the chronicle is important as a record of the political history of Kashmir under the Shāhmīrīs and the Chaks. It is the first comprehensive history of Kashmir written in Persian. On the political affairs of the period, it is indeed a mine of information, especially on some of the most controversial matters, like the obstructions to Shamsu'd-Dīn Araki's mission and the elimination of Nūrbakhshiyya sect, Ḥaidar Dughlat's religious policy, emergence of Baihaqī Sayyid's as a political force, and Mughal imperialistic designs in Kashmir.

The work amply reflects the feudalistic character of Kashmiri society during the rule of the Sulṭāns. The system was more or less a continuation of the system which existed under the Hindu rulers. Feudal lords were the props of the kingdom, enjoying power and influence. The landed aristocrats were called *Zamīndārs*; notable among them were the *Zamīndārs* of Bring, Chatr, Barthal, Nagam, Kother, and Kāmarāj. The *waqf* (endowment) institution under the

Sulṭāns may be compared to *agrahara* under the Hindu rulers. Alongside the feudal chiefs, other classes of landed aristocracy gained prominence during the rule of the Sulṭāns: *Ulema*, *Sayyids*, *Qāḍis* and men versed in religious learning. Sulṭān Sikandar created the post of *Shaykhu'l-Islām* and villages from each *pargana* were set apart for the perpetuation of the institution. The system continued down to the times of the author.[9] In special cases, the entire *pargana* was given as endowment; the *pargana* of Mattan was endowed to Sayyid Muḥammad Hamadāni. The relations between the landlords and the peasants could not be anything different from what they had been in traditional oriental feudalist society. The growth of religious institutions and increase in the number of religious intermediaries led to the disruption of the smooth functioning of the administrative machinery. The feudal lords who were converted to the new religion in the early period of Shāhmīrī rule became powerful and domineering because along with their political manoeuvrings, they also began to exploit religious feelings by showing obeisance to religious men and the divines.[10]

Bahāristān-i-Shāhī reveals that, apart from regular troops, private soldiers and mercenaries were also hired to take part in military operations. Most of the *Zamīndārs* raised private contingents of troops and provided them with provisions. No specific rules or practices of warfare were set forth; a victory over the enemy was usually followed by general loot and plunder of the properties of the defeated side. Twice did Zainu'l-'Ābidīn order destruction by fire of the residential complex of the defiant Pāndav Chak in Trehgam.[11] Kashmiri soldiers were adepts in mountain

9. P. 45 Infra.
10. P. 45 Infra. On this subject also see *Kashmir Polity* (600-1200 A.D.) Drabu, V.N., New Delhi, 1986, p. 199 *passim.*
11. P. 69 *Infra.*

warfare and made good use of natural defensive positions offered by mountain recesses and gorges. Each contingent was placed under a commander who acted and moved in unison with his soldiers. But a difference of opinion or interests with other commanders would not prevent him from taking his own decision and moving in a different direction. He could even make over to the enemy's side if it suited his own interests without having any qualms of conscience.

The work is also important because of its frequent references to the geography and topography of Kashmir. It mentions *parganas*, villages, towns, rivers, lakes, springs, routes, passes, mountain ranges, narrow gorges and extensive fields which tell us a great deal about Kashmir's topography, her boundaries and frontier military posts. The history clarifies how the territories beyond the northern and southern mountain ranges of the Valley shaped political events in Kashmir. In particular we see how regions of Tibet, Karnah, Drav (Baltistan and Darad lands) and those of Kishtwar, Rajouri, Poonch and Ghakkar lands were intimately linked with the history of Kashmir from early times. It also shows Kashmir's close relations with the northern plains of India, particularly with Delhi as the centre of the empire.

It should not go unnoticed that the chronicle paints a gloomy and dismal picture of Kashmir after the death of Sulṭān Zainu'l-'Ābidīn. His passing away let loose chaos and confusion in the land; each powerful chief or group tried to seize power in the kingdom, reducing the Sulṭān to the position of a nominal head. The chronicle also shows how the conditions prevailing in the vast country of Hindustan affected political developments in Kashmir, particularly from the beginning of the sixteenth century. The hostilities between various groups of Kashmiri Chieftains led them to establish contacts with Babur, Humayun, Sher Shāh and Akbar. Several other groups tried to get in touch with the powerful courtiers of the Mughals or their trusted generals. Kashmir gradually came under the Mughals; Shaykh Ya'qūb Sarfī's mission to Akbar's court clinched the process.

Calendar

The local Hindu calendar called Laukika was in use in Kashmir during the Hindu period. It continues to be used in *Bahāristān-i-Shāhī* alongside the Muslim calendar. The first time when the Muslim calendar is used is on fol. 8^b / p. 8, in connection with the death of Laxman Dev; it is A.H. 531 corresponding to A.D. 1136. The Laukika calendar has been used in the chronicle for the first time on fol. 58^b / p. 74, giving 46 Vivat 12 as the year of Sulṭān Zainu'l-'Ābidīn's death. It corresponds to A.H. 879 / A.D. 1473. Thereafter the Laukika calendar occurs intermittently and the last time when it is mentioned is 49 corresponding to A.H. 950 which is A.D. 1543.

It should be recalled that the Laukika calendar was used by all Sanskrit historians of Kashmir beginning with Kalhaṇa. The partial use of this calendar by the author of *Bahāristān-i-Shāhī* suggests that he had made use of a Sanskrit historical source at least for the portion of his work where Laukika calendar figures. Ordinarily, mediaeval Persian histories give dates only according to the Muslim calendar.

The following table gives the Laukika years (and their corresponding Christian dates) in the works of Jonarāja, Śrivara, Prājyabhaṭṭa and Suka:

Jonarāja

Name of the king	*Laukika*	*A.D.*
Rinchana	XXXVIII. 96	1320
Shamsu'd-Dīn	XXXIX. 15	1339
Jamsheed	XXXIX. 18	1342

‘Alāu’d-Dīn	XXXIX 19	1343
Quṭbu’d-Dīn	XXXIX. 30	1354
Shihābu’d-Dīn	XXXIX. 49	1373
Sikandar	XXXIX. 65	1389
‘Alī Shāh	XXXIX. 89	1413

Śrivara

Zainu’l-‘Ābidīn	XXXIX. 96	1420
Ḥaidar Shāh	XL. 96	1470
Ḥasan Shāh	XL. 48	1472
Muḥammad Shāh	XL. 60, 90, 92	1484, 1514
Muḥammad Shāh	XLI. 6	1516, 1530

Prājyabhaṭṭa and Suka

Fatḥ Shāh	XL. 62, 91	1486, 1515
Ibrāhīm Shāh	XLI. 4	1528
Nāzuk Shāh	XLI. 5	1529
Shams Shāh	XLI. 13	1537
Ḥabīb Shāh	XLI. 36	1560
Ghāzī Shāh	XLI. 36	1560
Ḥusain Shāh	XLI. 38	1562
‘Alī Shāh	XLI. 45	1569
Yūsuf Shāh	XLI. 54	1578
Lohar Chak	XLI. 54	1578
Yūsuf Chak (2nd time)	XLI. 55	1579
Ya‘qub Shāh	XLI. 63	1587

Kashinath Pandit

Chapter I

Hindu Period

Chroniclers[1] of the rulers of the domain of Kashmir, while recording in Kashmiri language[2] the events connected with their rule and also the affairs of people high and low, have written that in distant past the land we call Kashmir had remained submerged in water for two thousand years.[3] In those days, it was called Kashyap Sar. In its neighbourhood there dwelt a married hermit from India[4] named Kashyap. He made supplication to God Almighty for dry land where he could pray. Then God Almighty sent down three angels[5] commanding them to drain off the water to make dry as

---

1. The chronicles of Kashmirian kings are mentioned in Kalhaṇa's *Rājataraṅgiṇī:* Suvrata's handbook of historical poems, *Nilamata Purāṇa*, Kṣemendra's *Nṛpāvalī*, Chavillākar's work and the "eleven works of former scholars." See *Rājat.*, Vol. I, 'Introduction', p. 24, Vol. II, p. 365 *et seq*.
2. *ba qalam-i Kashmiri* of the text does not mean Kashmiri language as it is used now. It obviously means Sanskrit in Sārada script. The codex archetypus on which Stein based the text of *Rājataraṅgiṇī* is in Sārada script.
3. Regarding the calendar of "the people of Kashmir," see al-Bīrūnī's *India* (tr. Sachau), Vol. II, p. 8; Bühler's *Kashmir Report*, p. 38, *passim*; and *Rājat.*, Vol. I, p. 25.
4. The author considers India a foreign country throughout the text.
5. For the story of Satīsaras and the prayers of Kashyapa, see Bühler's *Report*, p. 39 and *Rājat.*, Vol. I, pp. 26-27 and Vol. II, pp. 388-89. Three angels referred to are Druhiṇa, Upendra, and Rudra.

much of land as was required by him. The land which they dried was named by them Kashshīle [*sic*], which means a 'chiselled stone'. It is said that subsequently [a person ?] Bekdarat [*sic*] by name sowed many kinds of seeds in the muddy soil and raised crops, and developed the place extensively. A large number of people came from India to settle on this land. Their king, the exalted Rājā, is Turkshil [*sic*]; Turkshil [*sic*] means 'unmatched in fortune and dignity.'

This land has been called Kashmir. The source of the Ganges also lies here,[6] [though] it is not accessible [to people]. Kashmir is protected by mountains. At their feet lie vast, clear and attractive lands; these are called *tāvar*. All these lands comprise seventy-two sectors and are spread over one hundred and eight *kruh*.[7] Amidst these lands is situated the city of Kashmir,[8] from which emerged people of sixty-four classes. Brahmans are one among them, all of whom are learned, and elderly theologians. After them is the class of Khatrish [*sic*]. Then come Vaish; they are artisans and peasants. Then follow Chandāls, the lowest among the masses; they resemble gypsies.

The ruler who first founded the city of Kashmir was called Pravarasen.[9] It widened under his stewardship. After his death, his sepulchre cracked and he rose to heaven

6. See *Rājat.*, i, 57n.
7. 1 *kruh* is approximately two miles.
8. The name Srinagar is nowhere mentioned in the text; instead we have the 'city of Kashmir' (*Shahr-i-Kashmir*). In Ferdawsī's *Shahnameh* also *Shahr-i-Iran* (sometimes *Iran-Shahr*) is used to denote the capital city of Iran. (Shahr = Shathra in Avestic).
9. Pravarasena II (3186-3248 Laukika) of Gonanda dynasty made extensive conquests in the south and the north. He built the capital town Pravarapura. See Cunningham's *Ancient Geography of Kashmir*, p. 91. The city contained thirty-six lakh houses. See *Rājat.*, i, 356.

near Maheshwar.[10] He was succeeded to the throne by his son Ratnāditya,[11] who reigned for sixty years. After him, his son Onta Dev reigned for forty years.[12] Lalitāditya[13] who descended from him ruled for eighty years. The people of Kashmir call him *Zu'l-Qarnain*. It is also said that he brought under his sway the entire world from the borders of China to the farthest west. Many of the idol-houses in Kashmir have been built by him. He also built a city named Parihāspora,[14] which means a 'peerless

---

10. See *Rājat.*, i, 374. It was in the temple of Pravareśa that King Pravarasena II attained spiritual perfection. A breach or an opening in the temple could be seen in Kalhaṇa's days. He writes that rising into the sky, King Pravarasena "joined in his body the assembly of the Lord of Beings (Śiva) Who is also called Maheshwara." Stein identified its ruins at a place now occupied by the *Ziārat* of Bahāu'd-Dīn Sāhib near the present Nowhatta locality in Srinagar, See *Rājat.*, i, 350-51n.
11. Pravarsena II was succeeded by his son Yudhisthira II and not by Ratnāditya. See *Rājat.*, iii, 379. Ratnāditya of the text is perhaps a reference to Ranāditya the son of Yudhisthira II and the younger brother of Narendrāditya (Lahkhana), the successor and son of Yudhisthira II. Ranāditya's reign lasted three hundred years, which appears to be an error in the text of *Rājataraṅgiṇi*. See *Rājat.*, iii, 470.
12. The succession list of Gonanda rulers in *Rājataraṅgiṇī* does not include any king by the name of Onta Dev. However, a silver coin of Lahkhana, the grandson of Pravarasena, bears the legend (Raja Lahkhana Udyāditya. See Cunningham's *Later Indo-Scythians*, p. 97. Onta Dev might be the scribe's mis-writing of Udyāditya who ruled for thirteen years (3286-3299 *Laukika*).
13. Lalitāditya Muktāpīd (377 *Laukika* / A.D. 700-736), the fifth ruler in the line of Kārkoṭa dynasty, ruled for thirty-six years, seven months and eleven days and not eighty years. See *Rājat.*, i, 136 and iv, 366.
14. On the site of Parihāsapura and the identification of its shrines with the ruins of Paraspor Udar, see *Rājat.*, Vol. II, Note F.

city'.[15] In it he built idol-houses, in which he installed huge idols. Each of these measured sixty yards in height.[16] It is said that in those days it was the usual height of human beings, and a man's shoulders were as broad as he was tall. Whatever *Zu'l-Qarnain*[17] asked of the idol, it was granted to him. The idol was worshipped ardently in his days.[18]

In those days there lived a man who possessed two jewels. The property of one of these was that if cast into an ocean it could dry up all its water, making it possible for anybody to walk across the dried-up path. The property of the other jewel was that when held in front of an ocean, the first one would be drawn to it and water would recede to its original level. *Zu'l-Qarnain* wanted to buy these two jewels, but the owner declined to part with them, saying that none but Shākyamuni was capable of taking them away from him. Shākyamuni means one who can transfer his soul into another body. [The owner of the jewels] said that he had

15. Kalhaṇa's version is that Lalitāditya built the town at, a time when he was given to merry jesting (*parihāsa*) and, therefore, its name. See *Rājat.*, i, 194.
16. Kalhaṇa mentions a great stone pillar, fifty-four spans high, on the top of which Lalitāditya installed the image of Garuḍa. *Ibid.*
17. The title *Zu'l-Qarniain* suggests that the author has drawn the material from some Persian or Arabic source. For speculations about the identification of *Zu'l-Qarnain*, whose mention is made in the Qur'ān, see *Dāiratu'l-Ma 'ārif*, Lahore, 1973, Vol. X, pp. 61-62 and Maulānā Abu'l-Kalām Āzād's *Tarjumānu'l-Qur'ān*, *sūra al-Kahaf*, 18.
18. It cannot be said with certainty which of the several idols installed by Lalitāditya was ardently worshipped. Kalhaṇa mentions several temples of his; Parihāsakeśava, Muktākeśava, Govardhanadhara, and Bṛhadbuddha. See *Rājat.*, i, 195 and *et seq*. However, the site of the temple Jyeṣṭharudra (present-day Zithyer) built by Lalitāditya is still visited by Kashmiri Pandits. See *Rājat.*, i, 113n.

been freed from all privations and hardships by means of these two jewels.[19]

After the sixth year,[20] he (*Zu'l-Qarnain*) returned to Kashmir and entrusted the city of Kashmir to his grandson named Ratnātīr.[21] Then he proceeded to conquer foreign lands; he did not return nor did anyone bring the news of how he died.[22]

His grandson Vinayāditya proceeded to conquer foreign lands and captured many cities. At last he came to a city in the East. Its king was made to fear Vinayāditya; he consulted his ministers and nobles to seek their opinion in this matter. His senior ministers submitted to him that Ratnātīr was a mighty king and they could not stand against him in battle. His chief minister said to him that it was difficult to repel his attack. But now that the king had asked for his counsel, he would advise him to surrender to Vinayāditya. This would enrage him and he would order that his nose be chopped off which would be followed by his expulsion from the city. After his nose would be chopped off and following his expulsion [from the city], he would join the enemy and devise some plan of destroying him.

When the enemy came to know of the minister's affairs and the news reached Vinayāditya, he made him his

---

19. This seems to be a distorted version of the story given in *Rājataraṅgiṇī* about Cankuṇa, the brother of the magician Kankanavarsa, whom Lalitāditya had brought from Tukhāra. See *Rājat.*, i, 246 *et seq.* For an explanation of the allegory, see verse 260. For Tuhkhārā, see *J.R.A.S.* (NE), Vol. VI, p. 94 *et seq.*
20. It is not clear whether it is the sixth year of his reign or of his expedition outside his lands.
21. No historical work lists this name among the successors of Lalitāditya.
22. Lalitāditya's last instructions to his ministers through their messenger indicate that he had taken a firm decision not to return to Kashmir from the extensive expeditions in the cold northern regions. See *Rājat.*, i, 337.

associate in conquering the neighbouring lands. The crafty minister, full of deceit and guile as he was, led Vinayāditya to take a route where no water was available for ten to twelve days [of their journey], and a fairly large number of his men and beasts perished. Seeing through the deceit and craftiness of the minister, Vinayāditya asked him what his objective was in [doing this]. The minister told him that he wanted to get rid of him so that the country of his king was spared the scourge that he was. When Vinayāditya heard this, he gave him a robe of honour and other rewards and also extended favour to his king.

From there Vinayāditya went to the countries of Kesh and Bahrain where he met with a disastrous defeat resulting in heavy loss of men and material. Along with a handful of his followers, the king fell into the hands of the king of Bahrain who placed them all in the custody of his mother, so that she could keep an eye on them. One day Vinayāditya threatened her with dire consequences for her son. Completely bewildered, she asked him how his capacity for retaliation had grown during his captivity.

Meanwhile, there blew a strong gale and he, as well as the mother of the king, embarked for Mabar.[23] In that place there was a man-eater and the king found himself unable to kill it. Vinayāditya put his left hand into the jaw of the lion and with his right hand rent it asunder, which surprised the king of Mabar. He summoned him to his presence and bestowed upon him robes of honour and other rewards and gave him his daughter in marriage.[24] A large contingent of

23. Muslim historians have generally used Mābār for Mālābār, which is a town on the south-western coast of India.

24. In *Rājataraṅgiṇī*, the story of the killing of a man-eater is associated with King Lalitāditya's grandson Jayāpīḍa. It was King Jayanta of Gauḍa who gave his daughter Kalyāṇa Devi in marriage to King Jayāpīḍa for his bravery in killing the lion. The village of Kalyāṇapura (present-day Kalampur) was founded by her. See *Rājat.*, i, 453.

troops was despatched under his command to conquer the country of Pārs.[25] He brought those lands under his sway and totally subjugated their people. Then he went back to Kashmir to continue with his rule over that land.

Once, while he was riding a horse, his whip slipped out of his hand. Thereupon he bade one of his attendants present there to reach him the whip. The attendant declined to oblige [him] saying that it was not his job. He was a courier called *Potkān* in Kashmiri. Enraged by his audacity, the king ordered that he be given a proper assignment forthwith. Then he wrote down a message, handed over the document to him, and directed [him] to carry it to the ruler of Gang? which is a big and famous city of India. The name of the ruler of this city was Dados [*sic*].[26] The message was that the king of Gang[?] despatch one thousand and five boats forthwith to him for the purpose of building a fort. Hardly had the messenger embarked when an enormous fish gulped down the boat along with all the passengers. The messenger had a sword with which he pierced the belly of the fish, which caused its death.[27] The carcass was cast ashore near the city of Kajendān. The messenger emerged from the belly of the fish, which amazed the people of Kajendān. They enquired of him about this happening. As a proof of what he had told them, they found the letters of command from [the king of Kashmir] on his person, and carried these to the king of Gang. On knowing all that had happened, the king of Gang despatched along with the *Potkān* a convoy of one

25. Focus is on reference to Pārs, the southern province of Iran.
26. According to Ḥasan, the name of the king was Vibhīṣṇa. See *TḤK*, p. 94.
27. There are several versions of this story. Kalhaṇa, for example, writes that king Jayāpīḍa once sent one of his envoys to bring five Rākṣasas from the king of Laṅkā. The envoy fell from the ship into the sea and was devoured by a great fish. He, however, freed himself by destroying it. See *Rājat.*, i, 503-4. Also *The Rājataraṅgiṇī of Jonarāja*, tr. J.C. Dutt, New Delhi, 1986, p. 94.

thousand and five boats. When he reached the outskirts of the city of Kashmir, he informed the king about the coming of the demons of the ruler of Gang. The ruler of Kashmir sent pulses and many thorny fruits for them. The daily quota of ration for the demons, consisting of pulses and cereals, was sent to them till the fort was completed at Andarkol.[28] Here the king reigned for seventy years. Then he handed over the reins of government to his son named Bardanatant[29] [*sic*]. The kingship then passed on to Kashshil [*sic*], and then to Rama Chand, and after his death to Onta Dev. He was miserly and so greedy for wealth that he ordered his daughters to take to prostitution in the streets to extract money from people.

There was a man, Brāhman by name, who was notorious for his licentiousness. After his death he was survived by his wife and son, who fell in love with the daughter of the king. On learning of her son's passionate love for the princess, his mother admonishingly told him that he had hardly inherited anything from his father which could help him in realizing his objective. All that his father had left behind was a *dinār*,[30] which had been put in his mouth at the time of his cremation. On knowing this, he visited the spot where his father's dead body had been cremated. There he was able to

---

28. Andarkot, the ancient ābhyantara Koṭṭa on the Sumbal lake was built by King Jayāpīḍa. See *Rājat.*, iv, 506-11n, and Bühler's *Report*, p. 13 *et seq*. The story in the text is perhaps a distortion of the event related to the raising of the castle called Jayapura. See *Rājat.*, iv, 506.
29. Possibly the corrupted form of Varman. If so, the possibility is that the author is alluding to the ascendency of the house of Utpala. 'His son,' therefore, refers to Avantiverman, the son of Sukhavarman. See *Rājat.*, v, 713. Another possible name could be Varnata who succeeded his father Yaśaskara in A.D. 948. See *Rājat.*, vi, 90-91. In *TMḤ* it is Barnadadat, the son of Raja Dowla Chand. MS. f. 11[b].
30. Sanskrit *dinnāra* is Kashmiri *dyār*. For details, see *Rājat.*, Note H.

find the coin which he, later on, presented to the princess and succeeded in fulfilling his desire. Next day, along with other girls, she went to see the king. He was delighted to see the standard coin, and bade his nobles to summon its owner. The Brāhman's son presented himself [before the king]. He asked him how he had procured the *dinār* and asked him questions about his passionate love [for the princess]. After knowing the whole story, he sought from his sagacious minister an answer to the question whether a person carried with him any worldly possessions after his death. The minister told him that a dead man carried with him nothing but memories of his good deeds, his even-handed justice to his subjects and of his acts of enduring benevolence. On hearing these words, the king repented over his deeds. He then ordered the building of schools, laying of the foundations of prayer-houses, and construction of bridges and roads. He distributed all his worldly possessions among the destitute and the mendicants. He then restored to his subjects their due rights. Of his line there were nine [persons], who ruled one after another over a period of three hundred and sixty years. During their reign they amassed three hundred and sixty treasures, which were ordered to be sealed.

In those days, there lived a distraught person, who held a stone under his arm and went to the king exhorting him to bury his treasure (the stone) along with his treasure. The king said to him, "O you mad person! What you have is a stone and not a treasure." He replied that a profitless treasure, a remorseless [*sic*] heart, and untimely anger were of a lesser value than that stone. The king uttered a cry, beat his head, and told him that he was right. He added that one should pay attention to words and not to the person who utters them. He opened his treasures and distributed their wealth among soldiers, destitutes and the poor. Soon after, the king breathed his last.

During his days, there lived a hermit who, on hearing the news of the king's death, expressed sorrow for the loss of his charitable acts. He transferred his soul into the body of the [dead] king and brought him back to life. The king expressed his thanks to God for having been revived to life after his death. This news spread through the lands of India. Learned men assembled to make a submission to the king that enquiries be made if someone had expired recently. These revealed that a hermit had died and his body had been burnt immediately lest the soul returned to it. Thereafter the king ruled for thirty-six years and then died.

His death led to dissension among the nobles. They resolved that whosoever entered the city gate first on the next morning would be proclaimed king. The first to do so next morning was a mendicant. He was made king and the crown and the throne were given to him. His descendants ruled for four hundred years. The last of their house was named Harshid [*sic*].[31] He invented the art of carving idols out of wood, stone, chalk and clay, [whereas] formerly these used to be cast in gold and silver[32] only. Another king[33] who lived in those days had two sons. Harshid [*sic*] decided to kill both of them because his nobles[34] were favourably disposed towards them. On learning of Harsha's intention, both of them fled for their lives.[35] He pursued them but was unable to lay his hands on them. However, he killed their parents and returned [to his place]. The boys received the

31. Perhaps Harṣa (A.D. 1089-1101), the last ruler of the first Lohāra dynasty.
32. That Harṣa was versed in "all the sciences" is attested to by Kalhaṇa in his lengthy account of Harṣa. But there is no reference to his ability to carve idols out of wood, etc. See *Rājat.*, i, 941.
33. Perhaps it is a reference to Malla, who was of the line of Harṣa.
34. It could possibly be Thakkanā, the most outstanding of Harṣa's nobles. *Rājat.*, vii, 1252.
35. The two brothers took refuge with the powerful Dāmaras of Utrāsa (Votrus). *Rājat.*, vii, 1254, II. 474.

news of the killing of their mother[36] and sought assistance from the rulers of neighbouring regions.[37] They marched against Harsha. In the fighting that ensued, he was defeated and killed.[38] His domain, crown and throne passed on to the elder of the two brothers, who meted out justice [to his people]. Twelve persons of his line reigned successively; the last of them, Shiv Dev by name, ruled in A.H. 750 (A.D. 1349(?)).[39]

During his days, there lived a king in India named Shri ⁓[40] who had a giant-like physique. He attacked the king of Kashmir, killed him and occupied his country. He [Shri ⁓] ruled for a hundred years. Towards the end [of his reign], he was attacked by Shri [Shir ?] Akramadit [*sic*][41] who wrested from him the city of Kashmir. He (Shri) was killed, leaving behind him his minor daughter and son, who fled to a foreign country. For many years they lived in the hollow of a tree. In due course of time their progeny increased numerically ⁓. When asked about their antecedents, they said that they were the offspring of the tree. They also said

---

36. If the allusion is to the sons of Malla, then it was the father (Malla) who had been killed and not the mother. See *Rājat.*, vii, 1481 *et seq.*
37. These could possibly be the rulers of Rājpuri (Rājouri) and the king of Kālinjar. See *Rājat.*, vii, 1256.
38. Perhaps the author refers to the struggle for power between Harṣa and the two sons of Malla, Sussala and Uccala, and the killing of Harṣa in A.D. 1101. See *Rājat.*, vii, 1254.
39. Suh Dev was the last of the Hindu rulers of Kashmir. He ruled for nineteen years and four months. See *TḤK*, p. 160.
40. There is a gap in the text. Subsequent gaps will be marked as ⁓.
41. He could possibly be the same Vikramāditya who is mentioned by Hiuen-tsiang as the predecessor of Śilāditya. He ruled in the first half of the sixth century. See Max Müller's *India*, p. 286, and *J. Bo. Br. R.A.S.*, 1861, p. 208. Kalhaṇa's chronicle does not record Vikramāditya's expedition to Kashmir. But he had decreed that Mātṛgupta would be the lord of Kashmir. See *Rājat.*, iii, 125, and *TMḤ*, MS. f. 14[b].

that formerly there lived a king in India Shri Harsha Dev by name, who had given Kashmir to their ancestors. Then they attended to the task of developing Kashmir. He and his descendants reigned for three hundred years. They were followed by the aforesaid Shri Akramadit [*sic*]. Then came Rāma, the paternal uncle of Shiv Dev. He was attacked by the Mongol army. Under the orders of Qāān[42] (Gur), the commander of the troops [of Qāān] besieged the city of Kashmir and plundered its people. Ram Dev tried to run away [on horseback] but was pursued by the enemy. He jumped into a river and crossed it.

The Mongols stayed on in Kashmir for six months, plundering and pillaging. After they returned to their native land, Ram Dev re-entered Kashmir. He gained control over the kingdom, defeated the Mongols, and later on raised an army. When Miku (Mangu) Qāān[43] came to know of it, he sent his troops under the command of Salinuyān to deal with Ram Dev. The city of Kashmir was once again besieged and its elders were put to the sword or taken prisoner. After Ram Dev's death, his brother, Laxma (Laxman) Dev, ascended the throne on the orders of Miku (Mangu) Qāān and Hulāgū Qāān.[44]

---

42. The allusion may be to an incursion by the troops of Chingiz or Hulāagū. For details of Mongols in Kashmir, see K. Jahn's "A Note on Kashmir and the Mongols," in *Central Asiatic Journal*, II(3), 1956, pp. 176-80. Also see *The World History of Rashīd al-Dīn*, (tr. Basil Gray), London, 1978, 6th Chapter, Plate 23.
43. Mangū Qā'ān (Khān) was the grandson of Chingiz, and these events took place during A.D. 1251 to 1256. During the reign of Mangū, two great, expeditions were sent against China and Persia. The Chinese expedition was entrusted to Kublai, a brother of Mangū. See Browne's *Literary History of Persia*, Vol. II, p. 452.
44. The Mongol incursion into Kashmir could have been a part of Kublai's expedition to China. But Hulāgū's consent to Laxman Dev's accession to the throne of Kashmir must have been given by him after he assumed power following the death of Mangū.

Laxman Dev died in A.H. 531 (A.D. 1136), and was succeeded by Zeyeh Sehm Dev[45] as the lord of Kashmir. During his reign in A.H. 535 (A.D. 1140), Malla Chand,[46] Rājā of Nagarkot, came to Kashmir and, after aligning himself with Zeyeh Sehm Dev, requested him to make him the commander of his troops.[47] Zeyeh Sehm Dev reigned for about twenty-seven years and died in A.H. 558 (A.D. 1163).[48] He was succeeded by his son Parmat Dev[49] who reigned for nine years and six months and died in A.H. 568 (A.D. 1172). After him, came his son Vanta Dev [Onta Dev], who reigned for nine years and two days and died in A.H. 577 (A.D. 1181). His son Bupeh (Vupeh) Dev remained in power for nine years, four months and two days, and died in A.H. 586 (A.D. 1190). Then came his son[50] Zaseh Dev[51] who reigned for eighteen years and thirteen days until his death in A.H. 604 (A.D. 1208). He was succeeded by his son Zageh Dev, who, after ruling for fourteen years and two months, died in A.H. 618 (A.D. 1221).[52] He was succeeded by his son Razeh Dev.

---

45. He is Jayasiṁha of *Rājat.* who ruled from A.D. 1128 to 1149. He is known as Jayasiṁha Dev and Jayasiṁha Rāj Dev. See *J.A.S.B.*, 1879, p. 281.
46. Mallaçandra, scion of Suśrama, the ruler of Trigarta, See *Jonar.*, p. 50, 2n.
47. Jayasiṁha's troops under the command of Mallaçandra fought the Turks. See *Jonar.*, p. 51, 2n. Also see *TMḤ*, MS. f. 31, and *TNK*, MS. f. 35.
48. He was slain by the Turks. See *TḤK*, p. 153.
49. Parmadeva is known variously: Parmānuka in *Jonar.* (p. 52), Parmāndi in *Rājat.* (viii, 1608), Parmāṇdadeva in Tāpar Inscription (S.P.S. Museum, Srinagar), and Parmadeva and Paradeva in the coins. See *J.A.S.B.*, 1879, p. 281.
50. According to Jonarāja, he was succeeded by his younger brother and not his son. See St. 56.
51. Jāssaka in *Jonar.*, p. 54.
52. Jonarājas version of this is different. According to him Jageh Dev was once forced by his ministers to relinquish power and abandon

(*Contd.*)

During the days of this Razeh Dev, Gaga Chand,[53] a descendant of the house of Chandās became the commander of his troops. Earlier rulers [of Kashmir] had confined themselves to the territories of Kashmir, and did not venture to annex the adjoining lands. But this Razeh Dev, on the advice of Gaga Chand, who also commanded his troops, subjugated and annexed the areas adjoining the kingdom of Kashmir. In the *pargana* of Lār, Gaga Chand built the fort of Gagangīr.[54]

Razeh Dev's reign lasted twenty-three years, three months and twenty-nine days. He died in A.H. 641 (A.D. 1243), and after him came his son Sangrām Dev. During his reign, Balād Chand,[55] son of Gaga Chand, assumed the command of his army. He founded the locality of Bardi Mar[56] in the city. When Sangrām Dev constructed Sangram Itoo [*sic*][57] in the town of Bejeh Belareh.[58] Balād Chand founded Chandpuryār[59] in that town.

Sangrām Dev's reign lasted sixteen years, and he died in A.H. 657 (A.D. 1258). His son Ram Dev succeeded him and ruled for twenty-one years, one month and twelve days and

---

Kashmir. See Stt. 67-68. About his death, he writes that he was secretly poisoned by Padma, the Lord of the Gate (*Dvārpati*), St. 74.

53. For detailed information on this, see *Rājat.*, viii, 43, 605 *et seq.*
54. For details see *Rājat.*, 'Introduction', Vol. I, p. 119.
55. According to Jonarāja, he was the Dāmara of Lahara (Kashmiri Lār), who belonged to the family of Malla. He occupied one half of the city of Srinagar and even proclaimed himself as king. See p. 56, 5n, and St. 83. Also see *Wāqa 'at-i-Kashmir*, p. 25.
56. Blāḍhyamaṭha in *Rājat.*, Vol. II, p. 448, and Baldi Mar in *TḤK*, p. 157. Also see *Jonar*, St. 82.
57. Setu (?), Sangrām mohalla. See *TḤK*, p. 158.
58. It is the present-day Bijbehara (Kashmiri Vejehbror).
59. Hariṣçandrapora in *Amarnāth Mahātmya*, ed. Nilakanth Gurtu and Dinā Nath Yachh, Srinagar, 1959, p. 41. Chandrayar in *TḤK*, p. 158, and Tsendradār/Tsandanyār in present-day Kashmiri.

died in A.H. 678 (A.D. 1279).[60] Then came his son Lachman Dev[61] who ruled for thirteen years, three months and twelve days. The command of his troops was in the hands of Balād Chand's son Sangrām Chand.[62] In A.H. 691 (A.D. 1293), Lachman Dev breathed his last,[63] and was succeeded by his son[64] Simha Dev who reigned for fourteen years and six months and died[65] in A.H. 705 (A.D. 1305). Then came his son[66] Suh Dev who ruled for nineteen years, three months and twenty-five days. Their commander was Rama Chand the son of Sangrām Chand.

---

60. Ram Deva's queen Samudra constructed a *maṭha* in Srinagar. It was named Samudramaṭha which has given its name to the present-day locality of Sudramar. See *Jonar*, p. 59 and *Rājat.*, Vol. II, p. 450.
61. Lachman Dev, according to Jonarāja, was Rām Dev's adopted son. See, Stt. 108-9.
62. Several historians have written about the valorous deeds of this powerful Dāmara. According to Jonarāja, he succeeded in repulsing the invasion of the Turks (Turuṣkas) led by Khajlak (Kajjala). See St. 116, 118. See also Eliot's *History*, Vol. III, pp. 525-27, and *TḤK*, p. 159.
63. His qeen Ahalā constructed a *maṭha* called Ahlāmaṭha, which gives name to the present-day Ahlamar locality. See *Jonar*, p. 60, 1n.
64. This relationship is not endorsed by Jonarāja. See St. 128.
65. He was assassinated by Darya with the support of Kāmasūha. See *Jonar*, St. 128.
66. According to *Jonar*, he was not his son but brother. See p. 60.

Chapter II

Zulchū and Rinchan

Shāh Mīr, now known by the title Sulṭān Shamsu'd-Dīn, a descendant of the rulers of Swādgīr,[1] came to the Kingdom of Kashmir during the reign of Suh Dev.[2] The reason for his coming to Kashmir was this: His grandfather [or ancestor] Waqūr Shāh was a pious and righteous man. He had received spiritual training from the saints of a recognized order and the Shaykhs who followed the path of truth. He had undergone severe penance which helped him to attain knowledge and a state of purity of the inner self. Through an intuitive observation of the world of the spirit, he had announced: "My son Ṭāhir will be given a son

1. Originally from pançagahvara in Rajouri region and not from Swādgīr. See *Jonar.*, p. 64. About Shāh Mīr's Pandava ancestors, see *Jonar.*, p. 62; *Āin-i-Akbarī*, Vol. II, p. 386; and *Tabaqāt-i-Akzarī* (Calcutta, text), Vol. iii, p. 424. Malik Ḥaidar is of the view that Shāh Mīr came to Kashmir as a dervish, which seems to put his royal ancestory in doubt. *TMḤ*, MS, f. 28b.
2. One of the very remarkable features of the reign of Suh Dev is that during his rule many outsiders came into Kashmir who played a significant role in its future affairs. Suh Dev seems to have been a very tolerant king. This is attested to by Jonarāja. Commenting on his account of Suh Dev (A.D. 1301-20), the learned Śrikanṭh Koul writes: ... it appears from Jonarāja's poetical language that Suh Dev was munificent in providing means of subsistance to outsiders who had entered the valley in search of employment. In fact the outsiders were mercenary recruits, refugees, and travellers patronized ... by the king...." *Jonar.*, p. 62.

named Shāh Mīr who will become the ruler of Kashmir and assume the title Shamsu'd-Dīn. The kingdom of that region and the government of those lands will remain entrusted to and confirmed in the hands of his descendants for a long time."

When Shāh Mīr came of age, he heard this story from his father and his relatives. He believed in the uncanny and extraordinary feats of his ancestors. Encouraged by the prophecy[3], he migrated to Kashmir along with his wife and children. When Suh Dev received the news of his arrival in Baramulla he directed that arrangements be made for his stay at Dwārksīl[4] where he be provided with means for his living.

Lankar Chak

It was during the days of Suh Dev that one Lankar Chak,[5] the forebear of the Chaks, abandoned the lands of Dārdu[6] and moved to Drāv because of a family feud. He then migrated to Kashmir with his wife and children and settled in the village of Trehgām.[7] As God willed, the same village became the seat of the Chaks [later on].

---

3. According to Jonarāja the goddess Mahādevī came to Śahmīra in a dream in which she told him that he would become the king of Kashmir. See *Jonar.*, Stt. 138-39. Ḥasan has reproduced the version of the story presented in the text from Ferishta's *Tārīkh*. See *TḤK*, p. 161. However, there is no mention of either of these two versions in *TMḤ*. It seems more a myth than reality.
4. Originally called Dvārvati. See al-Birūnī's *India*, (tr. Sachau), Vol. II, p. 313, and *Rājat.*, Vol. II, p. 480.
5. Lankarchak is a corruption of Alaṁkaracakra. See *Rājat.,* Vol. II, p. 341.
6. They actually came from the village Barshal in Dārdu. See *TḤK*, p. 217. For Dārdu and Drāv, see *Rājat.*, Vol. II, p. 282 and i, p. 93, vii, 201, 1130.
7. Now in Kupwāra district.

Rinchan

It was during the reign of Suh Dev that Rinchan came to Kashmir from the dominion of Tibet[8] on account of the hostility he faced from his enemies and adversaries.[9] On reaching Kashmir, he approached Rama Chand, the commander of Suh Dev's army, who gave him a dwelling place at Gagangīr.[10]

Zulchū's Ravages

Zulchū's[11] [Zulju's] incursion into Kashmir also took place during the reign of Suh Dev. Chroniclers of the events of Kashmir have not recorded an event more disastrous and catastrophic than Zulchū's raid. Its details are given below.

In the early spring of A.H. 727 (A.D. 1323), a king[12] Zulchū by name and confirmed as Zulājī by Mīrzā Ḥaidar[13]

8. There are conflicting views about Rinchan's status in Tibet. See *TḤK*, p. 161. Malik Ḥaidar states that he was just a noble person of his land. See *TMḤ*, MS. f. 28[b].
9. This is contradicted by Jonarāja and Malik Ḥaidar. Both of them state that he ran away because of the opposition from his relatives. See *Jonar.*, Stt. 149-52; and *TMḤ*, MS. f. 25[b].
10. Malik Ḥaidar makes no mention of such a request. But Ḥasan confirms that he sought military assistance from Rama Chand in the fort of Gagangīr. See *TḤK*, p. 161.
11. Jonarāja names him as Dulāça. See *Jonar.*, St. 142.
12. There are conflicting views about his status in the country of his origin. Ḥasan, who calls him Zu'l-Qadr Khān, states that he was a grandchild of Hulāgū from his daughter's line. See *TḤK*, p. 162. Malik Ḥaidar's opinion is more assured when he states that he was the ruler of Turkestān. See *TMḤ*, MS. 29[a]. Jonarāja, however, says that he was a general in the army of Emperor Karmasena. See *Jonar.*, St. 142. This seems to be correct because Śrikaṇṭha Koul writes that Dulāça (Jonarāja's version of Zulchū's name), is not the personal name of Zulchū, but a corruption of Darakechen, a military office under the Mongols. See *Jonar.*, p. 165.
13. Mirzā Ḥaidar Dughlat, the author of *Tārīkh-i-Rashīdī*.

entered [the valley] via Baramulla at the head of seventy thousand Mongol and Turk soldiers and horsemen.[14] From there he ordered his troops to carry out a wholesale massacre of the natives. Whosoever fell into their hands between the boundaries of Kāmarāj[15] and the extreme end of Marāj[16] was put to the sword. People who had run away into mountains and forests were captured. Men were killed; women and children were made prisoners and sold to the merchants and traders of Cathay who had accompanied his troops. All the buildings of the city and the villages [of Kashmir] were burnt. His troops consumed as much of foodgrains as they needed and whatever remained they destroyed The whole of Kashmir was subjected to destruction by their ungodly acts.

Suh Dev, the lord and ruler of Kashmir, was much disheartened and discouraged by the tyranny and corruption of Zulchū. With a handful of his close associates he fled towards Kāthwār. His commander Rama Chand shut himself up in the fort at Gagangīr[17] [*sic*] in the *pargana* of Lār. Zulchū's troops went on killing people and looting their possessions; nobody dared to come out of their hiding places in forests and mountains. The people of Kashmir were reduced to such a state of helplessness that they could not attend to their work of tilling the land. The result was that all arable lands in Kashmir remained unattended and uncultivated. Foodgrains stocked during the previous year were partly consumed and partly destroyed by his troops

---

14. The text obviously is silent about how the king of Kashmir reacted to his invasion. Malik Ḥaidar says that unable to resist Zulchū's attack, Suh Dev the ruler of Kashmir fled to Kathwār. See *TMḤ*, MS. f. 29[b].
15. See *Rājat.*, ii, 476-90.
16. *Ibid.*
17. The text is not clear. Ḥasan writes that the fort was that of Gagangīr. *TḤK*, p. 162.

who now faced hunger and famine and awaited death. In this way they "cast their boat of life into the whirlpool of disappointment and frustration."

[*verses*]

These alien troops resorted to indiscriminate bloodshed, killing and pillaging beyond all limits for a period of about eight months.

When the sun crossed the Capricorn in the zodiac, his [Zulchū's] soldiers were faced with an acute scarcity of foodgrains and hence decided to flee this land. They deliberated over the question of the route they should adopt to come out of this land, and enquired about the shortest route to India from the prisoners and the detenus who suggested the road via Tarbal.[18] They proceeded to India by the same route along with the prisoners. On reaching the top of the mountain, God's wrath hurled upon them a rain of destruction. Thunderbolts were let loose. Such was the onslaught of rain and snow that all the soldiers, the Turks and the prisoners met with their death and nobody survived.[19]

The lands of Kashmir were thus liberated from the ravages of the Turks and Zulchū. The people of Kashmir who had been forced to hide came out of their hiding places and went back to their homes and dwelling places in the hope of finding survivors among their kith and kin, their clan, or neighbours or well-wishers. They found that the

---

18. Name of a pass in the mountainous area of Divsar *pargana*. See *Jonar*., p. 69, 1n. The route over it led to Viṣalātā (Śrivara, i, 7. 206-7), identified with Bichlāri river valley by Stein. See *Rājat*., viii, 177n. Tarbal in *TMḤ*, MS. f. 29[b] and Khori in Divsar mountains in *TḤK*, p. 163. One more possible reading of this word can be Barbal. See *Rājat*., Vol. II, p. 399.
19. Fifty thousand Kashmiri captives perished in the disaster. See *TMḤ*, MS. Cat. No. 39, f. 56, and *TNK*, MS. Cat. f. 40[b].

domain of Kashmir had been totally destroyed.[20] They frantically searched from place to place, but could not find any of their relatives, friends, or acquaintances. They were so much overwhelmed by grief that they preferred death to life. For years on end, the lands in Kashmir remained barren, uncultivated and unproductive, so much so that though two hundred and seventy years have elapsed, every stretch of uncultivated and unattended land even now is traced to that period. Hence the saying: "Here Zulchū cultivated turf."

Finding that Kashmir was in a state of desolation, the depradators and robbers[21] living in the mountains poured [into it] from all sides; they plundered the remaining people and took their womenfolk and children as captives. In each *pargana*, forty or fifty villagers formed a group and chose one person as their leader. They procured various kinds of weapons and resolved to protect their families, their lives and their property. In due course of time they captured a fort in each *pargana*, appointed a *kotwāl* to take charge of it and claimed to be independent. None of them felt obliged to yield to the authority of others.

Rinchan's Plot

In the *pargana* of Lār, Rinchan raised a group of soldiers.[22] He aspired to be the master of the land and sent his men to

20. Jonarāja describes the ravages tellingly: "Depopulated, uncultivated, grainless, and gramineous, the country of Kashmir offered, as it were, the sight of primal chaos." See *Jonar.*, St. 162. Ḥasan says that out of a hundred persons only one person survived and the city (of Srinagar) shrank to eleven families. *TḤK*, p. 163.
21. The robbers belonged to the tribe of Khaśas of Khakhās. See *Rājat.*, Vol. II, p. 430 and *TḤK*, p. 164. Jonarāja describes them as Abhisāras, who lived between Vitastā and Chandrabhāga (the rivers of Jhelum and Chenāb). See *Jonar.*, St. 163. Also see *Rājat.*, i, 180n.
22. Ḥasan writes that Rinchan was provided soldiers by Rama Chand, who had proclaimed himself king, to suppress the Khaśas. See *TḤK*, p. 164.

the fort of Rama Chand in the guise of merchants with weapons concealed in their luggage.[23] They were instructed that as soon as he (Rinchan) arrived in the neighbourhood of the fort and signalled for attack and killing, they should throw open the gates of the fort from inside. Following his instructions his men entered into the fort of Rama Chand and he, too, proceeded thither the same night. He from outside and his men from inside of the fort resorted to killing and fighting [Rama Chand's men]. In the encounter that followed Rama Chand was killed.

Rama Chand's son Rāvan Chand and his wife and children were taken prisoner. Thus in A.H. 725 (A.D. 1324), Rinchan became the ruler and lord of this land. Not being a native,[24] he took the pragmatic view that it would not be possible for him to rule Kashmir unless he won over its people as his friends and supporters. Therefore, he bestowed favours upon Rāvan Chand to bring him closer to himself and married his sister (Rama Chand's daughter) Kotehren.[25] He conferred upon Rāvan Chand the *pargana* of Lār and the dominion of Tibet.

In those days the custom prevailing in this land was that if respect had to be shown to anyone, the title 'Renu' would be appended to his name. It was regarded as a mark of distinction. The meaning of the word 'Raina' is 'master and possessor.' For the same reason Rinchan conferred upon

---

23. This treacherous act is confirmed by Malik Ḥaidar and Jonarāja. See *TMḤ*, MS. f. 30[a] and *Jonar.*, Stt. 167-69. Ḥasan writes that arms were concealed in bags of charcoal which were unloaded by the Tibetan merchants in the cells of the fort at Andarkot. *TḤK*, p. 164.
24. Ḥasan writes that Kashmiris had shown their thankfulness to Rinchan for delivering them from the ravages of Khahān (Khaśas) by offering him presents in cash and kind. Some of these had been sent by him to Rama Chand also. See *TḤK*, p. 164.
25. From her he got a son named Ḥaidar Khān; Shāh Mirzā was appointed his tutor (*atālīq*). See *TḤK*, p. 165.

Rāvan Chand the title of 'Renu' which has been retained by that house to this day.[26]

Suh Dev, the ruler of this land, who had fled to Kāthwār[27] because of the threat posed by Zulchū, returned in the hope of recapturing his dominion. He confronted Rinchan, who, some time back, had been one among his inferior servants, but he could not match him on the battlefield and, after suffering another defeat, turned back to Kāthwār. In this way the government of his domain passed into the hands of Rinchan.

Rinchan's Wisdom

Rinchan was not bound by any religion or community.[28] However, during his rule, he tried to mete out even-handed justice to his subjects as far as he could, which helped the lands of Kashmir to achieve economic prosperity. In those days nobody would settle public disputes in accordance with the tenets of Muḥammadan religion. That is why Rinchan solved very difficult problems of his people with the help of his intelligence, understanding, sagacity, and wisdom.[29] The episode of the claim of two mares over a colt and the jumping of one of them into a stream is one of the examples of wisdom.[30] During his reign, a colt was suckled by two mares and thus had become intimate with both of them to such an extent that the onlookers could not make out its real mother. [This led to a situation in which] an imposter staked his claim of ownership of the colt and pressed it hard upon the real owner. Both of them were compelled to take their

26. Raina is the late version of Rajānaka. See *Rājat.*, iv, 489n.
27. Now called Kishtwār. See *TMḤ*, MS. f. 29^{b}.
28. Ḥasan contradicts this statement. According to him, Rinchan was a Buddhist. See *TḤK*, Vol. II, p, 166.
29. See *Jonar.*, Stt. 179 and 184.
30. Ḥasan associates this story with Malik Saifu'd-Dīn (Suh Bhat), the chief vizir of Sulṭān 'Alī. See *TḤK*, p. 186.

dispute to Rinchan. The judges of those days, though competent, were indecisive and hesitant in issuing a decree. Rinchan considered the case carefully and using his [gift of] wisdom ordered that both the mares and the colt be driven to the bridge over the canal passing through the city and the colt be hurled into the flowing waters. The two mares were left on the bridge. As soon as the colt fell into water, one of the two mares, moved by motherly instinct, also plunged into the stream and escorted its young one to the bank. The other mare remained impassive and did not budge from its place. In this way it was Rinchan's intelligence which established the genuineness of the real owner and rejected the false claim of the imposter.

Rinchan's Conversion

During the early stages of his career, Rinchan showed no inclination towards any of the existing religions.[31] It was in the fitness of things that he embraced one of these religions and vigorously prayed to God the Merciful.

At this time only a handful of people in Kashmir had embraced Islam. Most of the people were either infidels or dissemblers. But when Rinchan thought of embracing a religion and associating himself with a community he made enquiries about the principles and laws of their religion from the savants among the infidels and the learned men of the times. They beseeched him to join their fold.[32] The Muslims

31. Ḥasan's account of the religions prevailing at that time is amusingly incorrect. According to him they were: Khetri, Vaish, Kaisth and Pārsī. The first three are actually the classes within the Hindu community; The mention of Pārsīs is, however, interesting. Jonarāja has made a revealing comment about Rinchan's religious leanings by stating that "one Devasvami had scruples initiating Rinchana into the Śaivite faith. The refusal was made because Rinchana happened to be Bhautta by birth." *Jonar.*, p. 71.
32. Malik Ḥaidar is of the view that Rinchan was inclined to embrace the religion of the Brahmans. See *TMḤ*, MS. f. 31[a].

also put before him the principles and teachings of the Islamic faith and invited him to embrace their religion. But owing to serious differences between these two religions and the disagreement [prevailing] among the two religious groups, he was not able to reach any decision. Each community considered its religion the true one and each group induced him to embrace its religion. He was in a fix because of the serious differences and glaring contradictions in the views of these communities. Their heated discussions and discourses led him to no satisfactory conclusion. However, blessed as he was with a dispensation for justice, for 'God helps those who help themselves,' he found the right path. He firmly decided that he would embrace the religion of the first man he would meet in the street after coming out of his house the next morning. He also resolved to join the community to which that man belonged.

Next morning he came out of his house. The rays of the sun of divine guidance, bringing every object from darkness to light, liberated him from the darkness of ignorance and disbelief; for all of a sudden, in the neighbourhood of his mansion, he saw a dervish offering *namāz* (the Muslim way of praying), with full devotion. He went towards him. When the dervish had finished his prayer, Rinchan held him by his hand and brought him to his house. Then he called in an interpreter who knew their languages. He asked the dervish his name and then about his religion and the sect he belonged to. The dervish told him that his name was Bulbul Qalandar, that his religion was Islam[33] and that his community was that of Muslims. He disclosed to him that he was a member of the sect of Shāh Ne'matullah Walī. He then mentioned to him some of the miracles performed by the

33. According to Malik Ḥaidar, Bābā Bulbul's answer to Rinchan was: "*garībam*" (I am a stranger). See *TMḤ*, MS. f. 31[a]. Abu'l-Fazl writes that Rinchan accepted Islam because of Shāh Mīr. See *Āin-i-Akbarī*, Vol. II, p. 386.

Prophet, the virtues and superior qualities of 'Alī, the Imām, and lastly, the extraordinary feats of spirituality performed by Shāh Ne'matullah Walī.

[*verses*]

His (Rinchan's) heart had previously been blackened by the beliefs of a false community.[34] Now he subjected himself to the teachings of the religion of Musṭafa (Prophet), and the right principles of the truthful path of Murtaza (Alī), and embraced Islamic religion with sincerity and conviction.[35] He gave up once for all the false and corrupt religions.

In this way Rinchan became the first ruler of Kashmir to be admitted to the Islamic faith. He got a *khānqāh*[36] built for Bābā Bulbul Qalandar in the neighbourhood of his own palace and conferred upon him a *jāgīr*[37] from the income of which expenses could be met for his followers, kinsfolk, the mendicants and casual visitors to the *khānqāh*, who often stayed there. As a result of the abundance of good-will and purity of disposition of this dervish, the *khānqāh* continues to be in a prosperous state even to this day. The grave of Bābā Bulbul is also to be found there. Rinchan also built a mosque[38] for Friday prayers and congregations in the neighbourhood of his lodging and himself joined the Friday congregational prayers regularly besides joining the mass for all the five prescribed times of praying after the Muslim

---

34. This contradicts the author's earlier statement that "Rinchan was not bound by any religion ..." *Supra*, p. 20. See also note 28.
35. The event occurred in A.H. 726 (A.D. 1325). *TMḤ*, MS. f. 32[a]. This reveals that Rinchan was converted by Bulbul Qalandar to Shia' faith.
36. This was perhaps the first *khānqāh* built in Kashmir. *TḤK*, p. 166.
37. Ḥasan writes that a few villages in Nāgām *pargana* were given to him. See *TḤK*, p. 166.
38. Called Rentan (Renteh) Masjid. *Ibid.*, p. 167.

fashion.[39] The mosque built under his instructions caught fire but a smaller mosque made of solid stone was erected in its place [later on].

The first to embrace Islam from the house of Chandās was Rāvan Raina,[40] the younger brother of Kotehren. [Kota Rani], who was brought up by Rinchan.[41] Shāh Mīr, who later earned fame as Sulṭān Shamsu'd-Dīn, was made one of his chiefs and close associates by Rinchan. By Koteh [Rānī], Rinchan got a son and Bābā Bulbul gave him the noble name of Ḥaidar Khān. Rinchan entrusted him to the care of Shāh Mīr who was destined later to become Sulṭān Shamsu'd-Dīn.

39. Malik Ḥaidar is of the opinion that Rinchan's conversion to Islam was followed by mass conversions. See *TMḤ*, MS. f. 32^{b}.
40. A descendant of the house of Rājā Sushram Chand of Nagarkot. Before embracing Islam voluntarily, he held a debate with Bābā Bulbul. *Ibid.*
41. Rāvan Raina received the title Malik from Rinchan. *Ibid.*

Chapter III

Early Shāhmīrs

Sulṭān Shamsu'd-Dīn

Sulṭān Shamsu'd-Dīn was gifted with intelligence and sagacity and established cordial relations with all the leading personalities and chiefs of the domain of Kashmir. He also entered into matrimonial relations with them by giving his daughters in marriage to their sons[1] and by accepting their daughters in marriage to his sons. Thus he established harmonious relations with the nobles and the leading personalities [of Kashmir]. Sometime later, Rinchū (Rinchan), in accordance with the Qurānic saying that "all that lives must taste of death," left the "world of toil for the abode of eternal peace," having reigned for two years and six months. He died in A.H. 727 (A.D. 1326).

Koteh Rani

His widow Koteh Ren[2] (Rānī), with the consent of the chiefs of the day, recalled Uden (Udyana) Dev,[3] the brother of Suh Dev,

1. For details regarding these alliances see *Jonar.*, p 77. The chieftains with whom matrimonial relations were established by Shāh Mīr were of Shankarpora (Pattan), Bhāṅgila (Bengil), Bhṛṅga (Bring), and other places. See *Rājat.*, v, 156n., vii, 499 and Vol. II, p. 468.
2. Malik Ḥaidar says she was a descendant of the Rājās of Hind [*sic*]. *TMḤ*, MS. f. 32[b]. This, however, does not tell us anything about the ruling house to which she belonged.
3. Jonarāja says that Uden Dev was recalled to Kashmir by Śahmīra. *Jonar.*, St. 222.

who had fled to the lands of Swādgīr during the disturbances caused by Zulji (Zulchū). He was installed on the throne and she married him. This Uden (Udyana) Dev was weak and incompetent and given to monastic life. His wife Koteh Ren (Rānī) in effect held the reins of the government of Kashmir. She bore him a son whom she entrusted to the care of one of the chiefs of the land, named Tejeh[4] (Bhikshana) Bhat Kākehpūrī.

At that time, a group of Turk[5] soldiers entered into Kashmir from Hirpur. Coward and pusillanimous as he was, Uden (Udyana) Dev fled towards Tibet, but his wife Koteh Ren (Rānī) exhibited singular courage by infusing a heroic spirit in her brother Rāvan Raina, Sulṭān Shamsu'd-Dīn, and Bhikshana Bhat Kākehpūrī, and managing to rally round her all the *kotwāls* of Kashmir and the people [commandants] of the forts. Weapons for fighting [the enemy] were procured and the Turkish intruders were subjected to harassment. At last truce was made and they [the Turks] were made to quit the land. Negotiations of vital importance in connection with this event were largely conducted by Shāh Mīr. Thus his prestige and position were further enhanced[6] and most of the areas of the kingdom came under his control.[7] Koteh Ren

---

4. Ḥasan gives his name as Tejeh Bhat, but it does not appear to be correct. *TḤK*, p. 167. Jonarāja mentions neither of these names but his version of this seems to be correct when he says that it was Bhaṭṭā Bhikṣana. *Jonar.*, Stt. 274-75. When written in Arabic, the name Bhikhshana/Bhikhna (Kashmiri) can be misread as Pecheh or Tejeh. Malik Ḥaidar says that Tejeh Bhat was a foster-brother of Kotehren. See *TMḤ*, MS. f. 33[a].
5. The Turk invaders were commanded by one Urdun. *TMḤ*, MS. f. 33[a]. Ḥasan writes that he entered into Kashmir via Hirpur pass in A.H. 732 (A.D. 1331). *TḤK*, p. 167.
6. Jonarāja writes that during the disturbances created by Accala the people found a protector in Śahmīra. *Jonār.*, St. 245.
7. He subdued the chieftains of Bohurupa (Bīru): and Samala (Hamal). He burnt Vijayeśa and Cakradhara (Tṣakdar Udar), his

(*Contd.*)

(Rānī) recalled her imbecile husband from Tibet and re-installed him on the throne. In the year A.H. 742 (A.D. 1341), "the cup of his life tumbled upside down as a result of the rotation of spheres."[8] He ruled for fifteen years, two months and two days. Consequent upon his death, his wife Koteh Ren (Rānī) held the reins of kingdom for five months. Her headquarters were at Andarkol [*sic*].[9]

Shāh Mīr found that the realm of Kashmir lacked a government by men of ability. He was reminded of the words of his ancestor and began to nurse the ambition of capturing power and kingship. He took leave of Koteh Ren (Rānī) and settled in the city of Kashmir. Through his genial disposition, he succeeded in winning the favour of the chiefs and elders of the state. He got Bhikshana Bhat Kākehpūrī murdered because he refused to cooperate with him.[10] He assembled the chiefs and besieged Koteh Ren (Rānī) at Andarkol [*sic*]. After overpowering her, he bound her willy-nilly in a marriage contract with himself.[11] Two hundred and

---

stronghold. *Jonar.*, Stt. 252-55. Udyana Deva rewarded Śahmīra by granting him Kramrājya (Kāmrāz) and some other district in propriety rights to his sons Jyamisara (Jamshīd) and Allesera ('Alī Sher). See St. 225.

8. According to Jonarāja, his death was kept a secret by Queen Kotadevi for four days. *Jonar.*, St. 264.
9. Andarkot. For details see *Rājat.*, iv, 506-11n.
10. Jonarāja writes that Śahmīra assassinated Bhaṭṭa Bhiksaṇa (and not Tejeh Bhat) who was one of his political rivals. See note 4 *supra*.
11. The author of the chronicle gives the impression that the marriage of Koteh Ren with Shāh Mīr lasted for some time. This is refuted by several prominent historians. Malik Ḥaidar says that Koteh Ren rejected his marriage proposal because she did not want to marry her subordinate. But because she had been defeated by him, she committed suicide by driving a dagger into her belly. *TMḤ*, MS. f. 34[a]. Ḥasan gives the same story, but with a slight difference in detail. According to him she was compelled by

(*Contd.*)

eleven years elapsed between the beginning of the reign of Zayeh Dev and the time under reference. From Zayeh Dev to Uden (Udyana) Dev, thirteen rulers ruled over Kashmir, generation after generation. Koteh Ren (Rānī) was the fourteenth in order of succession and Rinchan fifteenth in the course of two hundred and eleven years.

In A.H. 742 (A.D. 1341), Shāh Mīr ascended the throne of Kashmir and assumed the title Shamsu'd-Dīn by which he is known even today.[12] He ruled for a period of three years and five months and died in the year A.H. 746 (A.D. 1345). He was survived by two sons, Sulṭān Jamshīd and Sulṭān 'Alāu'd-Dīn.

Sulṭān Jamshīd

Shamsu'd-Dīn was succeeded by his elder son Sulṭān Jamshīd who ruled for a year and two months, after which he fell out with his brother. In an armed confrontation which ensued in the village of Vantipore,[13] Sulṭān Jamshīd suffered a defeat,[14] following which Sulṭān 'Alāu'd-Dīn ascended the throne in A.H. 748 (A.D. 1347).

---

circumstances to agree to his proposal. On the day of their marriage she clad herself in gorgeous robes; but stabbed herself by ripping open her bowels, and said to Shāh Mīr, "This is my acceptance." *THK*, p. 169. Jonarāja, however, denies that they were married. He says that Śahmīra shared her bed for one night and then put her in prison. *Jonar.*, Stt. 305-306.

12. One of the significant acts of Shāh Mīr, which is important from the historical point of view, was his discarding the hitherto prevailing Saptrishi calendar in Kashmir and replacing it by the new Kashmiri calendar, which he invented himself, beginning with the date of accession of Rinchan in A.H. 725 / A.D. 1324. It continued up to the beginning of Mughal rule. *THK*, p. 169.
13. Avantipora. According to Ḥasan, Zenapora. *THK*, p. 170.
14. Ḥasan says that he suffered a defeat because his chief vizier Sirrāju'd-Dīn betrayed him and joined 'Alāu'd-Dīn. *THK*, p. 170.

(*Contd.*)

Alāu'd-Dīn

He ['Alāu'd-Dīn] had two sons, Shihābu'd-Dīn and Quṭbu'd-Dīn. During the reign of 'Alāu'd-Dīn it so happened that his eldest son, Shihābu'd-Dīn, in the course of a hunting expedition, strayed into a jungle in the mountains along with his three companions Chandar, Udsheh Rāwal and Ikhtājī.[15] Their other followers were left far behind. Suddenly there appeared a woman from the woods[16] who had signs of austerity and righteousness stamped on her face. She offered a cup of *sharbet* (drink) to Shihābu'd-Dīn and exhorted him to drink it. He took the cup from her hand unhesitatingly and drank it, leaving only the dregs for his comrades. Chandar drank half a draught out of it. So did Udsheh, leaving nothing for Ikhtājī. Then the woman told them that she would speak to them about the future events of their lives: "The throne and the kingdom shall pass into the hands of this Shihābu'd-Dīn and he shall conquer many more lands and territories which none of the rulers of Kashmir have ever commanded." She told Chandar and Udsheh Rāwal that they would become responsible for discharging vitally important duties in the shaping of [the future] events [of the kingdom]. She further told them that as a proof of what she foretold they would find that this Ikhtājī, who did not have the good luck to drink even a drop out of the cup, would go to the other world before reaching his present destination.

This is confirmed by Jonarāja who says that Sayyaraja (Sirrāj) was promised a reward and position by Allesera ('Alī Sher). *Jonar.*, p. 83.

15. This name does not occur in *TMḤ*. Jonarāja gives two names, Udayashri and Chandraḍārmara and the third man was a groom. J.C. Dutt, (tr.) p. 36.

16. This is confirmed by Malik Ḥaidar. *TMḤ*, MS. f. 34^{b}). But Ḥasan categorically states that she was Lala 'Ārifa. *TḤK*, p. 171. Jonarāja writes that a circle of yoginis appeared from the forest of Vākpushṭā. *The Rājataraṅgiṇī of Jonarāja*, tr J.C. Dutt. Delhi, 1986, pp. 35-36.

They returned from the hunt and, before actually reaching their destination, the messenger of death overtook Ikhtājī: from the world of matter he moved on to that of spirit. This confirmed the authenticity of the predictions made by that woman and they expected that the other items of her predictions would also come true. 'Alāu'd-Dīn's rule lasted twelve years and eight months. He founded the locality of 'Alāu'd-Dīn Pora where he himself lived.[17] In A.H. 761 (A.D. 1359), he breathed his last;[18] he lies buried under a tomb at 'Alāu'd-Dīn Pora.

Sulṭān Shihābu'd-Dīn

After the death of 'Alāu'd-Dīn, his eldest son Shihābu'd-Dīn succeeded him to the throne. Two of his nobles, Chandsar [*sic*] Dev,[19] a descendant of the line of Chandās, and Ujani Raina were the commanders of his troops. Udsheh Rāwal was his adviser and also held the charge of the collector of taxes, duties, and revenues of Kashmir. It was he who imposed *iki* [*sic*] on boatmen which meant that for one week in a month they were required to render service to the king without receiving wages, or remuneration. Many more practices [of extortion, besides the one mentioned] were initiated by him and of these some continue to this day. It was Sulṭān Muḥammad 'Alī Shāh, God Almighty pardon his sins, who discarded the practice of *iki* [imposed] on the boatmen.

---

17. Jonarāja states that he erected two palaces, one at Jayapīdapora, and the other at Rinchanpora (Buddhger). *Jonar.*, p. 84.
18. The date of his death is stated in the chronogram *makānash ferdows*. *TḤK*, p. 171.
19. In Malik Ḥaidar's work he is called Uchal [*sic*] Chand, the son of Rāvan Chand. This Malik Uchal [*sic*] settled in Chādūra where he built a fort, and thereafter his house was called Chādūri. He died while fighting in Laghmān near Kabul. His dead body was brought to Chādūra and buried there. *TMḤ*, MS. f. 36^{b}.

Sulṭān Shihābu'd-Dīn ruled for nineteen years during which he engaged himself mostly in subjugating and annexing adjoining territories to his kingdom. This kept him away from Kashmir and he visited it sparingly. The recounters of the events of kings and the chroniclers of mighty monarchs have recorded in their annals that Kashmir never saw a king of his valour and a warrior of his intrepidity. Details concerning this have been adequately recorded in the history of [illegible] written in Kashmiri (Sanskrit).[20] He [the historian] says that if the stories and anecdotes of his remarkable bravery are fully described, people are likely to ascribe them to his poetical exaggeration and as such would be taken as false. They would doubt their veracity. That is why only brief details are given here:

When Kashmir fell into a state of chaos and confusion because of Zulchū's ravages, it took her considerable time to repair the loss and gradually regain its prosperity. In each *pargana* villagers joined hands and strengthened their forts. They chose one among them as their leader and claimed to be independent and autocratic. They were not prepared to submit themselves to one another's authority. Although some of them did recognize the governor of the city as their overlord and sent presents and gifts to him, yet, strictly speaking, they did not observe the norms of loyalty and submission.

The first and foremost step which Shihābu'd-Dīn took after ascending the throne of his father was to coordinate civil administration of the *parganas* in Kashmir. Within a short time, he welded the whole of Kashmir into a single unit. Some of the defiant chiefs and lords of *parganas* were put to the sword and the others were brought under subjugation.

---

20. This sentence indicates that Jonarāja's *Rājataraṅgiṇī* was one of the sources for our chronicler as far as the history of early Shāh Mīrs is concerned. Also see *Jonar.*, p. 85.

Conquests

Having completed the aforesaid measures in Kashmir, he paid attention to the conquest of the neighbouring lands. At the head of a small contingent of troops he came out from Baramulla.[21] His first conquests were those of the lands of Paklī (Pakhlī) and Swādgīr, followed by the domain of Kakars (Ghakhars). Then he set out for the conquest of Multan. Later he headed towards Kabul and Laghmān[22] to restore order in those places. After the conquest and occupation of these lands, he marched towards Badakhshān, and conquered it. From there, he proceeded towards the mountains of Bulūr, Gilgit, and Dārdu. The next expedition was to Tibet, which he had firmly resolved to conquer. In those days, Tibet was under the suzerainty of the ruler of Kāshghar. On hearing of Sulṭān's expedition he gathered together a large number of soldiers and headed towards Tibet where, eventually, the two hostile forces confronted each other. In the ensuing battle each side showed feats of heroism and bravery. Although the troops of the ruler of Kāshghar outnumbered the Kashmiris, yet, as the saying goes "when God wills the smaller number shall prevail over the larger number," Shihābu'd-Dīn emerged victorious. The Kāshgharian army was routed and their soldiers dispersed helter-skelter. The victorious Shihābu'd-Dīn then proceeded via Tibet to conquer Nagarkot and restore order in those areas. He conquered those regions and from there he entrusted the campaign of Kothwār (Kishtwār) to Malik Chandar.[23] He took possession of the whole of the mountain

---

21. Ḥasan has computed their number at five lakh soldiers and fifty thousand cavalrymen. The command of the troops was put in the hands of Sayyid Ḥasan Bahādur, the son of Sayyid Tāju'd-Dīn, a cousin of Amīr-i-Kabīr Mīr Sayyid 'Alī Hamadānī. *TḤK*, p. 172.
22. Laghmān in Ḥasan, p. 172.
23. Candra, Śūra and Laula were the three Hindu Ḍāmara generals of the Sulṭān. *Jonar.*, Stt. 370, 402.

range right up to Jammu. From each town and land that fell into the hands of Sulṭān Shihābu'd-Dīn, he carried along with him their gallant and famous warriors, war-veterans and war-horses.

After the conquest of Nagarkot, Shihābu'd-Dīn resolved to conquer the lands of Hindustan. For this purpose, he assessed the numerical strength of his army, cavalry and foot-soldiers. The number came to fifty thousand horsemen and five lakh soldiers.[24] With this force, he proceeded towards Delhi to conquer the lands of Hind. The king of Delhi at that time was Feroz Shāh. Shihābu'd-Dīn reached the village of Sateh Ledar.[25] Feroz Shāh also arrived at the same place at the head of a large army. For some months the two armies confronted each other and no one could overpower the other. At last negotiations were started and hostilities ceased.[26] The lands lying beyond Sirhind right up to Kashmir came under the control of Sulṭān Shihābu'd-Dīn. Thus by the grace of the Creator of the World, he returned to Kashmir by Hirpur route carrying his banner of victory and beating the trumpet of his triumph.[27]

24. Ḥasan corroborates this statement. See note 21 *supra*.
25. Satadru (Sutlej) in *Jonar.*, p. 88. For further retails of his conquests, see *Jonar.*, p. 85.
26. Truce was concluded on the initiative of Amīr Kabīr Mīr Sayyid 'Alī Hamadānī. The Amīr proposed the marriage of three daughters of Feroz Shāh with the relatives of Sulṭān Shihābu'd-Dīn. The eldest daughter was married to Ḥasan Khān, the second one to Sulṭān Quṭbu'd-Dīn, and the third one to Sayyid Ḥasan Bahādur. *TḤK*, p. 173, Ḥasan further says that the Amīr came to Kashmir while Shihābu'd-Dīn was fighting with Feroz Shāh. It can be gleaned from Ḥasan that Mīr Sayyid 'Alī Hamadānī first came to Kashmir and then went to Ferozpur to bring about conciliation between Shihābu'd-Dīn and Feroz Shāh.
27. For details concerning the countries or town he conquered, see *Jonar.*, p. 185.

The town of Shihābu'd-Dīn Pora[28] founded during the reign of Sulṭān Shamsu'd-Dīn was re-built and considerably developed after the Sulṭān conquered the Indian lands. It was developed into a pleasure spot where people came for relaxation and enjoyment. He ordered the construction of a Jamia' mosque in that town.[29]

In order to ensure the safety of his country and the security of its borders, the Sulṭān sent there some of his nobles and chiefs. He conferred upon Ujani Raina – a descendant of the line of Chandas – the village of Chādūra as his place of residence.[30] He was sent to Kabul and Laghmān to consolidate gains [of conquest] and to enforce security [of those areas]. He first brought Kabul under control and then attended to the defence of Laghmān. But there he breathed his last and his dead body was carried all the way back to Chādūra where it was buried.

Sulṭān Shihābu'd-Dīn addressed himself to such works as would help him get peace in the world hereafter [illegible]. He arranged a tomb and a burial place for himself to be used after his death. Towards the fag end of his life, he was infused with a zeal for demolishing idol-houses and destroying the temples and idols of the infidels. He destroyed the massive temple at Beejeh Belareh[31] (Bijbehara). He had designs to destroy all the temples and put an end to the entire community of the infidels.[32] But death overtook him in the year A.H. 780 (A.D 1378). As he

---

28. Now called Shahāmpur. The locality comprised sixty thousand houses besides one thousand military camps. *TḤK*, p. 174.
29. Its foundation existed even in Ḥasan's days. See *TḤK*, p. 174.
30. A fort was built by Ujani Raina for himself at Chadūra which continued to be in the control of his descendants till the times of Malik Ḥaidar Chādūra. See *TMḤ*, MS. f. 36[a].
31. Present-day Bejbehara. For details see *Rājat.*, Vol. II, p. 463.
32. Malik Ḥaidar says that he brought many people within the fold of Islamic faith. *TMḤ*, MS. f. 36[b].

lay dying, the glory of kingship, the innumerable troops and a long retinue of liveried servants proved of no avail [to him]. The monarch of his soul that reigned over the realm of his body left his mortal abode and arrived in the everlasting world.[33]

Quṭbu'd-Dīn

He was succeeded by his brother, Sulṭān Quṭbu'd-Dīn,[34] who founded Quṭbu'd-Dīn Pora and made it his residential headquarters. Here he built himself a lofty palace the like of which had not been built by his predecessors, except the palace at Andarkol [*sic*]. The east of the city was selected for a graveyard where he built a tomb [for himself]. A large number of God-fearing men, saints and spiritualists lie buried in that graveyard.

Sayyid 'Alī Hamadānī

Sulṭān Quṭbu'd-Dīn ruled for sixteen years. During his time and in the year A.H. 783 (A.D. 1381), though some say in A.H. 773 (A.D. 1371), His Holiness arrived in Kashmir.[35] God knows better! The protector of the realm of spirituality, the holder of the position of guidance, the denizen of the hermitage where there is none but God, inmate of the Cloister where one merges with the Supreme, monarch on the throne of immortality, the peer of 'Alī, Amīr Sayyid 'Alī Hamadānī, God sanctify his soul, consecrated the land of Kashmir by planting on its soil his most august footsteps.

33. He was buried in the locality of Baldimar; a tomb over his grave was built by Pratāp Singh, a Dogra official under the rule of Mahāraja Ranbīr Singh. See *THK*, p. 175. For Baldimar, the ancient Balāḍhyamaṭha, see *Rājat.*, Vol. II, p. 448.
34. Ḥasan gives his name as Hindāl. *THK*, p. 175.
35. According to Ḥasan, Mīr Sayyid 'Alī Hamadānī visited Kashmir for the second time in A.H. 781/A.D. 1379. *THK*, p. 175. Malik Ḥaidar says that Mīr Sayyid visited Kashmir during the reign of Sulṭān Quṭbu'd-Dīn. *TMḤ*, MS. f. 37[a].

[This event] enhanced the prestige of the inhabitants of this land to supreme heights. Sulṭān Quṭbu'd-Dīn paid him the highest regard by receiving him [in person] with sincerity and conviction. Although Sulṭān Quṭbu'd-Dīn had been admitted to the Islamic faith, in those days none of the *'ulemā* and men of learning in Kashmir preached religion without hypocrisy. The Qāḍīs and the theologians of those days paid scant attention to things permitted or prohibited [in Islamic religion] and, because the teachings of Islamic faith had not been enforced fully, Sulṭān Quṭbu'd-Dīn had married two women who were uterine sisters. When Amīr Sayyid 'Alī Hamadānī came to know of it, he forbade him to do so. Sulṭān Quṭbu'd-Dīn divorced one of his two wives of his free will;[36] with the other he entered into a new marriage contract and made her wear his dress.[37] Sulṭān Sikandar, the Iconoclast, was born to her after this marriage.

In those days the majority of people was that of infidels and polytheists. The inhabitants of this land wore the common and popular dress of the infidels. Sulṭān Quṭbu'd-Dīn also dressed himself after their fashion. But at the behest of the Sayyid, he abandoned that costume and adopted the Muslim dress.

The Sayyid presented to the Sulṭān a cap from his personal wardrobe by way of a token; he considered it a mark of exaltation, and wore it under his crown. All the succeeding rulers of his line observed the practice of wearing it under the crown because they considered it a symbol of exaltation in this world and the other. This practice continued down to the times of Sulṭān Fatḥ Shāh; after his death, it was put in his shroud. A dervish who attended upon the people of that order learnt that the cap

36. This event has not been reported by Malik Ḥaidar.

37. This indicates that they were his Ḥindū wives. The name of Sulṭān Quṭbu'd-Dīn's wife who gave birth to Sikandar was Subhaṭṭā. *Jonar.*, p. 92.

of Amīr Sayyid 'Alī Hamadānī had been put in the shroud [of the dead Sulṭān]. He declared it as a sinister omen, an indication that kingship and authority would forsake that house for good.[38] And so it did happen. Up to that day the rulers of this house had enjoyed independence and were so powerful that they could dismiss anybody they wished from his official position or elevate anyone they liked to a position of command and prestige. But after the death of Fatḥ Shāh, the rulers of the house lost their power and authority. Thereafter each day witnessed a gradual decline in their authority till they were finally replaced by the dynasty of the Chaks, whose account will follow [at its proper place].

Again it needs to be recorded that for some of the time which the holy Amīr spent in Kashmir he lived in a *sarāi* at 'Alāu'd-Dīn Pora. At the site where his *khānqāh* was built, there existed a small temple which was demolished and converted into an estrade on which he offered *namāz* (prayer) five times a day and recited portions of the Qur'ān morning and evening. Sulṭān Quṭbu'd-Dīn occasionally attended these congregational prayers.

In those days there lived a chieftain (Sardar) called Ladi Māgray[39] who belonged to the clan of Māgrays. He came to the holy Amīr with all sincerity and humility, laying his head in humble submission at his threshold. The saint, bestowing upon him his love and affection, accredited him as his standard-bearer. On account of this distinction, the clan of Māgrays stole a march over the rest of the clans of chieftains (Sardars) and chiefs of Kashmir. Sulṭān Quṭbu'd-Dīn failed to propagate Islam in accordance with the wishes and aspirations of Amīr Sayyid 'Alī Hamadānī and as such the latter found himself reluctant to stay on in this land.

38. This story is not found in *TḤK*.

39. Ladda Mārgeśa in *Jonar.*, St. 617. By birth he was a non-Brahman Hindu of a high caste. *Jonar.*, St. 617. 5n.

Consequently, after a short while, he left via Baramulla under the pretext of proceeding on a pilgrimage to Mecca. Bearing his standard,[40] Ladi Māgray accompanied him up to the banks (waters) of Panbeh [*sic*] Drang. The governors and rulers of those lands showed great respect to the Sayyid and each one of them expressed his sincere loyalty to him. They entreated him to make a halt at their respective places. In A.H. 786 (A.D. 1384), he died at Paneri [*sic*] in the *vilāyat* of Swādgīr on the sixth of Dhu'l-Hijja. In this connection Shaykh Muḥammad Berāi [*sic*] has found this chronogram:

chu shud az gāh-i Aḥmad khātim-e dīn
ze hijrat haft-sado shast-o thamānin
biraft az 'ālam-i fānī be bāqī
Amīr-e har do 'ālam zāl-i Yāsīn.

The year of his death has been recorded in another chronogram:

Murshid-i sālīkān Shāh-e Hamadān
kez damash bāgh-i ma'rifat bishguft
mazhar-i nūr-i haqq kih rūyash būd
'aqabat az jahāniyān benihuft
'aql tārikh-i sāl-i rahlat-i ū
Sayyid-i ma 'Alī-e thānī guft.

After his death, his sacred remains were carried by his followers and the faithful to Khatlān where they made a burial place for these. All the details concerning his death and the carrying of the catafalque have been recorded by Nūru'd-Dīn Ja' far Badakhshi in *Khulāṣatu'l-Manāqib*.[41]

---

40. This perhaps may be the beginning of the tradition of *'Alamdārs* in Kashmir.
41. A MS copy of the work exists in the State Research Library, Srinagar, under Cat. No. 658.

Sulṭān Sikandar

Sulṭān Quṭbu'd-Dīn died[42] in A.H. 796 (A.D. 1393) and was succeeded by his dear and fortunate son; I mean that the devout, just, the protector of religion, the wielder of good fortune, the recipient of special favour of Master Bestower (God), Sulṭān Sikandar, the idol-breaker, God enlighten him in the grave, became the king of the realm of Kashmir.[43]

Mīr Sayyid Muḥammad

During the period of this glorious king's reign, the holy Amīr Sayyid Muḥammad, the son of Amīr Sayyid 'Alī Hamadānī, graced this land with his footsteps.[44] To him [Sayyid Muḥammad] goes the credit of wiping out the vestiges of infidelity and heresy from the mirror of the conscience of the dwellers of these lands. Through sermonising and exhortations, he succeeded in enlightening the hearts of the people with the world-embellishing faith of the choicest among men – the faith of Islam. Despite the inexperience of a youth, he was gifted with remarkable piety and knowledge of sciences, esoteric as well as exoteric. *Sharḥ-e Shameh* [*sic*] is his work on logic.[45] He also wrote a tract on mysticism for Sulṭān Sikandar, in which he has clearly recorded that he was twenty-two years old at the time of writing that book.

Immediately after his arrival, Sulṭān Sikandar, peace be on him, submitted to his religious supremacy[46] and proved his loyalty to him by translating his words into deeds. He

42. He was buried in Langarhatta *mohalla* in Srinagar. *TḤK*, p. 176.
43. His mother, as Jonarāja has rightly pointed out, was a Hindū. See note 37 *supra*.
44. It is interesting to note that he came to Kashmir along with three thousand disciples. *TḤK*, p. 178.
45. Ḥasan makes no mention of this work.
46. Jonarāja says that it was owing to his political sagacity (and not because of his religious conviction) that Sulṭān Sikandar showed respect to the Sayyid. See *Jonar.*, St. 574.

eradicated aberrant practices and infidelity.[47] He also put an end to the various forbidden and unlawful practices throughout his kingdom. Thus during the entire period of his rule, lasting nearly twenty-six years, all traces of wines and intoxicants and instruments of vice and corruption, like the cord of canticle, lyre, or tamborin were wiped off. The clamour of the drum and the trumpet, and the shrill notes of the fife and the clarion no longer reached people's ears, except in battles and assaults.[48] After the end of the rule of that king, the supporters and upholders of disbelief and darkness, who, helped the growth of infidelity and polytheism, revived their practices. Day after day the customs of religious innovators and polytheists gained currency more than what they had in previous times.

During the days of the late Sulṭān Sikandar, Malik Suh Bhat the chief and general of the king, embraced Islam on the initiation of Amīr Sayyid Muḥammad. He discarded the faith of the infidels and aberrant practices and accepted Islam with purity of heart and sincerity of conscience. Amīr Sayyid Muḥammad conferred upon him the title of Malik Saifu'd-Dīn.[49] Thus Sulṭān Sikandar and Malik Saifu'd-Dīn, God bless them both, joined hands to gear their full effort towards the eradication of infidelity and other aberrant

---

47. Also see *Jonar.*, Stt. 575 and 591. Ḥasan has given revealing details about Sulṭān Sikandar's attempts to do so by destroying Ḥindū temples some of which were Mārtāṇdēśvara near Mattan, three at Parihāsapura, Maha Shri, and Tārāpīṭha [*sic*] temples in Iskandarpora, Srinagar. For details see *TḤK*, pp. 178-80.
48. For details of forcible conversion of Hindūs to Islām and their massacre in case they refused to be converted, see *TḤK*, pp. 178-80. One significant detail is that three *kharwārs* (one *kharwār* is approximately equal to eighty kilograms) of Hindū ceremonial thread (*zunnār*) were burnt by Sulṭān Sikandar.
49. The Sayyid's marriage to Suh Bhata's daughter Baria is confirmed from *TḤK*, p. 178; *Tārīkh-i Sayyid 'Alī*, MS. f. 44 and *Fatahāt-i-Kubrawiyyeh*, MS. f. 157[a].

practices.[50] They raised the banner of Islam and the standard of the faith of the chosen among people to the highest pinnacle of glory and exaltation. Through the blessings and support of Islam and by the propagation of the commands of the *sharia'*, they were rewarded with victories wherever they led their armies, confirming the saying that "God helps those who help Muḥammad's religion."

During his (Sulṭān Sikandar's) days, Khāqān-i Ṣāhib Qarān, Mīrzā Tīmūr Gorkān conquered India. He showed love and affection to the above-mentioned Sulṭān and sent him a pair of elephants as a gift.[51]

It was also during his time that the Sayyids of Baihaq arrived in Kashmir. They had left their native place Sabzewār owing to the invasion of Mīrzā Tīmūr Gorkān and had got scattered over India. But unable to find a safe and tranquil abode in Kashmir, they returned to the plains of India, where they ultimately settled in the town of Jārīchah near Delhi. Details of this event will be recorded at the relevant place. They came to Kashmir again along with their entourage during the reign of Sulṭān Zainu'l-'Ābidīn, and finally settled here.

Baihaqī Sayyids

What follows now is the story of this clan. Mīr Sayyid Maḥmūd Baihaqī, son of Sayyid Muḥammad Baihaqī and a grandson of Sayyid Jalāl, did not adequately reflect on

50. The story of persecution of Hindūs by Sulṭān Sikandar is vividly recorded by Jonarāja in Stt. 657-669. Also see Stt. 597, 601-2, 606 and *TMḤ*, MS. f. 44[a].

51. Jonarāja's statement that the elephants were presented by Tīmūr out of fear of Sulṭān Sikandar is difficult to accept. See *Jonar.*, St. 562. Ḥasan's version is that Tīmūr was pleased to be informed at Attock that Sulṭān Sikandar of Kashmir accepted him as his overlord and would strike coins and read the *khuṭba* (homily) in his name. *TḤK*, p. 182.

finding solutions to the problems arising out of the emergence of Mīrzā Tīmūr. Resigning himself to the will of God and relying on his [quality of] steadfastness, he fought the overwhelming army of Tīmūr.

[*verses*]

His troops suffered defeat and he fled towards India. On his way he visited the shrine of Imām Rezā – salutes and respect to him – to offer his respects. In order to be blessed with knowledge, he retired to a secluded corner in the shrine, and after five days, with awakened mind and vision, saw the Imām in his dream. He prostrated before him as a mark of respect and made a humble submission to him that in his childhood, he had not read anything from books of learning nor had he tried to acquire knowledge. The Imām rubbed his saliva on his tongue which gave Sayyid Maḥmūd such eloquence that he became one among the learned. The saliva of Imām Rezā [also] gave him mystic powers. When he woke up from his dream, he found himself a wise and discriminating person. He found that he had been gifted with wisdom and powers of discrimination to a degree that was neither possible nor imaginable.

After that he left the holy town of Meshhad and arrived in the prestigious city of Delhi during the reign of Sulṭān Ghiāṭhu'd-Dīn. On being informed of his arrival, the Sulṭān showed him due respect by receiving him in person. He sat in his company for a while during which he showed all possible respect to him. The learned and scholarly men of the city would discuss their problems with him and he, with the help of his inspired knowledge, would solve their difficulties.

[*verses*]

After a few days, Sulṭān Ghiāṭhu'd-Dīn ordered a grand celebration. Peals of music sounded forth from the harp and the dulcimer; the lute and the organ; the tamborin and bell-hanging staff; the violin and the comet. The harp, the rebeck, and the *sīkh-i-khatāī* were played upon; and a quaint melody in Irāqī[52] was raised. The sunlike drum (*daf*) and the moonlike violin (*kemāncheh*) also came into play. The learned and the celebrated and the elite and the noble from all parts [of the country] living in Delhi gathered together. Up to that day, the sun – the headless and footless globetrotter – had never cast its rays on such a galaxy of brilliant people. The sky, which, through a hundred thousand eyes of its stars and comets, watches closely men and their affairs on this earth had never caught sight of such an assembly.

[*verses*]

Mīr Sayyid Maḥmūd composed two panegyrics in praise of Sulṭān Ghiāṭhu'd-Dīn with *sham'* and *chirāgh* as *qafiyas*. Historians have feared the length of the panegyrics and have recorded only the following verses:

[*verses*]

That night Sulṭān Ghiāṭhu'd-Dīn heard many strange and sensational things from Mīr Sayyid Maḥmūd. As the sun donned his golden crown and raised its head in the East, Mīr Sayyid Maḥmūd composed this extempore panegyric in praise of the Sulṭān:

[*verses*]

Sulṭān Ghiāṭhu'd-Dīn greatly trusted the words of Mīr Sayyid Maḥmūd. He permitted him to retire to his resting place so that the crowds left the royal palace.

The aforesaid Sulṭān had a daughter of unparalleled beauty. With regard to the matter of her marriage, he, first of all, held consultations with his courtiers and privy counsellors. They unanimously opined that none but the

52. A tune in classical Iranian music.

noble Mīr Sayyid Maḥmūd was qualified for this high favour; any other suggestion would amount to indulging in an exercise in futility. The suggestion of the courtiers was approved by the Sulṭān and they were entrusted with the mission of negotiating this matrimonial alliance. But when they made this suggestion to Mīr Sayyid – of venerable lineage –, he declined saying that in the holy shrine of Imām Rezā, he had received a message from the Inscrutable World that he had been honoured with the title of a dervish, and his entering into matrimonial alliance with the royal house was impracticable. He suggested to them that they could perhaps consider his nephew, Mīr Sayyid Ḥasan, the son of Mīr Sayyid Shāh, for this alliance and that this special favour could be granted to him. He further told them: "I shall consider this development as an inexhaustible good fortune. I vouch for Mīr Ḥasan's intelligence, merit, loyalty and sincerity. It is likely that this may create doubts in the mind of the Sulṭān and he might impute motives to my suggestion. But the fact is that after lighting the overwhelming forces of Sāhib Qirān, I retired to the holy city of Meshhad and in the shrine there, the invisible tongue of the Imām conferred upon me the title of dervish. This fact is known to every one."

Sulṭān Ghiāṭhu'd-Dīn's courtiers conveyed these words to him. Dismissing all doubts and controversial inferences, he told them that he would fulfil the wishes of a 'pure person' (*mūmin*), as both the honourable Sayyids were two pearls from one shell.

After a few days, the privy counsellors of the Sulṭān made elaborate arrangements for collecting gorgeous robes commensurate with their status and worthy of being presented to the royalty and also procured swift horses and camels and an unimaginable quantity of provisions, and then set up a grand feast. Then they carried the chaste betrothed one to Mīr Sayyid Ḥasan Baihaqī. The whole of Sambal and Miān-do-Āb was conferred upon him as his *jāgīr*. The *pargana* of Dankur in the vicinity of Delhi was given to him as his dwelling place. Thus the group [of Sayyids] settled at Jārīchah. They subdued and suppressed almost all the headstrong and defiant people of that locality and exacted taxes and tributes from them. Between Sambal and Miān-do-Āb, they set up security posts at vulnerable points. If a traveller, for some reason, was forced to leave behind his luggage at one of these points, the militant people of the area, fearing this group, would carry it on their backs and heads and bring it to the town of Jārīchah.

However, the world and its denizens at large know full well that the turbulent spheres do not let the faithful live in peace and permanence, and [consequently] Sulṭān Ghiāṭhu'd-Dīn responded to the call of the inevitable.

After the death of Sulṭān Ghiāṭhu'd-Dīn, a dervish, after visiting Kashmir, passed through Lahore and Delhi and arrived in Jārīchah, where he was introduced to Sayyid Maḥmūd. He praised Kashmir before him and also recounted to him the tales of just dispensations of Sulṭān Sikandar, the Iconoclast. This excited in Mīr Sayyid a desire to visit that land. He and his warriors left their families – children and womenfolk – at Delhi and Jārīchah and set out for Kashmir via Hirpur. Sulṭān Sikandar came out to receive them in the city. Their association flourished so much that Mīr Sayyid almost forgot his desire of governing Sabzewār and Miān-do-Āb. The remaining part of the story of this group will be resumed at its proper place.

Men of Learning

During the reign of that devout king (Sulṭān Sikandar) eminent and well-known scholars arrived in this land from different cities and places.[53] A fairly large number of revered

53. Such as 'Irāq, Khurāsān, Transoxiana (*Māwarā'-an-Nahr*), etc. *TḤK*, p. 177.

Sayyids and generous noblemen who had various attainments to their credit graced this land with their august steps. Among them is the versatile and remarkable Mīr Sayyid Aḥmad bin Sayyid Muḥmmad Isfahānī whose work *Tanvīr* is based on the commentary on *Farāiz-i-Sirrājī*.[54] This book gives evidence of his sharp intelligence and powers of elucidating subtle truths and sublime realities. Besides this work, his epistles exhibit his superb command over rhetoric. Another man of erudition among the immigrants is Sayyid Muḥammad Khāwarī, Khawārī being his pen-name. *Khāwar Nāmeh* is one of his works. In the field of mysticism, he wrote a commentary on *Lum'āt*. Both these learned men were devoted and close followers of Amīr Sayyid Muḥammad Hamadānī. They have expressed their devotion and adherence to the Sayyid in some of their works. Yet another learned and true Sayyid and the upholder of the faith is Qāḍī Sayyid Ḥassan Shīrāzī, who had held the post of a Qāḍī in Shīrāz. On arriving in this country during the reign of the late Sulṭān Sikandar, he was appointed to the post of a Qāḍī. There is a tract in his own hand, in which the *Ratniyeh* [*sic*] *hadīth* have been collected. At the end of the tract, the Qāḍī has recorded that he had shown it to the exalted and venerable Mīr Sayyid Muḥammad Hamadānī, who had duly authenticated it. It should not remain unknown that though some of the learned men have raised doubts about *Ratniyeh hadīth*, yet most of the '*ulemā*', the grand doctors, and prominent scholars have accepted them as authentic. It is thus clear that in this matter the Qāḍī was among the pupils of Amīr Sayyid Muḥammad Hamadānī.

In the days of that devout ruler (Sulṭān Sikandar), a large number of exalted Shaykhs and respectable Sayyids, who were men of extraordinary attainments and of spiritual powers, arrived in this land. One of these was Amīr Sayyid Aḥmad Madanī, who had migrated from Medina along with

54. It is not clear from the text whether *Tanvīr* was a work other than *Farāiz-i-Sirrājī* or a part of its title.

his family and settled in this land. Many extraordinary spiritual feats are attributed to him. After his death, his burial place became a shrine which common people frequented to receive blessings and for the fulfilment of their desires. Another person is Shaykh Jalāl Bukhārī who had came to this land from Bukhārā along with a large number of his companions including the Sayyids of respectable status. His grave can be found in the graveyard of the native Sulṭāns. The burial places of the Sayyids who had accompanied him have become shrines visited by people. For instance, both Mīr Sayyid Taju'd-Dīn and Mīr Sayyid Burhān are buried at Iskandar Pora – a locality laid out by Sulṭān Sikandar.[55] Sayyid Nūru'd-Dīn, who is buried in Quṭbu'd-Dīn Pora locality,[56] was a companion of Shaykh Jalālu'd-Dīn. Another person is Bābā Ḥājjī Adḥam who had come from Balkh along with a large number of his followers and attendants. Bābā Ḥasan Manṭaqī, father of Mīr Veys, is buried in the Mazār-i-Salāṭīn and he, too, was among the followers of Bābā Ḥājjī Adḥam. The great grandfather of the writer of these pages named Mullā Ḥasāmu'd-Dīn was also a follower of Bābā Ḥājjī Adḥam and had accompanied him from Ghazna. He served in the kitchen of that saint and his group of dervishes.[57] This Bābā Ḥājjī Adḥam lived to see the times of Sulṭān Zainu'l-'Ābidīn. After his death, his body was buried in the well-known garden called Bāgh-i Mīr Veys – an endowment property – at the foot of the *Khānqāh* of

55. Iskandarpora was laid out on the debris of the destroyed temples of Hindūs. In the neighbourhood of the royal palace in Iskandarpora, the Sulṭān destroyed the temple of Mahā Shrī which had been built by Pravarasena and another one built by Tārāpīḍa. The material from these was used for constructing a Jāmi' mosque in the middle of the city. See *TḤK*, p. 180.
56. Present-day Khānqāh-i-Mu'allā locality in Srinagar.
57. This sentence and the preceding one is all that the author says about himself in the present work.

Mullā Pārsā near Koh-i-Mārān.[58] His grave has become famous for visits [by the needy].

Mīr Veys

Bābā Ḥājjī Adḥam's disciple, Bābā Ḥasan Manṭaqī, though a married man, lived the life of an ascetic. Once Sulṭān Zainu'l-'Ābidīn requested him for a gift. A few days later the Bābā carried something in the sleeve of his leather coat[59] and came to Sulṭān Zainu'l-'Ābidīn. He asked him to stretch out the hemline of his gown to receive the gift. The Bābā put a month-old infant in his lap, saying. "This is my gift to you. Take proper care of him." The Sulṭān carried the infant to his private chamber and entrusted it to the care of his chief mistress, the daughter of Seydān Baihaqī. A nurse was engaged to look after the infant. It is said that the queen bore no child to the Sulṭān. When Mīr Veys[60] was given to her, out of extreme maternal love and affection, her breasts were filled with milk. Mīr Veys suckled on the milk of the queen as well as the nurse. Whatever portion of knowledge and learning fell to the share of Mīr Veys was through the care of Sulṭān Zainu'l-'Ābidīn, and whatever he acquired of asceticism and mysticism was inherited by him from his father and Bābā Ḥājjī Adḥam.

Another person among those who arrived in this land during the reign of the devout king (Sikandar) is Mullā Pārsā.[61] He too was gifted with piety and purity and had

58. Originally called Śārikāparvata. See *Rājat.*, iii, 349 and *TḤK*, Vol. II, p. 446.

59. Leather-coat was not a part of the dress of Kashmiris during the Hindu period. Perhaps it was introduced in Kashmir after the Central Asian practice. See my *Kashmir Shawl*, Srinagar, 1984.

60. The name given by Ḥasan is Muḥammad Amīn and not Mīr Veys. See p. 198.

61. Another saintly person of the same name was invited by Sulṭān Zainu'l-'Ābidīn to Kashmir. See *TḤK*, p. 195.

various attainments and virtues to his credit. At the foot of the Koh-i-Mārān, he built a *khānqāh* for himself.

Sikandar's Achievements

The august king and the upholder of the laws of religion granted villages, hamlets, habitations, and houses, commensurate with their needs and status, to each of the *'ulemā*, the learned, the ascetic, the pious, the noble, the Sayyid and the Qāḍī. These were by way of endowments and stipends so that they were provided with the means of subsistence. Villages and hamlets thus endowed were given as permanent holds to be inherited by their future generations, without any break. Thus their successors continue to hold these endowments down to his day.

The same king (Sulṭān Sikandar) created the post of Shaykhu'l-Islām in this land. A large number of hamlets and villages were selected from each *pargana* and set apart as endowed to that noble post so that stipends and alms could be provided through that source for distribution among the learned, the Qāḍīs, the Sayyids, the mendicants, the needy, the pilgrims and the travellers, in accordance with the needs and rights of each.

He also built a hospital, *Dāru'l-Shifā*, in this land, where food, medicines and other requirements were provided for patients and the ailing ones. The physicians and medical practitioners of this land were given stipends and financial assistance to enable them to attend to the sick. They were required to pay daily visits to the hospital, diagnose diseases and prescribe treatments and cures. These acts of charity, which have continued to this day, were the result of the august company and counsel of Amīr Sayyid Muḥammad Hamadānī. It was through his blessings that this noble and religious-minded king was able to support and strengthen the law of Muḥammad and to promote and advance his religion and community. So long as Amīr Sayyid Muḥammad Hamadānī lived in this land, the *pargana* of Mattan was provided for his subsistence. He built a two-storeyed mosque by the side of the spring of Bhavan, a spring of unparalleled clean and transparent waters.

Jāmi‘ Mosque

The late religious-minded king, Sulṭān Sikandar, built the locality of Navato[62] for his residence. There he built a magnificent palace, the like of which did not exist [before]. A lofty and imposing Jāmi‘ mosque was also built by him in the same locality where Īd festivals would be celebrated and congregations held. Throughout the lands of Hind and Sindh and the climes of Iran and Tūrān, one cannot come across a mosque of such grandeur and magnificence, though, of course such grand mosques do exist in the lands of Egypt and Syria. The architect of this mosque was Khwāja Ṣadru'd-Dīn who had come to this land from Khurāsān. A Jāmi‘ mosque and a lodge at Vejeh Belārah[63] were also among the architectural works executed under the orders of this king.

Mazār-i-Salaṭīn and Khānqāh

On the banks of the river which flowed through the city, he laid out a burial ground for the royal dead.[64] The lofty ideals and glory of this king are reflected in the magnificent buildings that he raised. The platform which the venerable Amīr-i-Kabīr Sayyid 'Alī Hamadānī had raised at 'Alāu'd-Dīn Pora for addressing religious gatherings was made use of as a foundation for the *Khānqāh*, for the maintenance of which he allotted a few villages by way of endowment and

---

62. Present-day Nowhatta.
63. Sulṭān Sikandar ravaged and looted the temple of Vijayeśvara. See *Toḥfat.*, MS. f. 138[b].
64. Present-day Mazāri-i-Salāṭīn on the right bank of Jhelum near Zaina Kadal in Srinagar.

provided means of subsistence for its employees and inmates.

Some people are of the opinion that Amīr Sayyid Muḥammad Hamadānī possessed a jewel which he gave to the late Sulṭān Sikandar. The Sayyid bought the villages of Talāl (Trāl) and Vachi, which he later gave to this *khānqāh* by way of an endowment to provide for the recitors of the Qur'ān and the caretakers of the *khānqāh*. The foundation and the structure of the *khānqāh* as laid by Amīr Sayyid Hamadānī made it small and limited. Private houses of the inhabitants [of the locality] and the caretakers were so close to the walls of the *khānqāh* that if a fire would break out in the locality, its flames would engulf the entire *khānqāh* [complex].

Sulṭān Zainu'l-'Ābidīn rebuilt the *khānqāh*. In the days of Malik Kājī Chak, Amīr Shamsu'd-Dīn Muḥammad Araki – God bless the most pious one – graced this land with his auspicious footsteps and he undertook the reconstruction of this *khānqāh* afresh to make it spacious, lofty and imposing. Private houses in its periphery were pulled down and adjoining private lands were acquired against substantial cash payments. People who were not in need of money, such as Qāḍī Muḥammad Qudsī and the offspring of Mullā Bābā 'Alī, were given alternative sites in other localities, and thus the neighbourhood of the *khānqāh* was cleared so that in future it would be secure against accidental fires and other calamities.

During the days of Amīr Shamsu'd-Dīn Muḥammad Araki the endowments to the *khānqāh* increased considerably, so much so that during the life time of that venerable person, one hundred and twenty five *traks*[65] of rice were cooked in the kitchen of the *khānqāh* each day; sixty-five *traks* for dinner. There was hardly a day when meat was not

65. One *trak* is approximately equal to five kilograms.

cooked in the kitchen of the *khānqāh*. These works of public charity included a public kitchen and a pottage-house (*āshkhāneh*). These were destroyed in a fire. Later on, the employees built smaller ones in their place. Loftiness of the building of the *khānqāh* and the commodiousness of its store-house for paddy and other required articles speak of the magnanimity of Amīr Shamsu'd-Dīn Muḥammad Iraki.

Sayyid Muḥammad expires

It must not remain unknown that on account of the obduracy and the animosity of Sayyid Ḥiṣārī towards Amīr Sayyid Muḥammad Hamadānī, the latter found himself disheartened in this land. After seeking the permission of [the late] Sulṭān Sikandar, he set out on a pilgrimage to Mecca to perform *Ḥajj* and *'Umrah*. After fulfilling this wish of visiting the holy shrines of the venerable Imāms,[66] he reached the province of Khatlān,[67] his birth-place, and also the land where his illustrious father had been buried. There he breathed his last, and was laid to rest by the side of his father.

Let it be known that Sulṭān Sikandar, the Iconoclast, reigned for twenty-five years, nine months, and six days, after which he died.

[*verses*]

Muḥammad Baiḥaqī, who adopted the pen-name of dervish in his verses of which a *Dīwān* was compiled, composed many verses and eulogies in praise of Sulṭān Sikandar, and has also composed a chronogram suggesting the year of Sulṭān's death. The fragment is reproduced from his *Dīwān*:

[*verses*]

66. These holy shrines are at Najaf and Kerbala in 'Iraq and Meshhad and Qom in Iran.
67. Now the independent Republic of Tājīkistān.

Another poet of those days composed some verses to record the year of Sulṭān's death.

[*verses*]

Maḥmūd Baihaqī leaves Kashmir

The late Sulṭān Sikandar was succeeded by his eldest son Sulṭān 'Alī[68] whose reign lasted eight years and some months. He did not feel comfortable in the company of Mīr Sayyid Maḥmūd Baihaqī. The Sayyid thought that the garden of Kashmir was a land of calamities, and made a firm resolve to proceed to Delhi. Thereupon the idea of hosting a public feast struck his mind. All the high officials, the nobles, the Shaykhs, the Sayyids, the learned, and men of eminence were invited to the spacious grounds of Īdgāh.[69] Sulṭān 'Alāu'd-Dīn, the son of the late Sulṭān Sikandar, was also present in that assembly. Supper was followed by recitations from the Qur'ān. After this the invitees were made to remove their mourning weeds and wear robes of honour according to their rank. Then Mīr Sayyid Maḥmūd moved on to the burial place of Sulṭān Sikandar to pay homage to him and then recited the following elegiac verses in a doleful voice:

[*verses*]

Thence Mīr Sayyid took the Hirpur route and arrived at his former house in Dehli to settle down into a quiet life. He withdrew himself from the base material world and began to attend to pursuits for the world hereafter. He built a mosque with [adjoining] structures and laid a burial ground [for the holy]. An enormous public catering place was also built for

---

68. His family name was Mīr Khān and he ascended the throne in A.H. 820 / A.D. 1417. *TḤK*, p. 185.
69. On the left bank of Jhelum in Srinagar. It continues to be known by the same name.

the use of people who visited the mosque. His extraordinary spiritual feats are well-known among the intelligent people in Kashmir and Delhi. His grave has become a shrine for people who usually seek blessings and fulfilment of their desires. His death occurred in the month of Rabī'u'l-Ākhir.

Jasrath's Rebellion

Mīr Sayyid Ḥasan, the nephew of Mīr Sayyid Maḥmūd Baihaqī, had been permitted by him to settle at Nowshehr[70] in India. He was known for his bravery and valour. Within a short time he succeeded in obtaining tributes from the stiff-necked chieftains of the mountainous regions of Kashmir[71] with which he met the expenses of salaries and provisions of his troops. With a firm hand he suppressed rebellions whenever they were reported and he (ruthlessly) put the miscreants to the sword.

During this time, it was reported to him that Rājā Jasrath, with the support of a group of infidels and wicked persons, had become so haughty as to defy his authority in his own fort.[72] He had misled the people to rally round him. On

70. Parts of Nowshehra area are now under Pakistani-occupied Kashmir.
71. South of Pir Panṭṣāl range.
72. Jasrath Khān Ghakkar had escaped from Tīmūr's captivity in Samarqand and had established his authority over Panjab. Shāhī Khān (Zainu'l-'Ābidīn) had been given the throne of Kashmir when Sulṭān 'Alī decided to proceed on a pilgrimage to Mecca. But on reaching Jammu his father-in-law, Rājā of Jammu, dissuaded him from abdicating the throne. On his instance and with his material help, Sulṭān 'Alī changed his mind and returned to Kashmir via Pakhli to resume kingship. His brother Shāhī Khān resisted him, but was defeated and fled to Panjab where Jasrat Khān Ghakkar (Rājā Jasrat of the text) gave him shelter. Together they raised a large army, and in the second battle fought between Sulṭān 'Alī and his brother Shāhī Khān, the former was defeated

(*Contd.*)

hearing this news, Mīr Sayyid Ḥasan seized his sword, mounted his light-footed horse, and marched out of Nowshehr in India till he confronted the rebels. A fierce battle ensued:

[*verses*]

The fort occupied by the profane infidels was as lofty as the sky and was surrounded by a dark forest.[73] This was the reason why his warriors could not overpower the enemy. Although Mīr Sayyid Ḥasan could not coerce these ill-equipped insurgents into submission, he continued his fight with them acting on the saying "a struggle in the path of God is its own reward." He looked at his fight with that group as a holy war. In the course of a fierce battle which ensued he attained martyrdom on the second day of Rabī'u'l-Awwal of the year A.H. 837 (A.D. 1433).[74] The year of his death has been commemorated in a fragment:

[*verses*]

His grave is in Jasrot[75] [*sic*]. When the news of his martyrdom reached his relatives and children at Dehli, it was

---

and fell a prisoner in the hands of Jasrat Khān. The victorious Zainu'l-'Ābidīn marched on to Kashmir where he was warmly received by the people. *TḤK*, pp. 187-88. Jonarāja says that Rājā of Madra (Jammu) Billa Deva was slain in a battle against Jasrath Khukhura who had become his enemy because he had disclosed his place of hiding to the troops of Sayyid Mu'izzu'd-Dīn Mubārak Shāh (A.D. 1421-1434) of Dehli. See Eliot's *History*, *Tārīkh-i-Mubārak Shāh* IV, pp. 56-59; *Jonar.*, Stt. 711-16.

73. Probably it was somewhere near present Kathua. Ḥasan says that after suffering defeat in the battle at Uri, Zainu'l-'Ābidīn fled to Sialkot. *TḤK*, p. 188.

74. Malik Doom Chādūra, a local commander of Sulṭān 'Alī's troops and a descendant of the house of Chandās, also fell in this battle. He was succeeded by his son Malik Avtār. *TMḤ*, MS. f. 39[a].

75. Jasrot should not be confused with Jasrath. Jasrot is the name of a place.

mourned by all the nobles, the learned and the commoners of that city. Mīr Sayyid Nāṣir, the son of the late Sayyid Ḥasan, invited all the leading aristocrats, Sayyids, learned men, and other notable personalities of Dehli to a feast where they were lavishly entertained with varieties of food and *sherbet*. Recitations from the holy Qur'ān continued for several days and prayers for the peace of the departed soul were offered. He also sent enormous quantities of food and drinks to the houses of the Shaykhs, the divines, Sayyids and all the notable and elderly persons of the city. After fulfilling these obligations, he returned to the town of Jārīchah.

Sulṭān Ghiāṭhu'd-Dīn's daughter bore Mīr Sayyid Ḥasan Baihaqī seven sons. They were Mīr Sayyid Zainu'l-'Ābidīn, Mīr Mua'zzam Khān, Mīr Mūsā, Mīr Sayyid Jalāl, Mīr Sayyid Shāh, Mīr Bādshāh, and Mīr Sayyid Nāṣir. But none except the youngest among them ventured to take revenge on Rājā Jasrath. Mīr Sayyid Nāṣir, the youngest of his sons, despite his youth, exhibited undaunted courage in avenging his father's death. After procuring necessary weapons and provisions, he marched towards the domain of the worthless infidels. The nobles advised him to carefully weigh the consequences of his adventure. All his six brethren came to see him and advised him to drop the idea of an expedition against that wicked group in that year. The courageous prince took their advice and the execution of his plan got deferred for the next seven years.

Chapter IV
Later Shāhmīrs

Zainu'l-'Ābidīn

The late Sulṭān Sikandar was succeeded by his eldest son Sulṭān 'Alī in A.H. 817 (A.D. 1414).[1] It has already been said that his reign lasted eight years and some months. In the year A.H. 826 (A.D. 1422), he proceeded on a pilgrimage to Mecca[2] and entrusted his kingdom, government and property to his son Zainu'l-'Ābidīn. The later ascended the throne of Kashmir in the same year, and his reign lasted fifty-two years.

---

1. Sikandar died in A.H. 816/A.D. 1413. See p. 59 *supra*. But the chronogram *faut-i-Sikandar* recorded by Ḥasan puts the date as A.H. 820 A.D. 1417. *TḤK*, p. 185.
2. There could have been more than one reason for taking this decision: (a) Sulṭān 'Alī did not feel happy with Sayyid Muḥammad Baihaqī (p. 59 *supra*); (b) He had lost 'both the Tibets' to the ruler of Kāshghar whose troops had made an incursion into those regions. (*TḤK*, p. 186); (c) His younger brother Shāhī Khān (Zainu'l-'Ābidīn) had become very popular with the people of Kashmir, a fact proved by later events. *Ibid*; (d) Baihaqī Sayyids had become very powerful and interfered in the affairs of the state, pp. 44, 48-51, *supra*. The fact that his Hindu father-in-law, Rājā of Jammu, dissuaded him from abdicating the throne and going on a pilgrimage to Mecca indicates that it was his political and military weakness and not his intense religiosity which forced him to leave his kingdom. The works of his poet-laureate,

(*Contd.*)

Expedition Against Jasrath

During his reign Mīr Sayyid Nāṣir re-equipped himself with arms and supplies to confront Rājā [of ?] Jasrot. He paid no heed to the entreaties of his brothers, dear ones and elders to desist from the contemplated expedition and was inspired by the verse which says: "In the hand of God, the conductor of affairs, have we left the result of our actions; let us see what His grace will be." Setting aside their advice, he told his relatives that the year appeared to be auspicious for his victory. Since, with the grace of God Almighty, all the necessary means were available to him, he was disposed to translate his desire into action. In accordance with the dictum that 'whenever God wishes a certain thing to be done, necessary means appear', it was likely that victory would be theirs, and that group of wicked persons would become their prisoner. The aforesaid group [of well-wishers] found that the Sayyid was not prepared to change his decision. Hence they were left with no alternative but to remain silent and leave the consequences of his actions to God Almighty. They returned to their residence. In short, the above-mentioned Mīr Sayyid very humbly embarked on this expedition and uttered the verses:

[*verses*]

In a fit of anger, he (Sayyid Nāṣir) burnt the dwellings of the inhabitants of Jārīcha, and then turned towards Jasrath.

Mullā Nāderī, which reportedly contain details of the events of his reign, are lost to us. See *TMḤ*, MS f. 39[a]. However, Jonarāja says that the authority of the government was given to Shāhī Khān out of affection, and other considerations. See St. 691. In fact, the title Zainu'l-'Ābidīn was also conferred upon him by 'Alī Shāh, who was given jewels and horses by Shāhī Khān presumably to enable him to meet the expenses of outfit and transport for going to Mecca. *Ibid.* Stt. 707, 709.

Sayyid Qāsim[3] says that apart from his own troops, five thousand more soldiers of his old acquaintance, who were armed to the teeth and owed allegiance to Mīr Nāṣir Baihaqī, preferring death to life, marched from Jārīcha to seek revenge on Rājā [of ?] Jasrot [*sic*]. They passed through dangerous stages [of the journey] and at last were face to face with the troops of the Rājā. A fierce battle ensued in which people in large numbers on both sides were killed. At last, with the help of God, the troops of Islam emerged victorious over the infidels, whose innumerable soldiers were killed on the battlefield and many were taken prisoner.

Relation with Sayyids

After destroying the Satan's[4] party, he (Mīr Sayyid Nāṣir) proceeded to Nowshehr (Hind) to visit the holy shrine of Mīrān Sayyid Ḥasan. When the news of the advent of the victorious troops of Mīr Sayyid Nāṣir in Nowshehr (Hind) reached Sulṭān Zainu'l-'Ābidīn in Kashmir, he despatched experienced advisers to [meet] Mīrān Sayyid Nāṣir with the purpose of reviving cordial relations with Mīr Sayyid Maḥmūd which had been established during the reign of Sulṭān Sikandar.

To strengthen and to stabilize his authority, he (Zainu'l-'Ābidīn) invited him to a feast and duly fulfilled the obligations demanded of a host. Mīr Sayyid Nāṣir had three sons, all brave and valiant. One of them, Mīr Sayyid Ibrāhīm, attained martyrdom while fighting the infidels in the vicinity of the Doāb; his grave is at Jārīcha. With his death Ibrāhīm's line came to an end. The second son, Mīrān Sayyid Maḥmūd, succeeded his father. At the time of

3. It has not been possible to identify who Sayyid Qāsim was. Perhaps he was one of the chroniclers from whom the author has borrowed some details. It could be Muhammad Qasim Firishta author of *Tārikh-i-Firishta*.
4. Infidels or Hindu Rājā Jasrath.

leaving Nowshehr (Hind)[5] for Kashmir, he bade his son proceed to Jārīcha. Mīr Maḥmūd remains buried at Jārīcha and his descendants continue to live at that place. His third son was Mīrak Sayyid Ḥasan who was taken by his father along with himself. Relying on Sulṭān Zainu'l-'Ābidīn's promises of friendship and cordiality, Nāṣir entered Kashmir by the Hirpur route at the head of a sizeable entourage. Then he settled in Kashmir.

Zainu'l-'Ābidīn found that Mīr Sayyid Nāṣir was gifted with excellent qualities of head and heart; be entrusted him with the administration of justice in those lands.[6] A dwelling-house situated somewhere between Bāgh-i-Mīr Veys and Nowshehr was provided to him. The Sulṭān strengthened his relations with this group to add to his prestige and power. The wisdom and sagacity of Mīr Sayyid was well-known among the learned men of Kashmir.

Nāṣir's Death

Finding that Sulṭān Zainu'l-'Ābidīn held the Sayyid in high esteem, the materialistic people of that wretched country (Kashmir) conspired to put an end to his life, which was dedicated to public good, by putting poison into a pineapple, which was sent to him as a gift.

This foul deed was done by a wicked person. God grants special favours to His true and sincere devotees, and one among these is to elevate them to the heights of martyrdom

5. It shows that Nowshehr in Jammu region was not included in the kingdom of Kashmir then. But the Baihaqī Sayyids had made the town their stronghold. According to Shrivara, Nāṣir was the chief of Bahurūpa. See R.C. Dutt (tr.) Delhi, 1986, pp. 184-185.
6. The suggestion is that this portion of the chronicle was written by the author outside Kashmir. Shrivara writes that the king was married to one Vodhā Khatūn of Sayyid family. *The Rājataraṅgiṇi of Jonarāja*, tr. R.C. Dutt, p. 157 Mīr Ḥasan's daughter was married to Zainu'l-'Ābidīn's grandson. *Ibid*, pp 184-85.

at the last moments of their lives.[7] Despite his miraculous powers of anticipating dangers, Mīrān Sayyid ate the pine-apple. What appeared to be a fruit was in reality the fatal poison which went into his bowels, tearing them to shreds.

Sulṭān Zainu'l-'Ābidīn immediately went to see him at his place and came to know about what had happened. He asked Mīrān Sayyid about the ignoble wretch who had committed that crime, so that he might be brought to book. "He has snatched you away from us and we shall meet nowhere save in the next world," said the Sulṭān. The Sayyid replied that he would, in no case, disclose the identity of the detestable culprit because torturing him would only work towards his [Sayyid's] losing the lofty claim to martyrdom. It was enough that on the day of resurrection the sinner would be exposed to untold torture and the wrath of the Omnipotent. Mīrak Sayyid Ḥasan, his son, pointedly insisted upon him to disclose the facts about the poisoning, but to no avail. He asked for a pen and an inkpot and wrote these couplets as a recommendation for his sons, and gave [the paper] to the Sulṭān:

[*verses*]

Perceiving that the Sayyid's illness had taken a serious turn, Sulṭān Zainu'l-'Ābidīn felt greatly distressed and retired to his palace in a state of utter dejection. He continued to make constant enquiries about his health, and was overpowered by grief to such an extent that he could not rest even for a moment in his bed. The *Ḥātif* (the invisible messenger) brought this word from the unknown to the ears of the pure:

[*verses*]

On Wednesday, the twelfth of the month of Sh'abān, his condition became serious:

[*verses*]

7. Martyrdom has a special significance in Shia' faith.

On Thursday, the thirteenth of Sh'abān, A.H. 829 (A.D. 1522), he surrendered his soul to the messenger of death. The chronogram of this event has been recorded as follows:

khiradmand dānā-i dānish pazīr
ze man bāz pursīd tārīkh-i Mīr
dil-e dānish andūz-e ulwī sarisht
biguftā buwad Sayyid ahl-e bihisht

His death was mourned by all, high and low, friend and foe.

[*verses*]

The burial [of the Sayyid] and the accompanying rites of a dead person were performed in accordance with the traditions laid down by the Prophet [of Islam].[8] The body was laid to rest in the neighbourhood of the graveyard of Shaykh Bahāu'd-Dīn,[9] a lovely, alluring place of spiritual charm. To this day, the shrine continues to be a place of spiritual attraction for the devotees who visit it to seek the blessings of the departed [soul]. They offer prayers to seek fulfilment of their wishes and solutions to their difficulties. The shrine in that land is called *Mazār-i-Sādāt.*

Sulṭān Zainu'l-'Ābidīn and his nobles and elderly people condoled the death of the Sayyid for three[10] days and also fulfilled mourning obligations demanded by the sad occasion. Divines, priests and scholarly persons were summoned to recite the Qur'ānic verses round-the-clock. On the third day, he [the Sulṭān] served a sumptuous meal to them as well as to poor people. After visiting the graves [of the pious ones], he returned to his palace. Mīrak Sayyid Ḥasan, the son of the deceased, and other kinsmen and

8. This is a significant sentence in the sense that there are slight variations in the death-rites of Shias and Sunnis. A Sunni author would not need to insert "with the tradition...."
9. In the present locality of Nowshehr in Srinagar.
10. The custom of mourning the death of a person for three days was also prevalent among the Muslims of Central Asia at that time.

relatives of the late Sayyid were then summoned by him to his palace, where he entrusted the office held by the late Sayyid to his son. The rest of his associates were rewarded with different favours.

Insurgents Curbed

After Mīrak Ḥasan assumed the office of his father, the foster-brothers[11] of Sulṭān Zainu'l-'Ābidīn, adopted a threatening stance in Nowshehr by showing defiance of and disregard for his authority. They began to put hurdles in the way of Sulṭān's administrative officers in conducting their duties. Their insolent and base actions made him unhappy. It was generally believed by people in Kashmir that these very persons were instrumental in getting Sayyid Nāṣir poisoned. Thus the Sulṭān had sufficient reasons to be displeased with them. Placing a contingent of troops under Mīrak Sayyid Ḥasan, the Sulṭān directed him to suppress the insurgents. Supported by the unbounded grace of God, Mīrak Sayyid Ḥasan confronted them bravely. A grim battle ensued which resulted in the wholesale slaughter of those people.

[*verses*]

With the defeat of the enemy, Sulṭān Zainu'l-'Ābidīn's government in the lands of Kashmir became very strong and stable. People in those lands were delivered from the oppression and tyranny of the Sulṭān's foster-brothers and their accomplices. They all submitted to the authority of Sulṭān Zainu'l-'Ābidīn and spent their days in peace and security and prayed for his long life.

Arts and Crafts

Relieved of anxieties, Zainu'l-'Ābidīn took up his residence at Nowshehr and ordered the construction of lofty mansions

11. Ḥasan says they were Goorchis (*Goorchivān*), and had concentrated at Nowshehr. See *TḤK*, p. 191.

and imposing buildings in that locality.[12] Most of his generals and commanders were given houses in that area for residential purposes. Apart from these, some high ranking people among the Sayyids and the learned, like Sayyid Muḥammad Madanī, Mullā Pārsā and others were also invited to live in that locality so that their association and company would be easily available [to him].[13]

After this victory, people in this land enjoyed peace and prosperity. The Sulṭān made full efforts towards the development and progress of his kingdom and extended encouragement to artists and craftsmen. As a result of these, a number of novel arts and crafts developed and became popular. Whenever a traveller came to this country, he was asked searching and pointed questions as to whether he was proficient in any art and craft. In case he was, a couple of clever and intelligent persons were told to learn these crafts from him. In this way many arts and crafts came into vogue.

During those days, no one in this land knew the art of paper-making and book-binding. This king of excellent parts despatched two intelligent and sharp-witted persons to Samarqand. Their families and children were provided with means of subsistence from the state exchequer, and they themselves received all the expenses of their journey and other incidental expenses during their travel to Samarqand. They stayed in that city for some years. One of them learnt the craft of paper-making and the other book-binding. After

---

12. The Sulṭān built in that locality a twelve-storeyed pleasure-house, which had fifty rooms in each storey. Each of its rooms was large enough to accommodate five hundred persons. The mansion was a unique piece of architecture. In histories it is famous as *Zooneh Deb*, but was popularly known as Rāzdān in those days which means the royal palace. *TḤK*, p. 191.

13. The tutor of the Sulṭān, Maulānā Kabīr, who later on became Shaykhu'l-Islam, was also given a dwelling place in that locality. The Sulṭān also ordered the building of a *madrasah* for him in the neighbourhood of his house. *TḤK*, p 195.

attaining perfection in their respective crafts, they returned to their native land where they popularized their newly-learnt crafts among people.[14]

Patron of Learning

He (the Sulṭān) bestowed so many favours upon men of arts and learning that it is not possible to imagine that anything more could be done [about it].

During those days, the number of authentic and rare books in this country was very small. This patron of learning sent a variety of presents to the rulers of Fārs, Khurāsān and the governors of 'Irāq and Sijistān, with the request that they arrange for him a collection of genuine and rare books. The number of books thus collected was so large that it cannot be described here. When the Sulṭān learnt from *haji* pilgrims that the original manuscript of Jārullah 'Allāma's Kashshāf in his own hand was in the possession of the learned men of holy Mecca, he [immediately] summoned an excellent calligraphist and, placing more than adequate funds at his disposal, despatched him to Mecca where he stayed for some years and succeeded in making for him a true copy of this work. After collating and correcting his copies of the manuscript very carefully, he procured a certificate from the nobles and the elites of the 'Mother of Cities' to the effect that the scribe had copied from the original manuscript of Jārullah and had most carefully compared the two, making necessary corrections in his copy before carrying it with him

14. Malik Ḥaidar says that paper-makers and book-binders were brought by the Sulṭān and they were provided with stipends. *TMḤ*, MS f. 41[a]. Ḥasan says that the Sulṭān sent some intelligent and clever persons to different lands to learn the crafts of their people to bring these to Kashmir. Book-binders, paper-makers, carpet-weavers, pen-case makers, stone masons, seal-engravers and bolt-makers were brought from Samarqand. *TḤK*, p. 198. Shrivarā's reference to Kashmir woollen fabric called Soha (Shawl ?) is confusing. See R.C. Dutt's translation, ed., 1986, p. 151.

to those lands. On seeing the manuscript, Sulṭān Zainu'l-'Ābidīn once again bestowed upon the scribe gifts and robes of honour. The manuscript was put in the custody of the concerned office.[15] During the first uprising of Mīrzā Ḥaidar,[16] amidst loot and arson, this manuscript fell into the hands of Qāḍī Mīrzā Ḥaidar [or the Qāḍī of Mirza Haidar ?].[17] The Qāḍī, realizing that it was a valuable prize, carried it to his native land.

Sulṭān Zainu'l-'Ābidīn showed considerable respect for men of learning and attainment; he also gave prizes and stipends to them. During his reign, many learned men of great repute flocked to his court from foreign lands (*vilāyat*)[18] Maulānā Mīr Muḥammad Rūmī and Maulānā Aḥmad Rūmī, the two brothers with various attainments to their credit, arrived in this land [during this time]. They received lavish gifts and favours from the Sulṭān and ultimately settled here. On learning about Sulṭān Zainu'l-'Ābidīn's bounteous patronage to men of learning, a large number of them came to Kashmir; they were received and looked after with special care.[19]

Tolerant Towards Infidels

Whereas the Sulṭān showed considerable favour and regard to the Muslim nobles and their learned men, he also undertook the re-construction of the monuments of the infidels and the communities of the polytheists. He

15. Ḥasan writes that some works on Ḥadiṭh were brought from the holy place and constantly studied, but he makes no mention of this particular work. *Ibid.* By office is meant library.
16. A.H. 947/A.D. 1540.
17. The text is not clear.
18. Meaning Khurāsān, Central Asia (*Māwarā'-a'n-Nahr*) and other adjoining Islamic regions.
19. Ḥasan mentions these names: Maulānā Kabīr, Mullā Aḥmad Kashmīrī, Mullā Pārsā, Mullā Muḥammad, Qāḍī Ḥamīdu'd-Dīn, Maulānā Nāderī, Maulānā Ziyāī, and Mullā Nadīm. *TḤK*, p. 195.

popularized the practices of the infidels and the heretics and the customs of idol-worshippers and the people ignorant of faith. All those temples and idol-houses of the infidels, which had been destroyed totally in the reign of Sulṭān Sikandar, may God bless his soul, were re-built and re-habilitated by him.[20] Most of the unbelievers and polytheists, who had fled to the lands of Jammu and Kishtwār because of the overwhelming strength of Islam, were induced by him to return to Kashmir.[21] The sacred books of the infidels and the writings of the polytheists which had been taken out of this country were brought back, and thus the learning of the unbelievers and the customs of the polytheists were revived by him.[22] He helped the community of the misled idolaters to prosper. In every village and town, blasphemous customs connected with springs or temples were revived. He ordered that in every town and locality, celebration of special feasts and festivals by the infidels be revived in accordance with the customs prevalent in the past. He himself attended many

---

20. One such temple was that of Jyeṣṭhwara in the vicinity of present-day Srinagar. *TḤK*, p. 197. For Zainu'l-'Ābidīn's tolerance towards the 'infidels and the polytheists', see *Jonar.* Stt. 824-25, 879, 898-99, and Śrīvara, i. 5, 46 and 53. It is recorded in *Toḥfatu'l-Aḥbāb* that he built an alms-house for *Yogis* on the Dal lake which gave name to the locality of Jogi Lankar (now called Zooj Lankar or Zooj Lank) in present-day Srinagar. See *Toḥfat.*, MS f. 134[b].
21. Ḥasan says that apart from inducing those Hindus to return to Kashmir who had fled under Sulṭān Sikandar's persecution, Sulṭān Zainu'l-'Ābidīn also induced many Brahmans from India to settle in this land. *TḤK*, p. 197.
22. Copies of Vedās and Shāstrās were procured from India and got translated into Persian. Many Arabic and Persian books were got translated into Sanskrit. Particular mention can be made of Mullā Aḥmad's translation of *Rājataraṅgiṇī* and *Mahābhārata*. The Sulṭān also made Pandit Jonarāja to write a sequel to Kalhaṇa's chronicle which is the chronicle of events from the times of Jayasimha to his day. *TḤK*, p. 197.

of these festivities[23] and distributed gifts among dancers, stage actors, musicians and women singers so that all people, high and low, found themselves happy and satisfied with him.

Security of Boundaries

Sulṭān Zainu'l-'Ābidīn provided efficient and orderly administration during his reign and ensured safety and security of the boundaries of Kashmir from encroachments and forcible territorial occupation by foreigners. He extended the territorial limits of his domain to acquire some arable land in distant Tibet at a place called Li Shi and turn it into a private farm.

On the side of India, all the territories conquered by Sulṭān Shihābu'd-Dīn on the other side of Bahlūl Pora waters, the Salt Range and the boundaries of Swādgīr were put in the control of Sulṭān of India. Whatever fell on this side [of the geographical boundary] remained under the control of the Sulṭāns of Kashmir.[24] Sulṭān Zainu'l-'Ābidīn made secure and guarded these boundaries of his domain. These territories yielded tribute to the Sulṭān. If any ruler dared to launch an attack on these frontiers, he would despatch his commanders and generals at the head of a formidable force to ensure the security of his territory from such attacks. Sometimes he came out in person to command his troops.

---

23. Jonarāja tells us that the Sulṭān paid a visit to the Hindu sacred site of Amareśvara (Amarnāth). See *Jonar* (Bombay ed.), p. 1233 *et seq*. Another shrine of the same name is present-day Amburhër near Srinagar. See *Rājat*., vii, 183, 185 and Vol. II, p. 409.

24. The truce following the Sulṭān's fierce battle with the monarch of Dehli, across the river Sutlej, made him the master of the area up to Sirhind, as had been provided in the treaty with Sulṭān Shihābu'd-Dīn. *TḤK*, p. 192.

Tibetan Operation

Once, during his reign, an uprising took place in those regions, in which the ruler of Kāshghar attempted to occupy Tibet and Balti. Sulṭān Zainu'l-'Ābidīn summoned his nobles and chiefs and a strong force of twenty thousand horsemen and a hundred thousand footmen was raised in the *pargana* of Lār. These troops were put under local commanders: Muḥammad Māgray, Malik Mas'ud Thakkur,[25] who was a descendant from the line of Chandās, Helmat Raina, and Aḥmad Raina. Among the non-locals, Mīrak Sayyid Ḥasan also shared the command with them. [Along with these] the Sulṭān marched on to Tibet. Although Kāshgharian soldiers outnumbered their Kashmiri counterparts, yet the latter exhibited singular courage and valour. A fierce and bloody battle took place at Yashya[26] [*sic*], a place in Tibet. At this juncture, under the pressure of the enemy the Kashmiri soldiers began to show signs of fatigue and slackness. But that valiant chief of the Sayyids of Baihaq – Mīrak Sayyid Ḥasan[27] – exhibiting the traditional valour of the Hāshimites[28] advanced to confront the Turki soldiers.

[*verses*]

Turkish troops made a desperate attack. A day's relentless fighting wore out both the sides down and, by nightfall, they

25. See *Jonar.* St. 716, 3n.
26. Its location in the regions of Tibet is given variously. Shi Zi in *TḤK*, p. 191; Sheh Zi in *TMḤ*, MS f. 41[a], and Saya in *Jonar.* St. 834.
27. Malik Ḥaidar makes no mention of Sayyid Ḥasan; instead he writes that exceptional bravery was shown by Malik Avtār, Malik Helmat and Malik Aḥmad, who were later granted additional *jāgīrs* by the Sulṭān. See *TMḤ*, Ms. f. 41[a].
28. The chronicler tries to establish the Baihaqī Sayyids as the descendants of the Hāshimī line which is the line of the Prophet of Islam.

retired to their respective camps. Next day, at sunrise, the commanders and the stalwarts of the realm of Kashmir, taking inspiration from the unique valour which Mīrak Sayyid Ḥasan had exhibited on the previous day, struck so fiercely and slew the Turks so ruthlessly that the very sun in its high spheres sang [their] praises.

[*verses*]

A large number of soldiers was slain on either side. "When God wills, a few shall overpower many", so goes the saying. The happy news of the victory of Kashmiri troops spread [among the people] and was conveyed to Sulṭān Zainu'l-'Ābidīn. He returned to Kashmir in triumph from the Tibetan ranges and continued to rule over his realm in peace and security.

Works of Public Utility

During the times of the aforesaid Sulṭān, the people of these parts as well as of those falling under his suzerainty witnessed prosperous days and security of life and property; for, the Sulṭān paid full attention to the dispensation of justice and general welfare of his subjects. During his times, food and other eatables were so abundant and corn and cereals so cheap as they had been never before. Wholehearted efforts were made by the Sulṭān towards the promotion of works of public utility and other construction activities which led to the prosperity of the country. Many villages and hamlets and stretches of land which had been devastated and rendered fallow and stood in ruins on account of the ravages of Zulchū were rehabilitated and reclaimed. Some of these are Zainpora, Zainakot, Zainadab, and Zainagīr. Wherever land was reclaimed for cultivation and habitation, he ordered the construction of a spacious mansion or an attractive rest-house. He desired that the land at Zainagīr be reclaimed and made arable. For this purpose he got the old Pohru canal blocked by huge stones. Its water was thus diverted to the lands of Zainagīr which enabled the villagers to cultivate paddy. Income raised from the taxes and revenues of those lands was given to men of learning, eminence and piety, for their maintenance. Thus it was endowed in their name. [In Zainagīr] he ordered the construction of a magnificent palace. When it was completed, he also ordered that a garden with shady and fruit-bearing trees be laid around it.

Pāndav Chak[29] Destroyed

In those days there lived one Pāndeh (Pāndav) Chak, a descendant of Lankar Chak,[30] and head of the clan of Chaks. He conferred with his relatives and associates that in case Sulṭān Zainu'l-'Ābidīn stationed himself in Kāmarāj,[31] it would result in forced labour for their tribe. Men would be forced to do manual labour including carrying of loads and luggage.[32] On the eve of the Sulṭān's arrival in the town, no workers except carpenters, masons, and artisans were present. Pāndeh Chak took with him a group of his kinsmen and set that place on fire [where the Sulṭān had decided to stay in Kāmarāj]. After destroying all the buildings, he

29. The word 'Chak' as it figures in the translation should have been spelt as 'Chakk' because when it occurs in the verses in the text, it demands a *shadd* on the letter K. However, its Sanskrit etymology (Cakra) does not warrant the doubling of the letter k: hence Chak in the translation.

30. Lankar Chak (Alaṁkarçakra) was a Dāmara leader. For details see *Rājat.*, viii, 2482-83. He had sought Rājā Suhdev's assistance and had settled in the village of Trehgām. See *TḤK*, p. 217.

31. For Kāmarāj (Krāmarājya), see *Rājat.*, Vol. II, p. 436. In fact the Sulṭān occasionally rested at the health resort of Zenagīr in Kāmarāj were he had laid out spacious and attractive gardens, nearly two miles long. See *TḤK*, p. 193.

32. This suggests that forced labour (*begār*) existed during the reign of Sulṭān Zainu'l-'Ābidīn.

withdrew to the mountains of Trehgām,[33] but despatched his womenfolk to Drāv.[34] When the news was conveyed to the Sulṭān, he sent a large contingent of his soldiers who burnt the houses belonging to Pāndeh Chak at Trehgām. Pāndeh Chak fled to Drāv. Sulṭān Zainu'l-'Ābidīn got the palace re-built but only to be burnt by Pāndeh Chak and his men once again, when they seized a suitable opportunity to return from Drāv. Again Pāndeh Chak retired to Drāv. Later on Sulṭān Zainu'l-'Ābidīn tried to win the people of Drāv by offering gifts and extending many favours to them. In this way he brought them under his subjugation. They captured Pāndeh Chak along with members of his family and kinsfolk, young as well as old, and then handed them over to the Sulṭān, who issued orders of execution [*sic*] of Pāndeh Chak and also of such of his sons and relatives as were capable of fighting or resisting him. Their children and womenfolk were banished to a village called Kavarel[35] [*sic*] and situated on the other extreme of Kashmir. They took up permanent dwelling there. After some time, their infants came of age and cultivated acquaintance with local people. Their neighbours treated them with compassion and affection. At last the clan of the Nāyaks which had been enjoying superior position in that locality entered into matrimonial relations with the Chaks. Most of the other leading families of the area also established matrimonial alliances with them.

Of their line – a son of Pāndeh Chak – was one Ḥusain Chak whom God blessed with nine or ten sons. The clan of the Chaks of Trehgām increased and multiplied through the

33. Now in district Kupwāra, also see *The Rājataraṅginī of Jonarāja*, tr. R.C. Dutt, New Delhi, 1986, p. 102 *et seq.*
34. A tract of land on river Kishen Ganga. See *Rājat.*, viii. 2709 and ii, 282.
35. Heril, perhaps in *pargana* Votur. *TḤK*, p. 194. For its ancient geography, see *Rājat.*, Vol. 11, Note 26, p. 485 *et seq.*

progeny of this Ḥusain Chak and their tribe broke off into various branches.[36] We shall deal with them at their proper place in this work.

The Legend of Wular

Sulṭān Zainu'l-'Ābidīn had zest for raising buildings and mansions at places which commanded scenic beauty and had attractive surroundings. Lakes, full of clean and transparent waters, like of Dal, Bumeh [*sic*] and Wular were filled with stones and earth [at particular spots] to create artificial islands on which splendid buildings were erected. Such a big artificial island was developed in the Wular lake on which a mansion, a mosque and some houses were erected; it was given the name of *Lank*.

It is said that in ancient times there was no water at the present site of the lake and a big town[37] with dense population flourished there. The ruler of this city was called Sudarshan. The inhabitants of the city indulged in various kinds of immoral and corrupt acts and the king and his courtiers perpetrated cruelty and oppression [on people].

In the city there lived a pious and God-fearing potter; he was unhappy with the rest of the people for their corrupt and impious acts. One night he saw a soothsayer in his dream who bade him to exhort his compatriots to desist from all acts of impiety and ignominy, failing which their land would

36. Apart from the Chaks of Trehgām, Ḥasan speaks of the Chaks of Gilgit originating from the ancestor of Helmat Chak. This tribe settled at Kupwāra later on. Pāndav Chak and his descendants, Ḥusain Chak and Kājī Chak accepted *Shia'* faith by following Shams Araki, but the Chaks of Gilgit adhered to *Sunni* faith and were of Ḥanafī sect. Ḥasan also writes that he had heard his father saying that one of the Trehgām branch of Chaks came to Sardār A'zam Khān. He donned a Tartar cap (*kulāh-i-tatri*), wore Uzbek boots and was so tall that he lifted the Sardār from the *howdah* and placed him on the ground. See *TḤK*, pp. 217-18.

37. *Sanādatnagar* in *TMḤ*, MS f. 39^{b}.

get submerged under a sheet of water. When the potter conveyed this to the people, they did not give any credence to him; they called him a mad man and dismissed his words as nonsense. The following night the potter received afflatus directing him to roll his belongings [that very night] and abandon the city because an impending deluge was to wipe it out entirely. Till midday he made a public announcement of this imminent danger, but no one paid heed to him. Shortly after the afternoon prayers, he collected his belongings and fled to Kāmarāj. The following dawn he glanced back from the hill-tops[38] far across the city and found it submerged. He found no traces of its buildings.

In that city there was a big idol-house and a lofty temple.[39] The idol-house also got submerged under water. Since Zainu'l-'Ābidīn desired to raise an artificial island in the lake on which the *lank* could be created, he ordered the boatmen and the divers to locate a spot of minimum depth in the Wular over which it could be raised without much labour. All of them suggested the spot where the massive buildings had stood previously. They said that when the water receded to its lowest level in winter, the stones of the temple would become visible through the crystalline waters of the lake. Sulṭān Zainu'l-'Ābidīn took a boat and personally examined the spot. He ordered the divers to make an attempt at finding anything [of the relics] inside the temple in the water. The divers plunged into the lake and with utmost care made their way into the temple, wherefrom they pulled out two bronze idols. The Sulṭān then selected the very site for developing an island.[40]

---

38. The hill-top is known as Krāleh Sanger even to this day. *Ibid.*
39. It had been built by Rājā Sandhimat. See *TḤK*, p. 194. Also see *Rājat.*, ii, 132.
40. Ḥasan calls it Zenadab. *TḤK*, p. 194. There is no mention of the existence of a temple and its bronze images in Jonarāja. See *The Rājataraṅgiṇī of Jonarāja*, tr. R.C. Dutt, New Delhi, 1986, pp. 90-92.

Prior to that, this Sulṭān had got a boat built for use in the Wular lake after the design of boats found in Gujerat. A master architect, Duroodgiri by name, had been called from Gujerat and he supervised the construction of the boat[41] in which the Sulṭān used to make pleasure trips whenever he so desired. The boat moved with the help of sails. For developing the artificial island, *lank*, he ordered that the boat be brought to stand exactly over the site of the submerged temple. It was then filled with stones and sunk into the lake. Then more stones were dropped around it. This was followed by boatloads of loose earth and stones till the island came up. It was brought to a level higher than that of the water, so that the structure raised on it was made secure against floods and storms. The shape of this island is somewhat like a rectangle, with its length extending from east to west and [illegible] yards respectively and [illegible] yards from north to south.

The Sulṭān ordered that two buildings be raised on that island; one, a palace with its ground floor made of stone, and the upper two storeys of brick and timber; the other, a mosque raised solidly in the middle of the island. One of the poets of those days found the year of construction of *lank* in the chronogram *Khurram-Ābād*. The verse engraved on the top fore-part of the mosque is:

> *tā Zain-i abād andar ān jashn kunad*
> *paiwasteh chu tārīkh-i khudash Khurram bād.*

The Sulṭān got mulberry and fruit trees planted and flowers of different hues cultivated on the island. In fact, an attractive place with an airy mansion was raised in the middle of the lake. A picnic spot of such beauty is not to be found in the whole of Kashmir.

It has been seen that some of the rulers who attained power and authority ordered the pulling down of some ancient buildings. They raised new structures on these sites

41. The boat was made on the pattern of a ship. See *TMḤ*, MS f. 40[a].

to be ascribed to them. But the palace and the mosque of Sulṭān Zainu'l-'Ābidīn [in the Wular lake] cannot suffer such an alteration.

Pohru Canal

After the construction of the *lank* and the raising of structures on it, the Sulṭān paid attention towards the reclamation of land at Zainagīr and also towards the digging of the Pohru canal, as is evident from the chronograms about these two projects. The date of creating the *lank* has been derived from the chronogram *Khurram-Ābād* and that of Pohru Canal from *Jūy-e Khurram*.

Men of Learning

There flourished a large number of famous saints during the reign of this Sulṭān, such as Shaykh Bahāu'd-Dīn Kashmiri, Shaykh Sulṭān Kubrā, Shaykh Nūru'd-Dīn,[42] Maulānā Othmān Majzoob, Shaykh Zainu'd-Dīn Rishī, Mīr Veys Majzoob, Maulānā Nūru'd-Dīn, Mīr Sayyid Madanī, and Sayyid Ḥasan Bilād-Rūm. Some of them lived from the times of Sulṭān Sikandar, the Iconoclast, to the times of Sulṭān Zainu'l-'Ābidīn; some appeared and became known only during his (Sulṭān Zainu'l-'Ābidīn's) days. Apart from them, a fairly large number of men of erudition and eminence also lived at that time: for instance, Mullā Muḥammad Rūmī, Mullā Aḥmad Rūmī [of whom mention has already been made], Qāḍī Sayyid 'Alī Shīrāzī, Qāḍī Jalāl,[43] Maulānā Kabīr, Sayyid Muḥammad Luristānī, and Sayyid Muḥammad Sīstānī. By and large, his courtiers and

42. Called Rishi in *Ḥasan*. See *TḤK*, p. 199.

43. Qāḍī Jalāl came from India and stayed in the *khānqāh* of Amīr Sayyid 'Alī Hamadānī; people used to seek solutions to their religious problems from him and also got their letters written by him. The Sulṭān invited him to his court after he got a letter from him. Later he was made the Qāḍī of the city of Srinagar. See *TMḤ*, MS f. 40[b].

the men of learning of his times were of cheerful disposition, experts in the art of versification, and subtle in their discourses. These included Maulānā Aḥmad Kashmiri, Maulānā Nāderī, Maulānā Ziyāī, Maulānā Fathī and several others whose artistry can be found in their delightful verses. The Sulṭān himself was adept at writing verses and possessed a poetic sensibility. He adopted *Quṭb* as his pen-name and has left behind a *Dīwān* of his verses. Here is a verse from his composition:[44]

> *ay begird-e Sham-i rūyat ʻalamī parvāneh-ī*
> *vaz lab-i shīrīn-i tū shorīst dar har khāneh-ī.*

In short, he was a ruler who did his utmost for the progress and prosperity of his subjects; who took keen interest in the rehabilitation and building up of the state; whose benevolence and munificence prompted artists and craftsmen to gain excellence in their skills. [When] the Jāmeʻ Mosque in the city caught fire during his reign, he ordered the re-building of its western structures so that Friday congregations and prayers were not suspended. The front portion of the mosque remained charred. The ceiling as well as the roof had been completely burnt and except for the bare walls nothing remained. The mosque continued to be in this condition till the times of the government and ministry of Malik Mūsā Raina [and] Ibrāhīm Māgray. During the ministry of Malik Mūsā Raina, Malik Ibrāhīm Māgray undertook the task of re-construction of the three sides of the mosque, making use of timber and pillars and other material brought from Kitch-hāma and Kāmarāj and [in ?] it is, indeed, a big achievement of Ibrāhīm Māgray.

Revival of Idolatry

The only conspicuous defect and an over-all drawback of Zainu'l-ʻĀbidīn was that idolatry and heresy, which had been stamped out in the reign of Sulṭān Sikandar the

44. Ḥasan has given five verses of the *ghazal*. See *TḤK*, p. 207.

Iconoclast – God bless his soul – and of which there had remained no traces in the lands of Kashmir, were revived by him. The customs and practices of the polytheists and the heretics received fresh impetus and were given renewed currency. He ordered that particular days of festivity be celebrated in every town and village, in which innumerable vices and corrupt practices were let loose. In more than one way, these had a deleterious influence on the *sharia'* and Islam brought by the Prophet. The community of infidels and heretics called him the Great King[45] because they flourished under his rule and he was known by the name throughout his kingdom.

With the passage of time, the customs of the Hindus[46] and the infidels and their corrupt and immoral practices attained such popularity that even the *'ulemā*, the learned, the Sayyids and *Qāḍīs* of this land began to observe them without exhibiting even the slightest repugnance for them. There was none to forbid them to do so. It resulted in a gradual weakening of Islam and a decay in its cannons and postulates; idol-worship and corrupt and immoral practices thrived; It was only after the arrival of Amīr Shamsu'd-Dīn Muḥammad Araki and through the instrumentality of his generous acts and excellent efforts that those unholy practices were eradicated. Islamic religion and injunctions of the *sharia'* of the Holy Prophet were revitalized under the dispensations of that spiritual guide. Some of these events will be recorded at their proper place.

Death

Thus ruled Sulṭān Zainu'l-'Ābidīn over the kingdom of Kashmir and enforced laws through its length and breadth.

45. Bud Shāh in Ḥasan. See *TḤK*, p. 206. Hindu writers raised him to the status of god Vishnu. See *Jonar*. Stt. 935, 973.

46. The word Hindu (and not *kāfir*) is used here for the first time in the chronicle.

His reign lasted fifty-two years. Unable to protect his dear life from the claws of the angel of death, he passed away in A.H. 878 (A.D. 1473). This, according to the calendar of the people of Kashmir, was 46 Vivat 12. He was buried by the side of his father Sulṭān Sikandar, God's peace and forgiveness be on him.[47]

[*verses*]

Ḥaidar Shāh

After the death of Sulṭān Zainu'l-'Ābidīn, his son Ḥaidar Shāh succeeded him on the aforesaid date. He did not live long, and, after reigning for about two years, died in A.H. 880 (A.D. 1475).[48]

Ḥasan Shāh

Thus, in the aforesaid year, which according to Kashmiri calendar is 48 Vivat, he was succeeded by his son Sulṭān

---

47. His reign lasted fifty-two years. *TMḤ*, MS f. 41^{b}. According to Ḥasan, he died at the age of sixty-nine. Malik Ḥaidar closes the chapter on Sulṭān Zainu'l-'Ābidīn with the verse

    agar ṣad sāl mānī dar yakī rūz
    bebāyad raft azīn kākh-i dilafrūz,

    Shrivara's detailed account of agonising last days of his life stands in contrast to the author's sudden closing of the) chapter. See J.C. Dutt (tr.) Delhi, 1986, pp. 165-67.

48. It is curious that the author has dismissed Ḥaidar Shāh in one sentence. Malik Ḥaidar, too, has devoted hardly one sentence to this king. But Ḥasan gives him more space, alluding to the court intrigues resulting from Ḥaidar Shāh's indulgence in carnal pleasures, his soft policy towards Hindus, and his damaging of the mosques. See *TḤK*, p. 208. It is to be noted that Shrivara has given us the account of the rebellion of Ādam Khān, the eldest son of Zainu'l-'Ābidīn and his banishment from the kingdom. *The Rājataraṅgiṇī of Jonarāja*, tr. J.C. Dutt, New Delhi 1986, pp. 124 *et seq*.

Ḥasan Shāh.[49] During the tenure of his kingship, the Sulṭān gave himself up to carnal pleasures. Nearly twelve hundred Indian singers[50] of both sexes were inducted into his service. Apart from them, Kashmiri musicians, singers, cymbal-beaters, etc. were also in the employ of his household. During the entire period, of his reign, he never came out [of his palace] to lead his troops, though, of course, he did despatch his chiefs and commanders to lead them. The commander of his army was Malik Aḥmad Itoo. Sehej Raina, a descendant of the Chandās, and Aḥmad Māgray of the clan of Māgrays[51] were among his high-ranking officials.

Expedition to Sialkot

Up to his times, the inhabitants of Bahlool Pore and its adjacent areas paid taxes and tributes to the officials of Kashmir and subjected themselves to their authority. One of his (Ḥasan Shāh's) officers, Tāzī Bhat had proceeded to Bahlool Pora with a contingent of troops to collect taxes and tributes. The governor of Lahore and Panjab at this time was one Tātār Khān. He had moved his soldiers to a certain place for military exercises and the troops [stationed] at Sialkot and its suburbs joined him for the said purpose. Thus [at the time of Tāzī Bhat's arrival] in Sialkot

---

49. His queen, Ḥayāt Khātūn, the daughter of Sayyid Ḥasan ibn Sayyid Nāṣir Baihaqī bore him two sons, Muḥammad Khān and Ḥusain Khān. The former was brought up by the wife of Malik Tāzi Bhat (who later on became the commander of Ḥasan Shāh's troops), and the latter by Malik Aḥmad Itoo, the chief vizier of Ḥasan Shāh. *TḤK*, p. 208 seq.

50. This is corroborated by Malik Ḥaidar and Ḥasan. See *TMḤ*, MS f. 42[a] and *TḤK*, p. 210. For more details see *The Rājataraṅgiṇī of Jonarāja*, tr. J.C. Dutt, pp. 231-32.

51. Malik Ḥaidar does not mention Aḥmad Māgray, only Malik Sehej, Malik Avtār, Malik Aḥmad Itoo and Tāzī Bhat are mentioned. See *TMḤ*, MS f. 42[a].

and its adjoining areas only the peasants, artisans, and petty shop-keepers could be found. Tāzī Bhat launched an attack on Sialkot and subjected the people to loot and plunder, causing ruin and devastation. When Tātār Khān returned to Lahore and came to his dwelling place, he was told about the devastation suffered by his country. Forthwith, he turned towards Kashmir at the head of his army. However, no strenuous efforts were needed at that time to occupy Kashmir for the reason that the Sulṭān, the nobles, the commoners, as well as the soldiers were given to sloth and had become addicted to *bhang* (canabis sativa) and other kinds of narcotics. In the past the kings of Kashmir had enjoyed fame and reputation in the lands of India, and the territories from the ridges of Kājdārī mountains and the off-sides of the borders at Gagren, was lost by the Sulṭāns of Kashmir and passed into the control of [the kings] of India, still, the revenues from the peripheral areas of the domain of Kashmir from Kājdārī and Gagren [*sic*] to this side amounted to twelve crores [?] and one thousand horses [*sic*] annually.[52]

After this (Tātār Khān's invasion), the commanders and the chiefs of Kashmir adopted an attitude of bellicosity towards one another and took to mutual feuds and in-fighting. This naturally crippled their capacity to re-capture the out-flanking areas of Kashmir. They could not ensure the security of the country; the result was that those territories were lost by the rulers of Kashmir. Thus, except for bare midlands, nothing remained under the sway of the authorities in. Kashmir. Indeed, when friends begin to oppose and confront one another, the enemy enjoys the fruit [of their conflict] to his heart's content.

---

52. Text not clear. Ḥasan says that the Sulṭān continued to receive 12 lakh rupees in cash and a thousand horses by way of presents from foreign countries. See *TḤK*, pp. 210-11.

Shams Araki arrives

In the times of Ḥasan Shāh, Mīr Shamsu'd-Dīn[53] – the pioneer among the enquirers of truth – blessed these lands for the first time with his auspicious footsteps.[54] He had brought an affectionate letter of greetings for Sulṭān Ḥasan Shāh from Sulṭān Ḥusain Mīrzā[55] in which the latter had honoured him by addressing him (Sulṭān Ḥasan) as his 'illustrious son.' Apart from that he had sent Sulṭān Ḥasan a fur-coat of Kesh from his personal wardrobe.[56] Being addressed as his 'illustrious son' and supplemented by the presents sent by him, the ruler of Khurāsān certainly added to the honour and prestige of the kings of those lands (Kashmir).

After the death of Ḥasan Shāh, Amīr Shamsu'd-Dīn Araki got detained in Kashmir for about eight years on account of chaos and confusion which prevailed there.[57] It was during the reign of Sulṭān Fatḥ Shāh that he was permitted to leave and presents were offered to him. His second visit [to Kashmir] came off after a lapse of twelve years,[58] during the reign of Sulṭān Muḥammad Shāh.

---

53. For detailed account of his being a Sayyid, a descendant of the line of Imām Mūsā Kāzim, the Seventh Imām according to the *ithna 'ashriyya* faction of the *Shia'*, the reader may see the amusing 'Introduction' of *Bahāristān-i-Shāhi* edited by Akbar Ḥaidari (Kashmir, 1982), p. 28, *et seq*. See also *Toḥfat, passim*. In Shuka's Chronicle he is recorded as Merasheṣha. *The Rājataraṅgiṇī of Jonarāja*, (tr.) J.C. Dutt, Delhi, 1986, p. 339 *et seq*.
54. Araki's first visit to Kashmir was in A.H. 882/A.D. 1477. *Bahāristān-i-Shāhi*, ed. Akbar Ḥaidari, p. 38.
55. Ḥasan writes that Sulṭān Ḥusain Mīrzā, the governor of Khurāsān suspected Araki's intentions, and therefore, expelled him from his country. On the basis of his previous contacts, he once again came to Kashmir after a period of twelve years. *TḤK*, p. 220.
56. See *Toḥfatu'l-Aḥbābd*, MS ff. 6-8.
57. In Kashmir he became a disciple of Bābā Ismā'īl, and secretly prompted Bābā 'Alī Najjār to accept Shia' faith. See *TḤK*, p. 211.
58. In A.H. 902/A.D. 1496.

Ḥasan Shāh's death

During the time of the same Sulṭān Ḥasan Shāh, Shaykh Shihābu'd-Dīn Hindī, accompanied by his daughter, paid a visit to this land. He announced that at Medina, by the side of the grave of the Holy Prophet, he had been told in a dream that his daughter would be the future wife of Sulṭān Ḥasan Shāh of Kashmir. He further made it public that he had come from Medina only to give his daughter in marriage to the Sulṭān.

This Shaykh Shihābu'd-Dīn was a learned man who came to Kashmir in the middle of autumn. Sulṭān Ḥasan put off the marriage ceremony for a couple of months to allow them rest after a long and arduous journey. When the spring set in, he wanted the marriage to be solemnized. But the inevitable dispensation brought him his message of death before the contemplated marriage could take place, and he joined the world of the dead. Sulṭān Ḥasan Shāh reigned for twelve years and five days[59] and in the year 89 – corresponding to the sixth Vivat, 10th in Kashmiri calendar – he breathed his last. He was laid to rest by the side of his father and his ancestors. In the same year, his son, Sulṭān Muḥammad Shāh, ascended the throne at the early age of seven.

[*verses*]

Muḥammad Shāh under guardianship

At that time, the authority and control of the government rested in the hands of Sayyids of Baihaq. The foremost leader of this group was Mīrak Sayyid Ḥasan, the son of Mīr Sayyid Nāṣir. He wielded authority over other high officials [*sic*] in major administrative matters; he considered Kashmiri

59. *TMḤ*, MS f. 42ª. Shrivara records the years as 60. See *Rajat of Jonarāja*, J.C. Dutt (tr.) Delhi, 1986, p. 265. The subtle hint is that he was poisoned by the Sayyids.

chiefs and commanders as not a bit higher than his servants and attendants. He had it proclaimed that in the management of public affairs, he would not outstrip the limits of the *sharia'*, and that negligence in its observance [by people] would not be tolerated. He further said that he would not take for himself a single penny exacted under oppression, and promised to abide strictly by the commands of the Holy Book while dealing with the matters of state. "Justice is a provost that adorns the state: a ray that removes darkness and brings light."[60] Mīrak Sayyid Ḥasan put into practice what he said; he meted out justice to the oppressed and gave them solace.

[*verses*]

Conspiracy

[Such an] enforcement of religious law was resented by the miscreants and the wicked who feared him. Since Kashmiri chiefs were ignorant of the [superior] quality of administration based on the Muḥammadan law, they found it difficult to get adjusted to the authority of Mīrak Sayyid Ḥasan.[61] Hence they looked for pretexts to put an end to his life. The scheme they devised was to deploy three hundred well-equipped irregular warriors[62] in the royal place at night. When Mīrak Sayyid Ḥasan would come to his chamber where he used to dispense justice after offering morning prayers, the troops would rush from their

60. The sentence has been borrowed from *Lawāyeh* of Jāmī. But Shrivara gives a very disappointing account of the administration of the Sayyids. See *Rājataraṅgiṇī of Jonarāja*, tr J.C. Dutt, Delhi, 1986, pp. 252-253, and 260-61.

61. Apostasy among the Muslims had increased considerably in Kashmir during the reign of Sulṭān Zainu'l-'Ābidīn. Stories of re-conversion to Islamic faith have been vividly told in *Toḥfatu'l-Aḥbāb*, MS (transcript), ff. 6-8. See also *TḤK*, p. 207.

62. *nīm jarrār* in the text.

hiding places, and put him to the sword. The conspiracy was kept a top secret.

It has been written in Kashmiri (i.e. Sanskrit)[63] that on that particular night, while Mīr Sayyid Ḥasan lay asleep as usual, he had a dream in which he saw his father Mīr Sayyid Nāṣir informing him that since his enemies had joined hands in a vicious conspiracy of murdering him, it was advisable that he should not come out of his house next day nor should he ride his horse. But after rising from sleep he ignored to seek an interpretation of the dream,[64] and proceeded to his office chamber. Despite vehement entreaties made by his well-wishers and sincere friends not to come out of his house on that day, he came out, and regarded the previous night's dream as the work of an evil spirit.

[*verses*]

Mīrak Sayyid Ḥasan arrived in his office chamber without any hesitation. The murderers rushed out of their hiding place and made a sudden attack on him and his nephews. He had with him his bow and arrow. Forthwith he struck an arrow into the breast of one of his assailants with such force that, piercing his breast, it embedded into another man's side, killing both of them.

They [the Sayyid and his assailants] came so near to each other that there was hardly any chance for anybody to use an arrow or a lance. With swords and daggers, clubs and other weapons Mīrak Sayyid Ḥasan and his nephews got entangled in fight with their opponents. It led to many

---

63. This indicates that the history of Kashmir of this period written in Sanskrit also existed and was made use of by the chronicler through a translator or an interpreter. These could be the histories written by Śrivara and Suka. Śrivara clearly mentions about Mīr Ḥasan's dream. See J.C. Dutt's translation, p. 270.
64. This was common during the Hindu period and several examples can be found in *Rājataraṅgiṇī*.

killings in which Mīrak Sayyid Ḥasan and fourteen of his brethren and nephews attained martyrdom. The date of his death has been found in the chronogram:

Tārīkh-i faut-i ū ze khirad just murshidī
Dānā-i aql goft ki Mīrak shahīd shud.

Revenge and fighting

Of Mīrak Ḥasan's party only one servant, wounded and badly-mauled and drenched in blood, could manage to force his escape through an aqueduct in the fort of Nowshehr. He carried himself to Mīr Muḥammad, the son of Mīrak Ḥasan, and told him of the tragedy [that had befallen Mīrak Sayyid Ḥasan]. In spite of the fact that Mīr Muḥammad had not even crossed the seventeenth year of his age, he was not frightened by this overwhelmingly tragic event. He told his blood-brother, Mīr Sayyid Hāshim, that if they did not fight the enemy then and there, the result would be death to their supporters.

[*verses*]

He added that unless they fought their enemy, unless the valiant on either side were slain in battle, and unless streams of blood flowed between the royal palace and the fields, their score with the chiefs of Kashmir would not be settled.[65]

65. It is clear that the attack on Mīrak Ḥasan was politically motivated and had little to do with this strict enforcement of the laws of *shariat*, see p. 95, *supra*. The Kashmiri nobles were against the Baihaqī Sayyids because they were still considered as outsiders. However, from the sentence that follows in the text, it appears that Kashmiri commanders were divided on the issue of loyalty to the Sayyids. Ḥasan says that since the Sulṭān was still a minor, the Baihaqī Sayyids had concentrated power in their hands and did not allow any other person to exercise authority: they made it even difficult to meet the Sulṭān. This made the Kashmiri nobles join hands with Rājā of Jammu who had earlier fled to Kashmir for fear of Tātār Khān Lodhī, and then they put Sayyid Ḥasan to death along with his thirty other associates. *TḤK*, p. 212.

[*verses*]

This suggestion was liked by the entire body of seniors on their side. A force of three thousand troops, armed to the teeth, was raised and, relying on God's grace, mounted their horses, and headed towards the fort of Nowshehr. When Kashmiri nobles came to know of their [enemy's] ability to strike, they blocked the gates of the fort and deployed archers and catapulters all around it. They armed themselves and stood guard at different gates.

Sayyids Win

People, high and low, climbed on roofs and house-tops to have a view of the mighty battle which was being fought between soldiers [fighting] on foot and on horse-back. Mīr Muḥammad, along with his soldiers, engaged the enemy in front of the gate where the royal band played at regular intervals. Amīr Sayyid Hāshim and his warriors took position near the gate from which water flowed down. Both the brothers told their men in loud words that the onlookers expected them to fight like brave and valiant soldiers. Emotionally charged, the warriors were galvanized into heroic action and they fell upon the enemy like lions on their prey. With divine assistance, they put those wretched people to utter rout with a single onslaught. Many Kashmiri warriors were slain, and the rest, realizing that resistance was futile, left from the gate opening towards the Phāk *pargana*. They destroyed the bridges over the river running through the city, and assembled at Zāldagar[66] *maidān* and sought reinforcement and help from the people of that locality.

Raising the lofty banner of victory, Mīr Muḥammad arrived at the spot where his father lay slain. He saw the tragic scene of his father's dead body and those of his

---

66. The locality near Sayyid Manṣūr mosque in Srinagar, which bears the same name to this day.

relatives lying in dust and blood, like the martyrs of Kerbalā.

[*verses*]

Despite the overwhelming strength and power of the Sayyids, the situation slipped out of their control for some time, with the result that there appeared signs of slackness on their part. However, Mīr Muḥammad was able to recover the dead body of his father from the heap of dust and laid it to rest in his ancestral graveyard. In despair he expressed his thoughts as are embodied in these verses:

[*verses*[67]]

Thereafter they challenged the Kashmiris in loud words, accompanied by the shrill sound of the clarion and the beat of the drum. Fully equipped horsemen rallied round the Sayyids in group after group on their side of the river. They kept themselves in full readiness for an attack. But finding that crossing the river without boats and platforms[68] was difficult for the horsemen, he (Mīr Muḥammad) decided to encamp on the specious Īdgāh grounds with his soldiers and attendants. He ordered that all treasures of the governors of Kashmir be taken out of the fort at Nowshehr. Not troubling his officials to blacken their fingers by counting gold and silver coins one by one, he signalled them with his arrow that these be distributed among his soldiers in shieldfuls and skirtfuls, by way of prize-money and incentive to fight the enemy.

---

67. *bī rū-i tū zindeh mī tawān būd wali*
īn zindaqī az hazār murdan batar ast.

(It is possible to live without seeing your face, but that life is worse than a thousand deaths.)

68. The first boat-bridge (*Nāvsetu*) on the Vitastā was built as early as the 6th century A.D. by Pravarasena II of Gonanda dynasty at some distance from Mākṣikasvāmin (present-day Maisuma). See *Rājat.*, iii. 354n.

Negotiations

Mīrak Sayyid Ḥasan's murder gave rise to serious confusion and chaos among Kashmiri chiefs and commanders. The local people as well as the aliens (*mawālī*) living in the land were also faced with a similar situation of chaos and disorder. However, the wise and the sagacious opined that since it was not possible to put an end to the prevailing turmoil without resorting to brute force and a policy of repression, it would be better to send a delegation comprising the learned, the noble and the pious to Mīr Muḥammad for exploring means of putting an end to the prevailing state of anarchy. The members of the delegation were told to use such soft and appeasing words as would make a definite impact on him. They were to use friendly words and give wise counsel which could bring about conciliation. They were to plead that to err is human and that they were only human beings.

[*verses*]

After agreeing to this, the delegation proceeded on its mission to see Mīr Muḥammad. First, it offered condolence to him on the death [of Mīrak Ḥasan] and presented him with gifts. Then it conveyed to him the deep regret of the nobles for their acts of omission:

[*verses*]

They went on to say that they (nobles) found themselves at a loss to understand why they did things in haste, and therefore, reproached themselves for not having shown caution and consideration.

[*verses*]

The delegation impressed upon him that if the government [of the land] did not pass into the hands of a capable elderly person, there was a danger that a large number of people would fall victims to revenge and reprisals. Already innocent persons like the pious and elderly Mīr Veys had been murdered because of such a state of anarchy. They further told him that because of this magnificent buildings and prestigious localities had also been destroyed.

[*verses*]

Truce conclude

In short, senior members of the mission succeeded in conducting negotiations with poise and affability to pave the way for conciliation. Negotiations for truce stretched over a period of two days and conditions were laid down, and by slow degrees Mīr Muḥammad was brought round to agree to the promotion of peace. Kashmiri nobles felt obliged [to them] for success in their mission. Mīr Muḥammad, therefore, returned with his troops and entourage to India via Hirpur route.[69]

[*verses*]

After the peace treaty was concluded, the reins of power and administrative authority during Muḥammad Shāh's reign rested in the hands of Jahāngīr (Aḥmad) Māgray.[70] Mīr Sayyid Muḥammad joined Sulṭān Fatḥ Shāh, the son of Ādham Khān, and the grandson of Sulṭān Zainu'l-'Ābidīn, at Nowshehr in India.[71]

---

69. The old Surapura. For its geography and remains, see *Rājat.*, p. 394. Note II.

70. Jahāngīr Māgray, who stayed at Lohar Kot fort, did not agree to support the Sayyids. *TḤK*, p. 213. In Shrivara's chronicle he is referred as Margapatī. J.C. Dutt, tr., p. 320, *et seq.*

71. After remaining away from Kashmir, Fatḥ Shāh went to Rājaurī to re-capture his ancestral kingdom. Several groups of Kashmiri nobles went to meet him, and he won them over by giving them rewards. But Jahāngīr Māgray was not among them: in fact, he resisted and repulsed Fatḥ Shāh's troops when they tried to (*Contd.*)

Saif Dār

Before this event, Malik Saif Dār had fled to that (Hirpur) mountain region. After three years, Fatḥ Shāh and Mīr Sayyid Muḥammad Baihaqī brought him to Kashmir along with them. They (Fatḥ Shāh and Mīr Sayyid Muḥammad) together became the governing authority of the domain of Kashmir. Since Mīr Sayyid Baihaqī was a blood relation of Sulṭān Muḥammad Shāh, he joined hands with him after some time; and, after raising troops, regained control over the state of Kashmir. Sulṭān Fatḥ Shāh was again forced to flee to India. In the sixty-fourth year of Kashmiri calendar, Jahāngīr Māgray breathed his last.[72] Once again, Sulṭān Fatḥ Shāh and Malik Saif Dār succeeded in establishing their control over the domain of Kashmir.

In this adventure, Malik Mūsā Raina and Serang[73] [*sic*] Raina – the offspring of the clan of Chandās[74] – joined Malik Saif Dār and Fatḥ Shāh.

Shams Chak

Malik Shams Chak of the clan of Chaks was among the nobles of the land (of Kashmir). He was the son of Helmat Chak. Their tribe hailed from the regions of Gilgit and had settled down in the town of Kupwāra.[75] Their kinship with

re-enter Kashmir. For more details see *TḤK*, pp. 215, *et seq.* Also see Śrivara's history, tr. J.C. Dutt, pp. 270 *et al.*

72. Ḥasan says that before his death he was forced to flee to the mountains. *TḤK*, p. 215.

73. Ḥasan calls him Sarhanq Raina. *TḤK*, p. 215. Now the word *sarhanq* in Persian means an army officer of the rank of a colonel. He is *Sḥringārarājānaka* of Śrivara's chronicle Tr. J.C. Dutt, p. 313.

74. Malik Ḥaidar includes another general Malik Nuṣrat Chādūra among the descendants of the Chandās of Chādūra. See *TMḤ*, MS f. 42[b]. All the three shared power with Saif Dār.

75. The Chaks of Trehgām (originally of Gilgit) have to be distinguished from another family) of Chaks of Dārdu. Lankar

(*Contd.*)

the Chaks of Trehgām had become very distant and there was only mutual rancour and hostility between them. At first, Shams Chak was in the service of the above-mentioned Mīr Sayyid Muḥammad. But as the two were not able to pull on together, Shams, later on, entered the service of Malik Nowroz Itoo, the son of Aḥmad Itoo. Before long, he was able to establish his fame as a brave and valorous person. Intrepid by nature, Shams Chak had displayed exceptional feats of bravery in many battles. Later on, he wielded full authority during the days of Malik Saif Dār.

Ḥusain Chak, the son of Pāndav Chak, dwelt in the village of Kawarel [*sic*]. He gave his daughter in marriage to Shams Chak[76] and with that [alliance] the long-estranged kinship between them was revived. A few of Ḥusain Chak's progeny joined Shams Chak as his soldiers. Since bravery, heroism, and martial spirit were in the blood of the Chak tribe, Malik Shams Chak was able to acquire an authoritative and powerful position through his people.

After some time, Sulṭān Fatḥ Shāh wished to deprive Malik Saif Dār of his power and authority: To achieve this, he aligned with himself a faction of the chiefs and nobles, such as Shams Chak, Malik Mūsā Raina, and Serang [*sic*] Raina, destroyed bridges over the river in the city, rose in opposition against Saif Dār, and created conditions of strife. After some days, Fatḥ Shāh and his men crossed the river towards the lower section of the city. The opposing troops then clashed in Ramleneh [*sic*] village. After a hard-fought battle, Malik Saif Dār was killed in the 72nd year of Kashmiri calendar. On Fatḥ Shāh's side, Malik Serang [*sic*]

Chak (Alaṁkarçakra) was the founder of the house of Barshal in Dārdu. Pāndav Chak, Ḥusain Chak and Kājī Chak were the descendants of this line, and they had been admitted to Shia' faith by Mīr Shamsu'd-Dīn Araki. See *TḤK*, p. 217.

76. The descendants of Shams Chak were the followers of Ḥanafi school. They were *Sunnis*. *Ibid*.

Raina was slain on the battlefield. After emerging victorious in the battle, Fatḥ Shāh entrusted the ministry and administrative authority to Shams Chak. But as in the past, owing to mutual rancour, Mīr Sayyid Muḥammad Baihaqī and Shams Chak could not get along smoothly. Two and a half years later, the two openly confronted each other near the *khānqāh* of Bābā Bulbul in the heart of the city. This has already been recorded in [earlier] narratives.

[*verses*]

Shams Withdraws

Finding himself hard pressed in the battle, Shams Chak proceeded towards Zāldagar by crossing the river over the bridge lying at the far end of Bābā Bulbul's Lashkar/Langar [*sic*]. He waited there for some time. Malik Kājī Chak, following him close at his heels, reached the head of the bridge, He found that the hump-shaped bridge, built with a view to facilitating the movement of lofty and loaded boats along the river, had been dismantled. Its wooden planks had wide gaps in them and one could not imagine even a horse to cross the bridge by leaping over them. But Malik Kājī Chak besides being a veteran horseman was also a man of extraordinary heroic spirit. He whipped his horse fiercely and made it leap in one jump onto the roving platform. He cast a mocking glance at the enemy who came close at his heels, and joined the troops of Malik Shams Chak. A few horsemen – associates of Malik Shams Chak – followed the above-mentioned Kājī Chak and arrived at the bridge-head. In trying to follow the example of Kājī Chak, they made their horses to leap onto the platform, but failing to do so, fell into the river and got drowned.

Shams Retaliates

Confusion and disorder in the rank and file of his army forced Shams Chak to turn towards Kāmarāj, and the crown and sceptre, the kingdom and fortune passed into the hands of Muḥammad Shāh. For the second time, administrative and judicial control [over Kashmir] came to rest in the hands of Mīr Sayyid Muḥammad Baihaqī. Muḥammad Shāh aligned himself with Mīr Sayyid Muḥammad, Mūsā Raina, Ibrāhīm Māgray and other sirdars, and headed towards the district of Kāmarāj to see that Malik Shams Chak was totally destroyed. As he reached the village of Trehgām, Malik Shams Chak fled towards Drāv.[77] Muḥammad Shāh and Mīr Sayyid Muḥammad jointly destroyed the whole of that area by burning houses and localities. Thereafter, they returned to the town of Soipore (Sopor) where they encamped by the river bank overlooking Kāmarāj. On learning of their withdrawal, Shams Chak reappeared from Drāv[78] and proceeded towards Trehgām along with his senior army officers like, Malik Bahrām Dār, Malik Othmān and Dati [*sic*] Malik, and the host of Dāngars with whom he held consultations. The opinion of the veterans was that since the main body of their force consisted of nobles and chiefs and the number of soldiers and footmen was inadequate, it would not be advisable to deploy them in an open combat and, therefore, a night-assault would be the most appropriate strategy. This plan of Shams Chak's remained a secret for the troops of Muḥammad Shāh.[79]

Battle of Sopor

Malik Mūsā Raina took up his dwelling there along with his sons and relatives whose number was not large. Malik Shams Chak arrived in the town of Sopor in the early hours of the day. When Malik Mūsā Raina learnt of his arrival, be assembled his men and gave him a tough fight. Most of

77. Ḥasan says that Shams fled to Dārdū. See *TḤK*, p. 219.
78. Karnāv in Ḥasan. *Ibid.*
79. Ḥasan says that Muḥammad Shāh and Sayyid Muḥammad had come to know of their plan of a night-assault, *Ibid.*

Shams Chak's men indulged in acts of vandalism and plunder. With the help of a contingent of brave warriors, he launched an assault on the troops of Malik Mūsā Raina. A large-scale and bloody battle ensued between the opposing troops leading to the slaughter of a large number of men on either side. Malik Kājī Chak displayed such extraordinary feats of bravery as even heroes and warlords, like the legendary Rustam and Sām, would have felicitated him in laudable terms. He sustained so many wounds[80] on his face and all over his body that all the persons known and unknown to him in that group felt that there was no hope of his survival. Some of his near-ones carried him off the battlefield for dressing his wounds and giving him medical treatment. Since it was the Will of God that he should hold the reins of the government of this country as also be the recipient of happiness in this world and the world hereafter, God's all-pervading grace restored him almost to a new life through his rapid recovery and return to health.

After a great fight, Malik Shams Chak once again returned to Trehgām and thence to Nowshehr in India where he joined Fatḥ Shāh. Muḥammad Shāh and Mīr Sayyid Muḥammad triumphantly entered the city and later on, combining themselves with Malik Mūsā Raina, occupied the domain of Kashmir.

Shams Araki's second visit

[During] those very days, Amīr Shamsu'd-Dīn Araki was on his second visit to the land of Kashmir.[81] Malik Mūsā Raina became his ardent follower and accepted his faith.[82] But he

80. Fifty wounds, besides a cut on his ear. *Ibid.*

81. See note 55 *supra.*

82. For a fuller account of the numerous presents, such as orchards, gardens, ornaments, costumes, horses, jewellery, gold, etc. given by Malik Mūsā. Raina to Mīr Shamsu'd-Dīn Araki, see *Toḥfatu'l-*

(*Contd.*)

could not get on well with Mīr Sayyid Muḥammad Baihaqī, and not before long they came to loggerheads [over some issues],[83] as a result of which Shams Araki proceeded on his travels to Tibet. For this reason, Malik Mūsā Raina became dissatisfied, rather disgusted, with [his services to and companionship of] Mīr Sayyid Baihaqī, and strengthened his relations with Ibrāhīm Māgray and Ḥājjī Padar.

[*verses*]

Fatḥ Shāh vs Muḥammad Shāh

He then established liaison with Fatḥ Shāh and Shams Chak who were at Nowshehr in India [at that time], and through an exchange of letters with them, he prepared the ground for a renewal of their old bonds of friendship. Trusting in his promises and letters, they left the mountainous regions of India to come to Kashmir. On reaching Hirpur, they were joined by Malik Mūsā Raina, Ibrāhīm Māgray, and Ḥājjī Padar along with a large number of their associates. On the other side, Sulṭān Muḥammad Shāh and Mīr Sayyid Muḥammad Baihaqī collected all-available troops to give them a tough fight. The two armies faced each other at

---

Aḥbāb. MS (trans.), ff. 35-7. These were utilized by the Mīr for the construction of a *khānqāh* at Zadibal. The date of its completion can be found in the chronogram *kashf-i-ummatīn* which is A.H. 902 / A.D. 1496. See *TḤK*, p. 220.

83. *Toḥfatu'l-Aḥbāb* gives full details about the differences between the two which made Shams Araki to leave Kashmir for Tibet. These are of political and personal nature. The political differences were over Shams Araki's unwanted and high-handed interference in Mīr Sayyid Muḥammad's administration, and is illustrated in Araki's brutal treatment of Māntji, a state revenue officer. The personal differences were over Araki's refusal to give his daughter Bībī Āghā in marriage to him. For more details, see *Toḥfat*. MS (trans.), ff. 62-3 and 69-70. Ḥasan's version is that Araki was expelled by Sayyid Muḥammad because he did not like his activities. See *TḤK*, p. 220.

Tsenteh Kuji[84] [*sic*]. The troops of Fatḥ Shāh outnumbered those of Muḥammad Shāh, but the latter's army included a brave leader like Muḥammad Baihaqī, a lion-hearted warrior, a veteran of many a grim and bloody battle, in which he had surpassed everybody in feats of bravery, and had won many victories by sheer heroism. On this occasion he inspired the sons of war-lords and the chiefs of his troops by infusing in them a spirit of heroism and manliness. The battle that was fought on this day was so terrifying, that the like of it had never been heard of by people in this land.

[*verses*]

The fame of his (Baihaqī's) extraordinary bravery and imposing personality had reached the ears of the people of these lands much earlier. Therefore they did not dare to confront him. In these circumstances, Fatḥ Shāh addressed Shams Chak in these words: "O you veteran of many a battle and valiant and famous among the distinguished warriors! Spur on your charger and, with the Herculean strength of your frame, sever the heads of our opponents on the battlefield and avenge the death of your kindred."[85] But the aforesaid Shams Chak did not move [towards the enemy] and told him that though they had a satisfactorily large number of foot-soldiers and cavalry forces in their camp, they did not have sufficient number of light-footed soldiers who were needed for a swift attack on the enemy.[86] To this Fatḥ Shāh answered: "What fears does a lion have of a whole pack of foxen?" "If the enemy chose to launch a massive attack on our flanks with only two or three thousand of its intrepid warriors, fighting in harmony as they do, there is no doubt that they will put the very centre of our army to

84. Tsenteh Kuji (?) on Khampore ridge. See *TḤK*, p. 220.

85. Kindred refers to those relatives of Sayyid Muḥammad who had been slain in the battle of Sopor.

86. Text is not clear.

utter rout in no time," said Shams Chak. With these words, he rejected the emotionally-charged appeal of Fatḥ Shāh. As it had already become dark, he avoided fighting and with the blow of trumpets, both sides retired to rest [for the night].

[*verses*]

With the rise of the sun, Shams Chak, Mūsā Raina, Ḥājjī Padar, and their soldiers assembled like ants and locusts to fight the enemy.

[*verses*]

Decisive battle

On the other side, Mīr Muḥammad also made promises of special honours, robes of honour, and high posts and other favours to his warriors. Reposing full faith in God and detaching himself from the world and what lies in it, he surrendered to the will of God and moved towards the centre of Fatḥ Shāh's army.

[*verses*]

On they marched to the battlefield. A deafening tumult of war cries together with feverish commotion was raised in the camp of Fatḥ Shāh. A great battle was fought from dawn till midday in which warriors on either side displayed feats of valour. The centre of Fatḥ Shāh's army could no longer withstand the attack of the enemy. He was compelled to link the right flank of his troops with the left and once again gave a concerted fight to Mīr Sayyid Muḥammad. The last attack of Mīr Sayyid's soldiers could have given him final victory; his sword spat fire of revenge:

[*verses*]

He spurred his horse and dashed against the enemy's centre. But it so chanced that on that ground there was an abandoned well, the top of which was covered with rubbish, but was hollow from inside. During his charge, his horse's leg was caught in the hole. Many of his foot-soldiers rushed to the top of the well:

[*verses*]

When the enemy saw this, it took advantage of the opportunity, and made a lightening attack on them:

[*verses*]

Death toll

A group of [the enemy's] wicked persons encircled him (Sayyid Muḥammad Baihaqī) and made repeated attacks to throw off the soldiers who surrounded) him. Beholding that the enemy had encircled them and that a breakthrough had almost become impossible, though no doubt his men had been fighting with all their courage and determination and not at all afraid of death that hovered over their heads, all that Muḥammad Shāh could do in such circumstances was to pray for their deliverance. He himself was forced to flee towards Nowshehr in India. The date of his (Mīr Sayyid's) death has been found in the chronogram:

kard tārīkh-i wafātash chu khiradmand su'āl
guft pīr-i khiradmand kih sazāwār-i behisht.

This event is very well-known in Kashmiri (i.e. Sanskrit) history.[87] It took place in the eighty-first year of Ashushat 9. In this encounter, one thousand seven hundred and nineteen of Mīr Sayyid Muḥammad's associates, kinsmen and attendants lost their lives, besides the Mīr himself. This number included a thousand and two hundred troops who wore saffron-coloured stockings. The tradition in those days was that none but the brave were entitled to wear such saffron-coloured stockings. The dead bodies of Mīr Sayyid

87. The allusion is probably to the historical records of Śrivara or Suka.

Muḥammad and his kinsmen recovered from the battlefield, which was littered with slaughtered bodies, were buried in their ancestral graveyards. Down to this day, their graves are visited by the needy and the suppliant. Thus Sulṭān Fatḥ Shāh's power over the kingdom of Kashmir was confirmed and with that began the second tenure of Malik Sams Chak's ministry.

Destruction of mansions

Mīr Sayyid Muḥammad was survived by three minor sons, who were brought up in the house of Bahrām Dār at Soybug. They were Mīr Sayyid Murtazā, Mīr Sayyid Ibrāhīm, and Mīr Sayyid Ya'qūb. The eldest one, Mīr Murtazā got killed when he was hurled down a mountain on his way to Tibet. Sayyid Ibrāhīm Khān remained a prisoner of the governor of Tibet for a period of two years and six months. It was only after the army of Kāshghar got disrupted that he was freed from prison, by the grace of God and without incurring the obligation of any human being, and then returned to Nowshehr in India to rejoin Muḥammad Shāh. Further details about him will appear at their proper place in this chronicle. Mīr Sayyid Ya'qūb because of being a minor,[88] continued to live in the main city, unhurt [by the enemy].

Out of deep-seated malice towards Mīr Sayyid Muḥammad, Sulṭān Fatḥ Shāh totally destroyed his mansions. These magnificent mansions had been recently completed after several years of labour. Their dormitories and parlours were decorated with wall paintings of exquisite grace and workmanship and the figures drawn were indicative of the artist's unique novelty. This lent them a distinctive place in the buildings of those times. The ceilings and towers were loftier than what one could imagine and let in fresh air and

88. Ḥasan is of the view that as a child he hid himself in the house of his foster-mother. See *TḤK*, p. 221.

light plentifully. A notable feature of these mansions was that these were swept clean by silvery-bosomed slender damsels, holding in their soft and delicate hands fly-whiskers of blue horse's tail with handles set in gold. These mansions were totally destroyed, so-much-so that peasants brought their ruins under plough in which they sowed cotton seed. On seeing such cataclysmic changes in these palaces, the minstrels of those lands made it a theme for their Kashmiri [i.e. Sanskrit ?] songs which they sang to the accompaniment of the rhythmic beat of their feet and cymbals. They sang these songs in such doleful voices that sensitive listeners were reminded of the grandeur and magnificence of the lord of those mansions and were moved to tears. These memories broke them down. The verses they composed and sang were:[89]

shinav īn qisseh andar mulk-i Kashmir
na az man az zabān-i kūdak-o pīr

. . . .

nishasteh bā hazārān hūr-o ghilmān
ba khūbi har yakī māh-i jehāngīr
ze uqṭās-i du rang-i bahr-i jārūb
na kardandi kanīzān hīch taqsīr.

. . . .

Araki's reaction

After this event, the news of killing of Mīr Muḥammad was brought to Mīr Shamsu'd-Dīn by one of his disciples, who told him that the enemy who had driven him out of Kashmir and forced him to turn to Tibet, had been over-powered and killed by his followers: The messenger had hoped that Mīr Shamsu'd-Dīn would feel happy over it. But as he was

89. Nine verses in all have been recorded. The chronicler says that the verses were sung in Kashmiri language (*be zabān-i Kashmiri*). This has to be differentiated from the phrase *be qalam-i Kashmiri*, which we have translated as 'Sanskrit language in Ṣarada script.'

a believer in the Oneness of God[90] and a person who surrendered to His Will,[91] he ordered that the messenger be lashed. Himself he felt greatly sad like a bereaved person mourned the death of Mīr Sayyid, and kept chanting this verse:

ū nīz guzasht azīn guzargāh
ān kīst kih naguzrad azīn rāh

He felt sorry that the gracious and benevolent (Sayyid Muḥammad) should have been levelled with the dust. Tears rolled down his face and he offered a prayer for the salvation of the soul of the dead person. He prayed for the welfare of his children and also wished well for all the inhabitants of the locality where the late Mīr Muḥammad lived. Through the good wishes of Mīr Shamsu'd-Dīn, that locality was rehabilitated and became prosperous within a few years.

Shams Chak murdered

In the early spring of the same year, 12th Veshast [*sic*] a terrible earthquake was recorded in Kashmir. For [a period of] four months after this, Malik Shams Chak held the reins of the government of Kashmir. After that Malik Mūsā Raina and Ibrāhīm Māgray, in connivance with Fatḥ Shāh, imprisoned and chained him (Shams Chak) and later on killed him. He was held responsible for the murder of Malik Saif Dār, for the destruction of the riches of the Dāngars, and for having concentrated power in his own hands. For these reasons, Malik Mūsā Raina gave orders to Bahrām Dār and Dati [*sic*] Malik to put an end to the life of Shams Chak. Shortly after offering evening prayers, they led a party towards the prison to undertake the task. One of the legs of Shams Chak was in chains. He understood that they had

90. *muwaḥḥid.*
91. *mujību'd-da'wāt.*

come to take his life and he had no weapons with him except a small knife. With it, he attacked his adversaries, and within the prison walls, he killed thirty persons, besides wounding many more. He repeated his attack several times till that party found itself helpless and nobody had the courage to strike him with a sword. With a small knife and with stones and brickbats, he held his assailants at bay. None of them, in spite of being equipped with swords and axes, could muster courage to go near him. At last his assailants shot a volley of arrows at him from a distance and killed him and his son on the eighty-first of Kashmiri calendar.[92]

[*verses*]

Mūsā Raina

After the murder of Shams Chak and his son, the office of the Chief Vizier and the administrative authority of Kashmir was entrusted to Malik Mūsā Raina[93] in A.H. 907 (A.D. 1501). In agreement and collaboration with Malik Ibrāhīm Māgray, he took control of the domain of Kashmir and undertook its governance. He felt that in certain matters he was being opposed by the group of Dāngars.[94] He suspected their designs of fomenting trouble and disorder in the state; [therefore], he drove them away towards the mountains of India. Malik Mūsā held the reins of administration for about nine years, during which period the enforcement of Islamic laws and religious tenets of the Prophet reached the highest point. Under the guidance of the righteous Amīr (Shams)[95] Shaykh Muḥammad Araki, the pure religion of Muḥammad

92. Ḥasan says that he governed for four months. *TḤK*, p. 223.
93. A descendant of the line of Rājā of Nagarkot. *TMḤ*, MS f. 44[b]. Could he be the Somachandra of Shuka's Chronicle. See J.C. Dutt's translation p. 339.
94. For Dāmarās (Dāngars), see *Rājat.*, Vol. II, p. 304 *et seq.*
95. The fuller version is: *Shamsu'l-haqq wa'd-dīn*. That is 'the sun of truth and faith.'

and the prosperity of the Muslim community reached the highest pinnacle [of attainment]. Malik Mūsā Raina supported and advanced the mission of Mīr Shams Araki.

Persecution of Hindus

[It may be recorded] that the temples of idol-worshippers, which had been destroyed and razed to the ground by the religion-minded and justice-loving Sulṭān Sikandar – God bless his grave and bless him – had been rebuilt and rehabilitated by Zainu'l-'Ābidīn. He had permitted idolaters and polytheists to revive the practices of infidelity and they had propagated heresy (*kufr*) and false religion (*dīn-i bāṭil*). With the support of some more kings,[96] the infidels had flourished day after day. But with the support and authority of Malik Mūsā Raina, Amīr Shamsu'd-Dīn Muḥammad undertook a wholesale destruction of all those idol-houses[97] as well as the total ruination of the very foundation of infidelity and disbelief. On the site of every idol-house he destroyed, he ordered the construction of a mosque for offering prayers after the Islamic manner. The idolatry and heresy which had existed prior to his coming to this place were effectively replaced by his preaching and propagation of Islamic laws and practices. He brought honour to all the infidels and heretics (*zandiqa*) of Kashmir by admitting them to the Islamic faith and bestowed upon them many kinds of rewards and benefactions. It is publicly known as well as emphatically related that during his life-time, with the virtuous efforts and elaborate arrangements made by the fortunate Malik Mūsā Raina, twenty-four thousand families of staunch infidels and stubborn heretics were ennobled by

96. This might be an allusion to Muḥammad Shāh.
97. As many as eighteen big temples of Hindus in the city of Srinagar and in the rural areas of the valley were destroyed under the instructions of Mīr Shamsu'd-Dīn Araki and Malik Mūsā Raina. For details see *Toḥfat*. MS (trans.), ff. 155-212.

being converted to the Islamic faith.[98] It is difficult to compute the number of people who had hitherto indulged in corrupt practices of a wrong (false) faith and dissent and were put on the right track under the proper guidance of Mīr Shamsu'd-Dīn Araki.[99]

In fact the transmitter of (God's) grace (Mīr Shams Araki) conferred favours upon the righteous Malik Mūsā Raina and gave him blessings which enabled him to fulfil that cherished task. Indeed, fortunate is one who has been able to become the recipient of such special consideration at the hands of a highly venerable and elderly person like him (Amīr Shamsu'd-Dīn). After Sulṭān Sikandar – God's peace be upon him – no one among the Muslims who wielded authority over this country rendered as much service to Islam by its propagation and advancement as Malik Mūsā Raina did. Nobody was able to make as organized an effort as he did towards the advancement and furtherance of the Muhammadan religion.

---

98. The ennobling conversion of infidels to Islamic faith has been described in *TḤK* and *Toḥfat.* in this manner. Ḥasan says that twenty-four thousand Hindu families were converted to Araki's faith (of Shia'ism) by force and compulsion (*qahran wa jabran*). *TḤK*, p. 223. It is recorded in *Toḥfat.* that on the instance of Shamsu'd-Dīn Araki. Mūsā Raina had issued orders that everyday 1,500 to 2,000 infidels be brought to the doorstep of Mīr Shamsu'd-Dīn by his followers. They would remove their sacred thread (zunnār), administer *kelima* to them, circumcise them and make them eat beef. See *Toḥfat.* MS (trans.), f. 157. For a graphic description of forcible circumcision on Īdgāh grounds, see the same work ff. 190-91. Also see tr. of Tohfat by K.N. Pandit.

99. Since the reign of Sulṭān Sikandar, no ruler in Kashmir worked as much for the propagation of Islamic faith as Malik Mūsā. *TMḤ*, MS f. 45[a]. Ḥasan says that he repressed Sunni nobles also. Some of them were expelled to evoke fear among people. *TḤK*, p 223.

Chapter V
The Chaks

With the murder of Malik Shams Chak, the clan of Chaks fell on evil days and suffered a decline. Their disintegration touched such a low ebb that Malik Kājī Chak, Seh Chak and Serang (Sarhang ?) Chak were forced to join the service of 'Alī Raina, son of Malik Mūsā Raina. For some time they served as his footmen.

[*verses*]

When Malik Mūsā Raina planned to despatch his son [Malik 'Alī to Tibet at the head of a contingent, equipment for the expedition was provided by soldiers who had the ability to pay. The Chaks were so poor that they could not pay for the required equipment for these troops; they came to Mīr Shamsu'd-Dīn to request him for financial assistance. They had also brought along with them Serang (Sarhang ?) Chak, the son of Malik Shams Chak, thinking that he would grant them their request because of him. When they came to Mīr Shams Araki in a group of about five or six persons, they did not expect to get more than a gold coin each which, they had thought, would suffice them for paying the Tibet-bound troops.

Kājī Chak patronized

Mīr Shamsu'd-Dīn Araki granted them assistance in kind to the tune of a hundred *traks*[1] of rice and fifty *traks* of flour

1. One *trak* is approximately five kilograms.

and two lakhs of *pool* (money) in cash. He affectionately asked that Malik Kājī Chak, the prince with a clipped ear, be brought to his presence.[2] Malik Kājī Chak had suffered a clipped ear in the course of Malik Shams Chak's night-assault in the battle of Sopor. Mīr Shams called Kājī Chak to his presence and told him that the Omnipotent would give unto his command the government of that country; that he should adopt the path of justice and keep in mind the welfare of his people. He was also told to give his full attention to the propagation of Islam.[3]

Kājī Chak feared that these words might be carried to Malik Mūsā Raina. In confusion, he bowed his head before Mīr Shams in reverence, and told him: "I take an oath upon my honour that I shall strictly abide by your dictates. Should God Almighty choose me to wield authority, I shall neither deviate from your directive nor disregard your wishes." Thereupon, Mīr Shams Araki lifted his big turban from his head and put it on the head of Kājī Chak, telling him that he had bestowed upon him the crown of power and government which would soon be his.

After some time, the offspring of Ibrāhīm Māgray, whom wealth and influence had made so strong as to aspire control over the government of that land, aligned themselves with some chiefs of that time, and, with the concurrence of Fatḥ Shāh, planned to destroy Malik Mūsā Raina. In A.H. 916 (A.D. 1510), corresponding to 89th year of Kashmiri calendar, they destroyed the bridges over the river in the city and began fighting and killing in the vicinity of the royal quarters (*Dāru'l-Amāreh*).[4] Malik Mūsā Raina took position

---

2. This gesture reflected his wisdom to win over people to strengthen his religious mission. Shuka gives his name as Kānchana Chakresha or Kācha Chakra and says that he was an incarnation of Inḍra and Vishnu. See J.C. Dutt (tr.). pp. 347-48, 351.
3. Perhaps Chaks alone could restore order in the country at that time.
4. It was located at Iskandarpora. See *TḤK*, p. 224.

at Zāldagar, but finding that his friends and associates had completely gone back over their old promises and commitments, and had become openly hostile and taken to perfidy, he thought it advisable to flee and therefore abandoned the battlefield after a couple of days.[5]

Mūsā killed

Malik Uṯẖmān, Datī Malik and some members of the group of Dāngars, who had hitherto remained scattered over the Indian mountains, were taken into confidence by the Māgrays by establishing communication and rapport with them. They marched on to Kashmir and arrived at Hirpur. In view of this, Malik Mūsā Raina thought it inadvisable to flee via Hirpur. The other routes were either via Tsereh-Ḥār or Shamaz [*sic*]. But, by preordination, fate and divine decree, he fell from a horse during this flight and joined the ever-lasting world.[6]

Dāngars dominate

The ministry and authority [of this land] passed into the hands of Ibrāhīm Māgray, but this did not last beyond forty days. Shortly after, the group of Dāngars whose assistance they (Māgrays) had sought in winning this victory, overpowered them and took quick steps to install themselves in power and in a position of command. They succeeded in winning over most of the sirdars and rose against Malik Ibrāhīm Māgray, who was, ultimately, overpowered and

5. Ḥasan says that the nobles and commanders of the time became his adversaries because of his religion. See *TḤK*, p. 224.
6. Ḥasan describes his death in this manner: During his flight, he reached the village of Rāwalpora where his neck got entangled in the branches of a vine. He fell from his horse, and as he frantically tried to disentangle himself, the horse gave him a nasty kick on his head which broke his skull and scattered his brains on the ground. *TḤK*, p. 224.

destroyed. They declared their authority over this land and the ministry passed into the hands of Malik Uṯḥmān. They decided to imprison some of the chiefs of those times in order to consolidate their authority and leadership. Two months later, Malik Kājī Chak, Jahāngīr Padar, and Gadāy Malik joined hands with Fatḥ Shāh. In the court chamber (*Dāru'l-Amārah*), Datī Malik and Ghāzī Khān, who were dispensing justice, were murdered with dagger and knife [knives].[7] At that moment Malik Uṯḥmān was in the company of Fatḥ Shāh in his private apartment; he was detained and put in chains.

Fatḥ Shāh returns

Malik Jahāngīr Padar [now] declared his authority over the land. A month later, Malik Ibrāhīm raised a body of crack soldiers, equipped with effective weapons, and headed towards Kashmir. Some of the contemporary chiefs joined him. Because of this Malik Jahāngīr Padar and Fatḥ Shāh thought it advisable to leave the country.[8] When they had reached Hirpur, Ibrāhīm Māgray despatched somebody to bring back Fatḥ Shāh; Jahāngīr Padar and the other members of the party of Chaks continued their onward march to India.

Ibrāhīm Māgray installed Fatḥ Shāh on the throne. Malik Kājī [*sic*][9] Uṯḥmān was released from prison and he joined the Māgrays. For the second time the office of the Chief Vizir passed into the hands of Malik Ibrāhīm Māgray. At that time news was brought to Fatḥ Shāh from Nowshehr in India that Muḥammad Shāh had left his troops behind and had proceeded towards Maldayal [sic] mountains. He also learnt

---

7. According to Malik Ḥaidar, many leading Dāngars were also killed in this rebellion. See *TMḤ*, MS f. 45^b.

8. Ḥasan says that they had been overpowered and therefore were forced to flee to India. *TḤK*, p. 225. But Malik Ḥaidar says that Fatḥ Shāh stopped at Hirpur. See *TMḤ*, MS f. 45^b.

9. The text is incorrect. Malik Uṯḥmān was in prison.

that, except Ibrāhīm Khān,[10] whose mention has already been made, there was none close at hand with their families and relatives. This news intensified Fatḥ Shāh's hatred for that house; he hastened to arrange a strong force and ordered it to march towards those lands forthwith.

Fatḥ Shāh repulsed

The family members and close relatives of Muḥammad Shāh learnt of the movement of the troops [of Fatḥ Shāh], but they found no possibility of escaping from that place. Sayyid Ibrāhīm Khān unsheathed his sword and set out to meet Fatḥ Shāh. A fierce encounter took place at the village of Ghāzī Kot. The brave warriors of Fatḥ Shāh realised that it was not possible to gain victory through the strategy they had adopted; and, therefore, dismissing all hopes, turned back towards the capital. Sayyid Ibrāhīm Baihaqī gave them a hot pursuit and all those on whom he could lay his hands were slain. Then he and his party returned to Nowshehr in India.

[*verses*]

After that day, he strengthened his power and authority, and owing to the power and influence that he wielded, he dominated over the rest of the nobles. Details concerning this will be given at their proper place.[11]

Muḥammad Shāh reacts

A messenger brought full details of these developments to Muḥammad Shāh. He was told how Sayyid Ibrāhīm Khān heroically fought the foe and defended the locality in Nowshehr to prevent Fatḥ Shāh from entering that town and how a number of Fatḥ Shāh's soldiers were slain in the battle. He reacted happily to this and gave fatherly

10. Ḥasan says that he was the son of Sayyid Muḥammad Baihaqī. *TḤK*, p. 225.
11. This sentence can be interpreted in more than one way.

affection[12] and special favours to the state officials and chiefs of Kashmir.

Uṭḥmān's second ministry

During the year following this event, Malik Uṭḥmān and Malik Shankar Raina joined hands to oppose Malik Ibrāhīm Māgray and managed to secure the support of Fatḥ Shāh in this. They succeeded in imprisoning Ibrāhīm's two sons, Malik Abdāl and Malik Fëroz. Malik Ibrāhīm left for Poonch. With that Malik Uṭḥmān became the Chief Vizir for the second time. Malik Shankar Raina and his group gave him full support.[13] Five months later, Ibrāhīm Māgray in combination with a group of Chaks and Padars, who were scattered over Indian lands, proclaimed Muḥammad Shāh as king, and entered Kashmir via Baramulla, and encamped at Sopor. On the other side, Malik Uṭḥmān and Malik Shankar Raina took Fatḥ Shāh along with them and with a fairly large force at their command encamped by the bank of the lake (or river ?) outside the range of their arrows. At that time a musket or a gun was unknown in Kashmir.

Araki warned

It so happened that Mīr Aḥdī (Abdi, *sic*), the son-in-law of Mīr Shamsu'd-Dīn Araki, deserted Malik Uṭḥmān and joined the troops of Māgrays. At this, Malik Uṭḥmān held out threats to Amīr Shamsu'd-Dīn that "with God's grace the victory will be ours and on reaching the city (of Srinagar) the first thing for me to do would be to burn you alive, and then enter the city." Mīr Shams developed deep hatred for him.

12. Muḥammad Shāh conferred upon Sayyid Ibrāhīm the title of Khān for his bravery. See *THK*, p. 226.
13. Ḥasan says that Shankar Raina was made commander of the army. *TḤK*, p. 226.

Fighting in Sopor

Shortly afterwards, Uṭhmān realized that on account of the obstruction posed by the river, it would not be possible for him to make any headway. Proud of his bravery and valour, he left behind Fatḥ Shāh and Malik Shankar Raina with their troops to confront the enemy and took the Khuihāmā route to make a surprise attack on them from the rear. On the other side, Lohar Māgray and Regī Chak, accompanied by innumerable troops, sealed off his way by occupying the top of Bosangari[14] hillock. When Uṭhmān reached near them, he made a valorous attack and succeeded in defeating and repulsing them. The defeated troops somehow managed to rejoin their main force. Malik Uṭhmān halted at the top of Bosangari for the night. The news of his occupation of Bosangari and the defeat of the troops of Māgrays reached the city. When Mullā Muḥammad Ganāī, the tutor of Fatḥ Shāh, came to Amīr Shamsu'd-Dīn Araki, he asked him the latest news about 'his'[15] Fatḥ Shāh. The tutor told him that the top of Bosangari had been captured, the enemy defeated, and that the victorious troops were at the hillock. Mīr Shams told him that even if he would move up to the top of the sky, God Almighty would hurl him down upon earth and not grant him freedom to oppress the helpless (*faqīrs*).[16]

Malik 'Alī's treachery

During those days there lived a very shrewd and intelligent man, Malik 'Alī by name, in the group of Malik Kājī Chak. He sensed that Malik Uṭhmān was in a strong position to overpower them in the battle that would be fought the following day. By nightfall he came to the bank of the lake

14. The hillock on the right bank of Wular lake, and situated between Khuihāma and Zenagīr.
15. 'this' is obviously a sarcastic reference.
16. Mīr Shamsu'd-Dīn Araki called his followers *dervishes*, *sufis* and *faqīrs*. See *Toḥfat*. MS *passim*.

and loudly announced like this: "I am Malik 'Alī, the son of Mullā Ḥusain ـٮٮـ (illeg.). A couple of trusted men among the closest courtiers of Fatḥ Shāh may come here as I want to speak to them about something important." When Fatḥ Shāh heard it, he ordered two or three of his trusted courtiers to proceed to the bank of the lake. Malik 'Alī spoke these words to them in a subdued tone: "I have had the honour of being a ward of your king. It was his benevolence which lifted me high from nowhere. I want to show my goodwill towards him. Let it be known to you that Malik Uṯẖmān has been slain and his entire army has been crushed and dispersed [by the troops of Kājī Chak]. They have drawn a plan to ferry the troops across the lake tomorrow morning and capture Fatḥ Shāh and hand him over to Muḥammad Shāh. I beseech you a hundred times that this very night Fatḥ Shāh should move away to Poonch by Havel [*sic*] route,[17] otherwise he will be captured. Since I have enjoyed the patronage of that house – having been brought up in it – I cannot help showing good – will towards it."

This story was carried to Fatḥ Shāh by persons nearest to him. He decided to set out the same night towards India via Havel taking with him a few of his belongings and leaving behind the rest. Malik 'Alī succeeded in wrecking their (Fatḥ Shāh's) army through his intelligence and his skill for contrivance.

[*verses*]

Next day, Malik Uṯẖmān learnt that the treacherous act of Malik 'Alī had led to the destruction of the troops of Fatḥ Shāh and Shankar Raina. He was left with no alternative but to retrace his steps from Bosangari and withdraw to the city. By nightfall, he arrived at the banks of the waters of Lār[18] which he managed to cross and then halted there for the

17. In Ḥasan it is Tos Maidān. See *TḤK*, p. 227.
18. Probably the Ānchār lake.

night. At sunrise, he resumed his flight towards the village[19] [illegible] (illeg.) Malik Ibrāhīm Māgray was unrelanting in his pursuit; ultimately, he captured him at Neev and put him in prison. Later on, he was put to death in that prison, and the fury of the flames of dervishes' anger took a concrete shape.[20] The chronogram denoting the year of his (Uṭḥmān's) death is the word *tarkash*.[21]

Muḥammad Shāh's third term

Thus Muḥammad Shāh wrested the throne for himself, and for the third time, the high office of the Chief Vizir went to Malik Ibrāhīm Māgray.[22] The rule of Muḥmmad Shāh and the ministry of Ibrāhīm Māgray lasted nine months.

Fatḥ Shāh's third term

After the expiry of nine months, Fatḥ Shāh turned from India towards Kashmir, but, before entering it, he despatched his son Ḥabib Khān to Mongehnār [*sic*]. Malik Jahāngīr Padar fled from Pir [*sic*][23] to join him (Fatḥ Shāh). When Path entered into Kashmir, most of its people rallied to his side. Malik Kājī Chak also joined him along with his troops. Muḥammad Shāh, Ibrāhīm Khān, Mīr Muḥammad Baihaqī and Ibrāhīm Māgray fled to India, leaving the domain of Kashmir to Fatḥ Shāh. For the second time, the administrative authority of Kashmir passed into the hands of Jahāngīr Padar. Apart from the state-owned lands, Kashmir

---

19. This could be Akhāl. See *TḤK*, p. 227.
20. By dervish, the author probably means Shamsu'd-Dīn Araki.
21. The year is A.H. 920/A.D. 1514.
22. Ḥasan writes that Ibrāhīm Māgray did not at all trust the promises and pledges of Kashmiri nobles. He considered Muḥammad Shāh and Fatḥ Shāh like pawns on a chess-board, and handled them as he liked. See *TḤK*, p. 228.
23. It could probably be Padar. Ḥasan writes that Jahāngīr Padar deserted Muḥammad Shāh and joined Ḥabīb Khān. *TḤK*, p. 229. This is also corroborated by Malik Ḥaidar, *TMḤ*, MS f. 46[a].

was now divided into three zones allotted each to Jahāngīr Padar, Malik Shankar Raina and Malik Kājī Chak.

Muḥammad Shāh defeated

The spring breeze from the pious breath of dervishes[24] blew in the vernal garden (of Kashmir), and the fruit-yielding tree of the rule of Chaks began to grow. A year later, Malik Ibrāhīm Māgray brought Muḥammad Shāh along with him to Kashmir. At Brengil[25] [*sic*] a fierce battle took place between them [the troops of Muḥammad Shāh and Fatḥ Shāh] in which Ibrāhīm Māgray and his two sons[26] were slain; Muḥammad Shāh fled towards Poonch.

Desertions

Two years after this event, Muḥammad Shāh went to Sulṭān Sikandar Shāh[27] for help; he treated him with regards and courtesies befitting a king and also placed at his disposal a large force for his assistance.[28] With army, he reached Rājver and encamped at Dānorā[29] grounds. Malik Jahāngīr Padar and Malik Shankar Raina despatched a number of messengers, one after the other, to him, and through them conveyed to Muḥammad Shāh their promises of loyal submission and unconditional obedience. They repeatedly sent him letters[30] in which they expressed their allegiance

24. These are the followers of Shamsu'd-Dīn Araki and members of the Nūrbakhshiyyeh order.
25. *Pargana* Bengil. See *TḤK*, p. 229.
26. They were Malik Feroz and Malik Abdāl. *TḤK*, p. 229.
27. The Lodhi ruler of India. See also *TḤK*, p. 230.
28. Malik Ḥaidar and Ḥasan estimate the number around thirty thousand soldiers. See *TMḤ*, MS f. 46[b] and *TḤK*, p. 230.
29. Ḥasan's version is Wāthora plains in Rajor which is not correct. See *TḤK*, p. 230.
30. Malik Ḥaidar says that letters of submission to Muḥammad Shāh were also sent by Kājī Chak, Malik Serang (Sarhang) and Malik Nuṣrat Chādūra. See *TMḤ*, MS f. 46[b].

and submission to him. They declared that his orders and directives would become articles of faith for them.[31] Malik Kājī Chak and Shankar Raina and Nuṣrat Raina separated from Fatḥ Shāh and returned to the fort of Tarsh [*sic*]. Malik Jahāngīr Padar joined hands with Fatḥ Shāh and fighting broke out between the two sides. In the fight, he (Fatḥ Shāh) suffered reverses and fled towards the mountains. This news was brought to Muḥammad Shāh who expressed his full appreciation of their loyalty and sincere submission.

It was Muḥammad Shāh's considered opinion that stationing of such a large and foreign army in those lands would lead to its spoliation and desolation. Thirty thousand cavalrymen accompanied him; he sent back some of them from Dānorā, but some more were left behind at Rājverī (Rājourī) and Dānorā. He picked only two thousand horsemen for his entry into Kashmir. Malik Kājī Chak and Malik Nuṣrat Raina[32] preceded Muḥammad Shāh in order to welcome him on his arrival in Kashmir.

On arrival in Kashmir, he (Muḥammad Shāh) found it proper to elevate Malik Kājī Chak as the Chief Vizir of this land to the exclusion of the rest. Consequently, Malik Kājī Chak became a minister and the administrative head of the land. Malik Shankar Raina was detained.[33] The Indian army contingents were persuaded to return home. In order to make a formal show of compliance to Sulṭān Sikandar, Muḥammad Shāh accompanied the returning troops in person up to Nowshehr and then bade them farewell. Winter had already set in and behind them lay mountains freshly covered with snow, making the passage difficult for them.

---

31. On receiving these reassuring letters of support, Muḥammad Shāh sent back the Indian troops. See *TMḤ*, f. 40[b].

32. Malik Shankar Chādūra and not Malik Nuṣrat Chādūra. See *TMḤ*, MS f. 47[b].

33. Malik Ḥaidar says that under some pretext he was detained at Nowshehr. See *TMḤ*, MS f. 47[a].

Muḥammad Shāh was thus left with no alternative but to pass the winter at Nowshehr in India.[34]

Kājī Chak's victory

Taking advantage of a long winter and bitter cold, Malik Lohar Māgray and Malik Nuṣrat Raina together raised troops and led insurrections defying the authority of Malik Kājī Chak in the fort at Nowgām. At this time Malik Jahāngīr Padar emerged from Kohistān (Indian mountains) and joined Malik Kājī Chak. Malik Lohar Māgray and Malik Nuṣrat Raina now realized that an open and direct fight with the adversary would not be a judicious step, and, therefore, resolved to make a night-assault on them. Taking the enemy by surprise would perhaps yield them success. But before leaving the fort of Nowgām, Kājī Chak had received information about their impending move, and consequently he had taken all precautionary measures to foil their attempt by keeping his troops in full readiness. With the war-cries raised by the assaulting troops and the deafening tumult over the battlefield, the troops of Kājī Chak rushed out of their camps and quarters to cross swords with the enemy. On the grounds of Zāldagar, a grim and bloody battle was fought, in which many brave soldiers and warriors were wounded or killed on either side. Malik Nuṣrat Raina lay among the

---

34. Ḥasan has recorded a tragic happening connected with the severity of that particular winter. Nearly ten thousand Pandits met with their death while going to Harmukat Ganga to immerse the ashes of their dead. At the top of Mahalesheh Marg mountain, they rose at midnight and following a call from the invisible moved along a wrong track which led to steep precipice named Heprudan [*sic*] from which they fell down one after another and were killed. The dead included men, women and children. The date of this event has been recorded in this chronogram:

    az bayābān kashīdeh sar tārīkh
    ghul guftā tabahi-e Panditān.

    which yields the year A.H. 925/A.D. 1519. *TḤK*, p. 230.

slain. Malik Kājī Chak himself received wounds in that battle and also lost one of the fingers of his right hand. On seeing that most of his associates had been either killed or wounded, Lohar Māgray was forced to flee.

Thus with the blessings of God the Benevolent, the flower of victory and triumph blossomed in the rose garden of the clan of Chaks. The pious breath blown by Ḥazrat Amīr Shamsu'd-Dīn had brought fragrance to their clan.

When the bitter winter came to an end and the sun reappeared with its full lustre, Muḥammad Shāh and Sayyid Ibrāhīm moved into Kashmir along with their army. With the good wishes and to the pleasure of Amīr Shamsu'd-Dīn Araki, Malik Kājī Chak occupied the ministry and held the administrative authority of the kingdom. During the whole period for which he held the reins of the government, he was always guided by Amīr Shamsu'd-Dīn Araki's instructions, directives, and commands. It was during this regime that Amīr Shamsu'd-Dīn Araki ordered Malik Kājī Chak to reconstruct the *khānqāh* of Amīr (Sayyid 'Alī Hamadānī). At this time Fatḥ Shāh reigned over Kashmir. On the day they were laying out the plan of the structure of the *khānqāh*, an altercation took place between Amīr Shamsu'd-Dīn and Fatḥ Shāh with the result that, a few days later, Fatḥ Shāh was deposed and expelled from the country. Muḥammad Shāh was recalled and put on the throne. Fatḥ Shāh never came back to Kashmir afterwards. Malik Shankar Raina, too, was languishing in the Indian mountains at that time. In A.H. 925 (A.D. 1519), both Fatḥ Shāh and Shankar Raina died somewhere in the mountains of India.[35]

35. Ḥasan says that Fatḥ Shāh died in A.H. 925/A.D. 1519, somewhere in Nowshehr mountains and the cap of Mīr Sayyid 'Alī Hamadānī which had remained in the possession of the Sulṭāns from the times of Quṭbu'd-Dīn was buried with the dead body of Fatḥ Shāh. The year of this event was found in the chronogram *Fatḥ Shāh fanā* (A.H. 925) A.D. 151. See *TḤK*, p. 232.

In the year [illegible] when Muḥammad Shāh was the king and Kājī Chak his vizir, the *khānqāh* of Ḥazrat Hamadāniyyeh caught fire.

Massacre of infidels

One of the big tasks completed by him and one of the major commands of Amīr Shamsu'd-Dīn Muḥammad Araki carried out by him was the massacre of infidels and polytheists of this land. It happened like this.

During the government of Malik Mūsā Raina, all the depraved heretics of this land had been converted to Islam. [But] with the help of some of the chiefs of this land, some of them had reverted to the customs of the infidels and polytheists. These apostates had resumed idolatry. Some of the infidels related that during the hours of offering prayers and worshipping of idols, they would place a copy of the holy Qur'ān under their haunches to make a seat to sit upon. Thus idol-worshipping proceeded even while they sat on the divine book. When the news and details of these doing were brought to Amīr Shamsu'd-Dīn Muḥammad Araki, he summoned Malik Kājī Chak to him. Accompanied by Malik 'Alī and Khwāja Aḥmad, his two counsellors and administrators, Malik Kājī Chak presented himself before the venerable Amīr Shamsu'd-Dīn Araki, who declared to them: "This community of idolaters has, after embracing and submitting to the Islamic faith, now gone back to defiance and apostasy. If you find yourself unable to inflict punishment upon them in accordance with the provisions of *sharia'* and take disciplinary action against them, it will become necessary and incumbent upon me to proceed on a self-imposed exile and in that case you shall not stand in my way at the time of my departure."

Since the above-mentioned Malik, prior to his assumption of power and authority, had promised him that he would never deviate from or disregard his wishes and injunctions, therefore, in deference to his wishes, he held consultations with his counsellors and administrative officers, and decided upon carrying out a wholesale massacre of the infidels. Their massacre was scheduled for the days of the approaching *'Ashūrā*.[36] Thus in the year A.H. 924 (A.D. 1518), corresponding to 94th year of Kashmiri calendar, during the *'Ashūrā*, about seven to eight hundred infidels were put to death. Those killed were the leading personalities of the community of infidels at that time: men of substance and government functionaries. Each of them wielded influence and sway over a hundred families of other infidels and heretics. Thus the entire community of infidels and polytheists in Kashmir was coerced into conversion to Islam at the point of the sword. This is one of the major achievements of Malik Kājī Chak.

Padar's revolt

In the year A.H. 926 (A.D. 1519), Kājī Chak placed a large force under the command of his son Mas'ūd Chak and sent

---

36. Tenth day of the month of Muḥarram. There is a short reference to the massacre of Hindus in Shuka's Chronicle. He writes, "Now in times gone by Shiryya a twice-born had planted * * * as it were the creeper of his karma. On the approach of winter * * * it was watered by the good Brāhmaṇa Shri Nirmmalakaṇṭha. Then at the time of the mlechcha oppression, Kaṇṭhabhaṭṭa and others held a council and was able to avert the disgrace which such oppression beget. Khujjāmerahmada, on the other hand, by devoting his life to the service of Kācha Chakra and by giving him wealth, induced him, who was alarmed at the work of Nirmmalakaṇṭha and others, to give him permission to act against them; and actuated by the mlechchas, caused them to be murdered. * * * O Brāhmaṇas where in this Kaliyuga are your Brahmanical spirit and practice? It was for want of these that the sorrowful and affrighted Nirmmalakaṇṭha and others were killed. The oppression of the Mausulas which began in the time of the Saidas (Sayyids) was made prominent by Somachandra (Mūsā Raina – (*Contd.*)

him to capture Jahāngīr Padar.[37] But Malik Jahāngīr received the information of Malik Mas'ūd's move in advance. He fled towards Kāmarāj[38] where he aligned himself with Gadāy Malik and the people of [illegible] (illeg.). In A.H. 927 (A.D. 1520), Malik Abdāl, Lohar Māgray and Malik 'Idī Raina[39] rallied round Iskandar Khān, the son of Fatḥ Shāh, and captured the fort of Nāgām to lead an insurrection against Malik Kājī Chak. Jahāngīr Padar and Gadāy Malik also appeared from Kāmarāj and Drāv to join hands with Iskandar Khān. They reached the *pargana* of Lār where Kājī Chak had despatched his son Mas'ūd Chak to offer resistance to them and himself came out to confront Iskandar Khān. He went a little ahead of his son Mas'ūd Chak and took position near Shihābu'd-Dīn Pora, where he got engaged in a fight with Gadāy Malik. In the battle that ensued,[40] Gadāy Malik was slain by Malik Daulat, and Mas'ūd Chak fought Jahāngīr Padar. By chance an arrow struck Mas'ūd Chak in his eye; he fell from his horse in front of Jahāngīr Padar and was killed.

After killing Malik Gadāy, Malik Daulat proceeded towards Lār thinking that he had emerged victorious. Both the parties [which fought each other] headed onwards in a happy and joyous mood towards Lār and did not know about the losses they had suffered.

On reaching Shihābu'd-Dīn Pora, Malik Daulat's party came to know of the death of Malik Mas'ūd: On the other hand, on reaching Krehmu, the troops of Jahāngīr Padar

---

translator's inference) and was perfected by Kāka (Kacha) Chakra." *The Rājataraṅgiṇī of Jonarāja*, tr. J.C. Dutt, Delhi, 1986, pp. 353-54.

37. At Pampore. See *TḤK*, p. 232.
38. Both Ḥasan and Malik Ḥaidar say that it was Dārdū. See *TḤK*, p. 232 and *TMḤ*, MS f. 47[b].
39. Malik 'Idī Chādūra. *TMḤ*, MS, f, 47[b].
40. Ḥasan says that it was fought at Shihābu'd-Dīn Pora. *TḤK*, p. 233.

learnt of the killing of Malik Gadāy. Malik Daulat then crossed the lake[41] at Shihābu'd-Dīn Pora and joined Ibrāhīm Khān and Malik Tāzī Chak both of whom had come to extend their support to Malik Mas'ūd. They carried with them Malik Ḥusain Raina, son of Serang (Sarhang ?) Raina, as their captive, and put him to death before heading towards the city. Jahāngīr Ḥusain also set out for the city by the Lār route with the intention of crossing the lake and joining Iskandar Khān. But several attempts of his to cross the lake at a place of his choice were foiled by Ibrāhīm Khān, Malik Tāzī Chak and Malik Daulat, all of whom had control of the opposite bank. A few days later, Iskandar Khān and his associates decided to withdraw towards India after ceasing hostilities.[42] Malik Jahāngīr Padar followed suit. In this way Malik Kājī Chak rose to the heights of glory. He bestowed special favours and choicest benefactions upon Malik Daulat. He placed the office, the *jāgīr*, the *harem* and the establishment and household of Malik Mas'ūd Chak under his complete control.

In A.H. 930 (A.D. 1523), Malik 'Alī, Malik Abdāl, Malik Lohar Māgray and Malik Regi raised the banner of revolt,[43] and with the cooperation of the Māgrays, Muḥammad Shāh and Nowroz Chak left the city and proceeded towards Lār.[44] Finding that most of the people in the city had broken their promises and revoked their commitments and come out in

41. Throughout the text *āb* is used for lake or pond and *nahr* or *nahr-i-shahr* for the river Jhelum.
42. Ḥasan says that he sued for peace and then withdrew to Panjab. See *TḤK*, p. 233. Malik Ḥaidar says that Iskandar Khān and his allies concluded truce with Kājī Chak. See *TMḤ*, MS f. 48[a].
43. Ḥasan says that it happened in Tsereh-Vudar fortress. The reason for their revolt was the autocratic style of Kājī Chak's administration. He did not care even for Sulṭān Muḥammad Shāh. See *TḤK*, p. 233.
44. It is not clear what compelled them to leave the city and go to Lār. It could possibly be owing to their initial reverses.

open opposition, Malik Kājī Chak picked up his associates and followers and, with necessary equipment and supplies, left for the Indian mountains. The party stationed itself at Nowshehr in India where it camped for some time.

Mughals repulsed

At this time, two of Bābur Pādshāh's generals, namely Kūchak Beg and Shaykh 'Alī Beg, moved towards Nowshehr with a strong contingent of Turki soldiers with the intention of conquering Kashmir. But he (Malik Kājī Chak) collected the sturdy men of the mountains and of neighbouring areas,[45] and stationed them on the top of Kājdārī mountain to block the routes. Tāzī Chak and Ghāzī Khān[46] had moved their contingents a little ahead of Malik Kājī Chak, and got involved in a skirmish with the Mughals. This was followed by a battle between them, in which Tāzī Chak succeeded in killing a couple of Mughal soldiers. Ghāzī Khān struck his lance at a Mughal soldier which sent him reeling down from his horse. The soldier rolled down the slope and collided with another Mughal horseman who also came hurtling down, and both of them got killed there and then. Ghāzī Khān was

---

45. It is significant that instead of befriending the generals of Bābur, he decided to resist them. One cannot be sure whether he did it out of political expediency or because of his feeling of belonging to a local polity. The latter seems to be more probable because it is a fact that the Chaks though of non-Kashmiri origin identified themselves with the Kashmiris. It is also significant that the attitude of Chaks towards the Kashmiris is different from that of the Baihaqī Sayyids. The latter, according to the present chronicler, looked upon the Kashmiris as their servants. No such thing has been said about the Chaks. Śrivara says, "...they (Sayyids) regarded the people of Kashmir scarcely even as grass". *The Rājataraṅgiṇī of Jonarāja*, (tr. J.C. Dutt, Delhi, 1986, p. 252.
46. Ḥasan's version is that Kājī Chak sent only two sons: Ghāzī Khān and Ḥusain Khān. See *TḤK*, p. 234. Malik Ḥaidar's version is that he sent Ḥusain Khān and two other persons. See *TMḤ*, MS f. 48[b].

hardly seventeen or eighteen years old at this time. He achieved fame for having killed two Mughal soldiers with a single thrust of his lance.[47]

Kājī Chak returns

At last the Turki and the Mughal[48] troops were defeated and the hardy men of the mountains put a large number of them to the sword down the farthest extremities of the mountains. A few months later, Malik Kājī Chak arrested Iskandar Khān because he had been responsible for inviting the Mughal army. Iskandar's arrest by Kājī Chak prompted Muḥammad Shāh to revive old bonds of affection and unity with Kājī Chak and to forget their mutual rancour and animosity. Through letters he assured him of his friendship and cooperation and requested him to return to Kashmir. Thereupon Malik Kājī Chak came to Kashmir along with Iskandar Khān. He was ultimately handed over to Muḥammad Shāh, who got his eyes gouged out.[49] In collusion with Malik 'Alī, a group of Māgrays rose in revolt against the army [of Muḥammad Shāh] in the Village of Kichhāma,[50] which led to hostilities between them. Muḥammad Shāh, Malik Kājī Chak and Sayyid Ibrāhīm Khān Baihaqī proceeded to tight them. The Māgrays were ultimately defeated, their soldiers took to

---

47. Ḥasan does not mention this exploit of Ghāzī Khān. He narrates the following story about Ḥusain Khān: He forced his way into the tent of Shaykh 'Alī Beg and dealt three successive strokes of his sword at him. The first stroke was warded off by 'Alī Beg by shielding himself with a cushion, which, however, was cut into two; the second by shielding himself with a metallic tray, and when the third stroke was about to be delivered, 'Alī Beg hid himself under a bedstead and begged for his life. See *THK*, p. 234.
48. The combination of the Turki and Mughal perhaps implies the soldiers speaking Turkish and Chaghatāī languages.
49. Ḥasan says that he died a few days later and was buried at Zāldagar. *THK*, p. 234.
50. The site of ancient Kṛtyāśrama Vihāra. See *Rājat.*, i. 147n.

their heels and Malik 'Alī fell a prisoner in the hands of Malik Kājī Chak.

Ibrāhīm Shāh

A few months later, Malik 'Alī, a prisoner in the house of Malik Tāzī Chak, managed his escape to India. A little later, Malik Kājī Chak deposed Muḥammad Shāh and interned him in the perilous mountain-village called Lud along with his soldiers. Ibrāhīm Shāh[51] was installed on the throne in place of his father and Kājī Chak now committed himself to serving and bringing him up. Malik 'Alī and Malik Regī Chak thought that the time was ripe for action, and, therefore, collected a large number of Māgrays at Nowshehr.

Māgray's seek Bābur's help

After arriving at a decision through consultations with them, Malik Abdāl Māgray went to Bābur Pādshāh to seek his help, who received him with full courtesy bestowing such special favours upon him as befitted the dignity and status of monarchs; he also issued commands to Shaykh 'Alī Beg and Muḥammad Khān[52] to help him. Forthwith they proceeded towards Kashmir. In A.H. 935 (A.D. 1528), the group of Māgrays, in collaboration with Malik 'Alī and Regī Chak and with the assistance of Bābur's troops[53] entered into Kashmir via Havel[54] [*sic*]. Malik Kājī Chak learnt about their advancing columns and, therefore, marched out to meet them. They confronted each other at village Nangil in Bengil

51. Ḥasan says that Ibrāhīm Shāh was the son of Kājī Chak's sister. See *TḤK*, p. 235.
52. Neither Ḥasan nor Ḥaidar Malik has mentioned the name of Ḥasan Khān.
53. Ḥasan puts their number at twenty thousand. See *TḤK*, p. 235, but Narāyān Koul Ājiz says that they were only eight thousand. *TNK*, MS f.
54. Juel (?). This place could not be identified. Its correct version could not be established.

pargana. Malik Tāzī Chak, the backbone of their force, took the lead and attacked the enemy. As God willed it, he suffered defeat and disaster, and death tightened its unrelenting grip on him. This was followed by a direct encounter between Malik Kājī Chak and the Turki troops.

Kājī Chak's bravery

The Mughal troops included a warrior, a veteran of many grim and bloody battles, and renowned in his days as the bravest of the brave. He had sustained many wounds and had won many laurels on the battlefield. From the first day of the movement of Mughal troops from Agra until the time they reached Kashmir, he had been making repeated enquiries about Kājī Chak. During the battle he sought the help of his friends to identify Kājī Chak for him. He announced that he wanted to fight that brave man to find out how much daring and courage he possessed. His challenging words had reached Kājī Chak before the actual fighting had broken out. At the moment when Kājī Chak's troops were suffering reverses, this gallant Mughal warrior came closer to the troops of Malik Kājī Chak and said in loud words: "Who among you is Kājī Chak? Where is he? I want to tight him. Let him come out and let us try who is braver of the two?"

[*verses*]

On hearing these challenging words of the Mughal warrior, he turned back from his retreating troops and slowly moved towards him. The latter too spurred his horse and came closer to Malik Kājī Chak. He attempted a lightening blow of his sword on Malik Kājī Chak's head. The Malik lifted his shield to protect his head and face; with great alacrity he dodged the blow aimed at his head. Then making an offensive charge, he struck his lance at the chest of the Mughal warrior with such force that, in spite of his being clad in a coat of mail, it pierced [the warrior's chest] and came out from his back about a span, and with that he lifted him from his saddle and hurled him down on the ground, uttering in Kashmiri language:[55] "This is the very Kājī Chak you had been looking for from Agra to Kashmir to take your life." After uttering these words, Kājī Chak turned towards the city. The Mughal troops came to the wounded warrior. With a slender breath of life in him, he warned them that one who ventured to pursue that man (Kājī Chak) would certainly endanger his life because a fight with him would only be suicidal. The Turki soldiers looked at the condition of their fallen warrior and also at the wounds he had sustained, and gave up their attempt of pursuing Kājī Chak, though, of course, they continued their onward march at an easy pace.

Daulat Chak's heroism

In this battle, Malik Daulat Chak first wielded his sword to fight the enemy, but when it broke, he pulled his heavy mace out of its holder. When a Turki soldier confronted him, he struck a blow of his mace on his head which sent the soldier reeling on the ground. But in the process, the mace slipped from Malik Daulat Chak's hand. A Mughal warrior saw that he was without a weapon and took the opportunity of striking at him with a sword, but with alacrity Malik Daulat held back the assailant's striking hand and then wrested the sword from his grip. Since his right hand was wounded [in the scuffle], he held the sword in his left hand and dealt a severe blow to the Mughal warrior. However, it did not prove fatal. As Malik Daulat had sustained many wounds in that battle, he made his way into the house of a soldier and closed the door from inside.

55. The author's use of the word 'Kashmiri' at this place does not mean Sanskrit language as stated earlier. There is historical evidence to prove that by this time colloquial Kashmiri language was in use.

In this battle a number of Kājī Chak's veteran soldiers and famous warriors like Malik Tāzī Chak, Malik Serang (Sarhang) Chak and Malik Suh Chak[56] were slain along with their followers, near ones and subordinates who had braved many a misfortune with them. In the same battle, the group of Baihaqī Sayyids, under the leadership of Sayyid Ibrāhīm Khān, retraced their steps among the fleeing troops of Kājī Chak and made a second daring attack on the enemy. In the encounter he (Sayyid Ibrāhīm) excelled as a brave warrior. With a stroke of his lance, he struck down Bābā Beg [illegible] (illeg.) from his horse.

[*verses*]

Sayyid Ibrāhīm's imprisonment

These assaults caused harassment in the rank and file of the enemy, who in desperation rained arrows on him (Sayyid Ibrāhīm Khān). Not being able to withstand the volley of enemy's arrows, his horse sank into the dust of the battle-field. Mīr Sayyid Ibrāhīm fell a prisoner into the hands of the enemy.[57]

After the Turki troops captured Malik Daulat and Ghāzī Khān – the veterans and celebrities of the Kashmir army – Malik Kājī Chak, along with a handful of his associates, succeeded in disentangling himself from the battle and turning towards the mountain range called Kakru (Ghakru).[58]

Malik Daulat's escape

When Ibrāhīm Khān and Malik Daulat Chak were being escorted to the city as captives, Malik Daulat, despite a

56. One more name in the list of Kājī Chak's fallen warriors is of Masīḥī [sic] Chak. See *TḤK*, p. 236.
57. According to Ḥasan he and his allies, Ghāzī Chak and Daulat Chak were put in chains. *TḤK*, p. 236.
58. Ḥasan says that they fled to the land of Ghakhars. *TḤK*, p. 236.

number of wounds on his body, jumped to the bank from a boat after the evening prayers had been offered, and went to a nearby lake. His guards deployed forty to fifty boats all around the lake and searched for him till midnight. Malik Daulat Chak had hidden himself in the waters of that lake by taking cover under large leaves of waterlily plant, keeping only his head out of water so that he could breathe. When the search for him proved futile, the boats withdrew after midnight. Thereupon Malik Daulat came out of the lake and ran for safety. Ibrāhīm continued to be their prisoner.

Mughal Troops leave

The victorious group triumphantly entered the city. The domain of Kashmir was divided into four parts, which they shared among themselves. Muḥammad Shāh was recalled from the mountains and was installed on the throne. The authority of the government and the ministry was given to Malik Abdāl. With the setting in of autumn, Shaykh 'Alī Beg and his Turki troops were permitted to proceed towards India. Malik 'Alī accompanied them up to Nowshehr in India, where he bade them farewell and returned to Kashmir. Four persons who divided Kashmir among themselves and rapaciously appropriated their respective portions were Malik Abdāl, Malik Lohar Māgray, Malik Regī Chak of Kupwāra and Malik 'Alī.[59]

In A.H. 938 (A.D. 1531), corresponding to the 17th of Kashmiri calendar, Mīrzā Kāmrān planned to occupy Kashmir.[60] He stationed himself at Nowshehr in India, but sent a strong force of well-equipped three thousand horsemen

---

59. The statement is corroborated by Malik Ḥaidar. See *TMḤ*, MS f. 49^b.

60. The immediate reason of Kāmrān's incursion into Kashmir is not known. Ḥasan says that since Kashmir had no powerful governing authority, the neighbouring rulers coveted the land. *TḤK*, p. 237.

under the command of Maḥram Beg[61] and Shaykh 'Alī Beg with instructions to march on to Kashmir. Kashmiri nobles were left with no time to obstruct them in the mountains and to engage them in sporadic fighting in narrow passes leading into Kashmir. In this way the Turki troops entered into Kashmir unopposed and unhindered, and camped in the city. Kashmiri chiefs assembled in the fort at Tsereh Vudar. Malik Kājī Chak emerged from Kakru (Ghakru) mountains and along with his sons and allies joined the Kashmiri chiefs. Maḥram Beg conveyed the date of the event in the under mentioned verses to Kāmrān Mīrzā in Nowshehr (Hindustan):[62]

. . . .

chu kardam fatḥ-e nīm-e ū'be tārīkh
khirad quftā kih fatḥ-e nīm-e firdaws

The news of victory contained in the despatch delighted Kāmrān Mīrzā and, having been freed from all anxieties, he left for Lahore.

Kashmiri nobles assembled in large numbers at the village of Athwājan[63] and took position on mountain heights. Maḥram Beg and his troops crossed the river and engaged them in that village. In the battle that ensued a large number of soldiers on either side was slain. As God willed it, the Mughal faced reverses and, withdrawing from Nowshehr, turned towards the western quarter of the city

---

61. Maḥram Beg Tāshlīqī and Shaykh Alī Beg Uzbek. See *TḤK*, p. 237.

62. *be hukm-i pādshāhī kez harīmash*
be fahm asan shawad tafhīm-i ferdaws
safar kardam be sū-i mulk-i Kashmir
kih az khubī dihad ta'līm-i ferdaws
chu kardam fath-e nīm-e ū be tarīkh
khirad gufta kih fath-e nīm-e ferdaws.
fath-e nim-e ferdaws yields A.H. 938/A.D. 1531.

63. Southern quarter of Srinagar between Pāmpora and Batwāra.

where they had set up their headquarters. Kashmiri troops appeared on the heights of Koh-i-Suleymān and came down slowly towards the east of the city to establish their camp.[64] There was sporadic fighting with the Mughals for some time. At last, Maḥram Beg got sick of this and entered into negotiations with Kashmiri chiefs and made firm promises of peace and conciliation to them.[65]

Kājī Chak and Maḥram Beg meet

All the nobles [of Kashmir] assembled in the *khānqāh* of Amīr Sayyid 'Alī Hamadānī. Malik Kājī Chak took a boat which had been tied with ropes. From the side of the Turks, Maḥram Beg also took a boat of the same kind, and both the boats were rowed simultaneously to reach the midstream. As the boats drew close, Malik Kājī Chak leapt into Maḥram Beg's boat and sat beside him. Maḥram Beg was greatly delighted and felt obliged to Kājī Chak for this extraordinary gesture. They talked and deliberated for nearly an hour and then, taking each other's leave, rowed back to their respective camps. On rejoining his party of Kashmiri nobles, Malik Kājī Chak was asked by them why he had left his boat and gone to Maḥram Beg's boat. His answer was that he felt convinced that Maḥram Beg was incapable of doing him any harm because he was not as agile and clever as he himself was. This prompted him to move into his boat without entertaining any fears, he added.

A few days later, he arranged presents for Kāmrān Mīrzā and bade farewell to Turki troops, who left Kashmir via Baramulla. Malik Daulat Chak and Jahāngīr Māgray accompanied them up to Pakhli.

It had been decided [by Kājī Chak and Maḥram Beg] that Muḥammad Shāh would be given the state lands of

64. Ḥasan locates it at present-day Gupkār. See *TḤK*, p. 238. For more details see *Rājat.*, ii, 290 and 454.
65. He sued for safety. See *TMḤ*, f. 50[a]

Kashmir as his *jāgīrs*. Out of these a *jāgīr* was allowed to Sayyid Ibrāhīm Khān for his maintenance.[66] They divided Kashmir into five zones. Kājī Chak set up his headquarters at Zenehpore. Another zone and the ministry went to Abdāl Māgray with his headquarters at Bengil.[67] Malik Regī Chak stationed himself at Kāmarāj. The fourth share went to Malik 'Alī who occasionally shifted between the *parganas* of Ular and the village Tursh [*sic*]. They stuck to this arrangement for about a year.

Ḥaidar Dughlat's invasion

In the year A.H. 939 (A.D. 1532), Sulṭān Sayyid Khān[68] came to Tibet from Kāshghar. It took him some time in subjugating and plundering those areas. Meanwhile the passes leading to Kāshghar got blocked. He was, therefore, forced to spend the winter in Tibet. But as Tibet did not have provisions sufficient to meet the requirements of his troops, he decided that his son Iskandar Sulṭān and some senior commanders proceed to Kashmir with an army under the overall command of Mīrzā Ḥaidar.[69] They took the Lār route and reached the outskirts of Kashmir. In the *pargana* of Lār, Kashmiri commanders suffered serious reverses at their hands, and withdrew to the fort of Hānjeek.[70] Mīrzā

66. Ḥasan says that Lohar Māgray was also one of the shareholders and his headquarters were at Bengil. See *TḤK*, p. 239.
67. At Kichhāma not Bengil. See *TḤK*, p. 239.
68. Sa'īd Khān in *TMḤ*, MS f. 50ᵃ and *TḤK*, p. 239.
69. Ḥasan says that he was a nephew (sister's son) of Sulṭān Sayyid (Sa'īd ?) Khān. *TḤK*, p. 240. The number of Mīrzā Ḥaidar's troops has been estimated at fourteen thousand soldiers and seven thousand horses. Describing the chaos caused by the Kāshgharian troops in Kashmir, Ḥasan writes that people fled their homes and hid in caves and remote gorges. Men of learning and scholarship and of respectable status retired to the island of *Lank* in Wular lake. The nobles shut themselves up in the fortress of Hanjeek. See *TḤK*, p. 240.

Ḥaidar encamped at Nowshehr and finding that the fort of Hānjeek was strong, they turned towards Marāj, where they burnt the whole city and fanned out in the entire *pargana*. Wherever the Turki troops halted, Kashmiri nobles also stationed themselves close to them, and pursued them with their groups. The, Mughal troops indulged in large-scale killing, loot and plunder of household goods, property and other materials. They took children and womenfolk as captives to be enslaved. Unscrupulous and extremely irreligious as they were, they converted the Islamic city [of Srinagar] into enemy's country (*dāru'l-ḥarb*), and considered the shedding of the blood of Muslims as lawful as 'sucking milk from one's mother's breast.'[71] The Qāḍī the learned, the jurisconsults and scholars left their homes and took shelter on the island of *lank*.[72] Muslim nobles, officials and chiefs approached the Qāḍī, the eminent doctors of religious learning, the jurisconsults and also the Sayyids for their opinion on the outrage perpetrated by the Turki hordes. They asked them as to what, according to the tenets of Islam, would be the position of a Muslim and a faithful who got killed in fighting on the side of Kashmiris and also what the Muslim law said about those of the persons who were killed on the side of the Mughals. A unanimous decree issued by the learned, the divine, the jurisconsults observed that, according to the doctors of religion and [*Shia*'] theology, those killed on the side of Kashmiris, high or low, were to be considered as martyrs

70. Malik Ḥaidar says that they hid themselves in the fort at Tsereh Vudar. See *TMḤ*, MS f. 50[a].
71. It is interesting to note that the Turki soldiers are considered by the author as irreligious though Islam had made a footing in Central Asia (Kāshghar, Khotan etc.) much earlier than in Kashmir. The epithet 'Islamic City' for Srinagar has been used for the first time in this chronicle.
72. The island was raised by Sulṭān Zainu'l-'Ābidīn. See pp. 71-72 *Supra*.

and the oppressed. [They further said that] the powerful and the overbearing who subjugate and dominate Islamic lands and subject its Muslim men and materials to wholesale rapine and plunder are usurpers according to Islamic ecclesiastical authorities and prelates. According to the religion of Muḥammad their killing was not merely permissible, but necessary. It had a legal sanction and was considered an act of virtue.

Kashmiri nobles carried these decrees in their hands and bravely searched for them [the Turks] from place to place till that winter came to an end. In early spring, Kashmiri troops and Mughal soldiers clashed in the neighbourhood of the barren lands of Babul.[73] Both sides used weapons like bows and arrows in the battle that followed. Loud war cries were raised by warriors on either side and the tumult of the striking swords virtually extinguished the life-breath of the young and the old.

[*verses*]

Kashmiri troops, who were commanded by Malik 'Alī, came into direct confrontation with Turki soldiers, and a big battle followed. The Mughal troops, commanded by Bābā Sirāgh Mīrzā and numbering about five hundred, were all armed and clad in coats of mail. Realizing that much blood would be shed in the course of fighting, Malik Alī produced the decree which had been obtained from the divines and learned men and, showing it to the people, implored them to stand witness to the fact that it was on the basis of this

---

73. Near the present-day town of Matan. The town was built by Rājā Rām Dev. The plains of Babul and Bāgh-i-Suleymān figured in an encomium which the Qāḍī of Kāshghar composed in praise of their victory in Kashmir. It runs as this:

kez maqdamash shud sarsabz-o khurram
sehrā-i Babul Bāghī Suleymān.

See *TḤK*, pp. 178 and 242.

decree that he had taken up arms against Mughal troops.[74] Putting the decree under his armpit, Malik 'Alī spoke the opening words of the Islamic prayer 'In the name of Allāh, the Compassionate the Merciful.' After this, the son of Malik Mūsā Raina, Malik Shaykh 'Alī Bhat, and many other brave warriors attacked the Turks. They exhibited feats of singular courage and extraordinary valour on the battlefield and inflicted severe wounds on Mughal soldiers; the heads of many of them were cut off. A brave Kashmiri soldier struck such a deep wound on the horse of Beg [sic] Sirāgh Mīrzā that the charger was forced to gallop back to the 'background'. Sirāgh Mīrzā took another horse and turned to flee. Beholding that the centre of their army had started cracking, Dāyam 'Alī Beg from the right flank and Mīrzā Ḥaidar from the left flank of their army, dashed out, each with about a thousand soldiers, and attacked with a total strength of two thousand strong. This was met by Malik 'Alī, Malik Ḥusain Raina, son of Mūsā and Malik Shaykh 'Alī Bhat. Kashmiri commanders and soldiers fought with great intrepidity and displayed their excellent fighting qualities. However, since God Almighty's grace did not favour them, their efforts were of no avail. Despite the rare courage and prowess shown by Malik Ḥusain Raina, son of Mūsā Raina, Malik Shaykh 'Alī Bhat, and the rest of the warriors, they could not defy what was predestined; and, therefore, fell in the battlefield. Since they were the senior commanders and

74. It seems necessary to point out why the Kashmiri commanders were forced to invoke the teachings and traditions of Islam because it is unusual that decrees had to be obtained from men learned in Islamic theology for purposes of fighting. The possible reason is that Turks were of Sunni faith whereas most of the Kashmiri nobles professed Shia' faith. In order to win over the Sunnis of Kashmir and register their support in fighting the Turks, the Kashmiri commanders felt it necessary to get the decrees issued which justified their fighting and killing Turki (Muslim) soldiers.

the backbone of their army and fell as martyrs, their soldiers turned their back on the battlefield. About a thousand and five hundred soldiers were slain in the Lidar valley through which flows the Khovurpāra[75] stream. The rest of the commanders and their troops fled the field. Malik Kājī Chak together with a party of his sons and soldiers ascended the heights near Babul slopes. Ibrāhīm Khān continued to resist his opponents bravely. He carried in his hand a fire-spitting sword, and excited his charger so as to make furious dashes all over the battlefield and struck blow after blow to the enemy on the battlefield.

[*verses*]

Reverses

When the opponents saw that the troops of Ibrāhīm Khān, whose sword spat fire, had met with defeat and that he was fighting single-handed, they encircled him. But when Ibrāhīm Khān saw that Kashmiri troops had been defeated and had withdrawn to the barren lands of Babul, he pierced the encircling troops of the enemy and joined Malik Chak's soldiers. The rest of the defeated soldiers also assembled at the above-mentioned heights. They held on to that elevated spot for some days till their ranks were reinforced by the defeated and dispersed soldiers in the neighbouring areas. Once again, they took up arms against the Mughals to avenge their earlier defeat.

At this time, Mīrzā Ḥaidar sent[76] to Sulṭān Sa'eed Khān, then encamping in Tibet, a despatch stating that on the 4th of Sha'bān, a fierce battle had been fought with Kashmiri army on the slopes of Babul in which a large number of troops were involved. God had blessed his triumphant army with victory. The date of this victory was found by a Qāḍī

75. For its ancient history, see *Rājat.*, ii, 465.

76. 'and' (*wa*) in the text.

[or by Qāḍī] in the army of Sulṭān Sa'eed in the epithet *roz-i chehārum az māh-i Sha'bān* (the fourth day of the month of Sha'bān). He incorporated the chronogram in a verse which he composed and despatched to him:[77]

[*verses*]

But Mīrzā Ḥaidar regretted that though it was he who had composed the phrase, he had not computed the date which it yielded.

In spite of the defeat inflicted on them [Kashmiris] Malik Kājī Chak and all of the remaining Kashmiri commanders still ventured to harass and to create obstacles for the Turki and the Mughal soldiers. Wherever the Mughals encamped, Kashmiri commanders contrived to lay in ambush close by. The helplessness of their army was intensified by a rupture in the relations between Mīrzā Ḥaidar and Dāyam Alī Beg. The latter proposed truce and cessation of hostilities with Kashmiri commanders to which Mīrzā Ḥaidar agreed reluctantly.

Muḥammad Shāh's niece[78] was given in marriage to Iskandar Khān and presents and gifts were sent to Sa'eed Khān. With this they chose to withdraw by the same route in Lār which they had taken [for entering into] Kashmir.[79]

Famine

By the time autumn set in, Kashmir was liberated from the presence and also, the ravages of the Mughals. Despite the lateness of the season, farmers and peasants cultivated their fields, but because of the onset of winter, crops could not ripen and çorn fields were damaged. Consequently in the 41st year, corresponding to the 10th year of Kashmiri

77. See note 73 *supra*.

78. Ḥasan says daughter. *TḤK*, p. 242.

79. The date of this event in Ḥasan is 10th of Har, the 14th year of Kashmiri calendar. *TḤK*, p. 242.

calendar,[80] Kashmir suffered a severe famine, the like of which had not been witnessed by anybody in the land. Whosoever among the inhabitants of this country escaped the sword and slaughter by the Mughals found himself locked in a grim battle with starvation. Many young and old people of this land perished in the famine. A *kharwār*[81] of grain was not available even for a thousand *tankas*.

Aftermath

Let it not remain unknown that after the Mughal troops quit Kashmir, her chiefs and nobles compromised to forge unity among themselves and pledged to set aside dissensions and rancour that had bedevilled their relations in the past. They now promised to respect their mutual pledges of solidarity.

Malik Kājī Chak took up his abode in Kāmarāj *pargana*; Malik Lohar Chak dwelt in the *pargana* of Bengil and Malik Abdāl Māgray moved between the city and the *parganas*. This arrangement lasted a few years.

Muḥammad Shāh died in the year A.H. 944 (A.D. 1537), after reigning for nearly fifty-one years. In the aforesaid year, his son Sulṭān Shams Shāh ascended the throne, but his reign did not last for more than a year, and he was succeeded to the throne by his brother Īsmā'īl Shāh in A.H. 945 (A.D. 1538).[82]

Kājī Chak's activities

In the preceding year (i e., A.H. 944 /A.D. 1537), Malik Kājī Chak had aligned some of the chiefs with himself and entered the city despite resistance and Opposition from the Māgrays, who along with Malik Regī Chak had assembled at Baramulla. Malik Kājī Chak also moved along with his

80. A.H. 941/A.D. 1534. *TḤK*, p. 243.
81. One kharwār is approximately eighty kilograms.
82. He was the second son of Muḥammad Shāh and son-in-law of Kājī Chak. *TḤK*, p. 244.

troops out of the city and confronted them there. A few days later, Malik Daulat and Malik Zetu [*sic*] Chak,[83] who had deserted Malik Abdāl Māgray, were summoned by Malik Kājī Chak. Truce was concluded with the Māgrays and Kājī Chak returned to the city. But those of the chiefs who had formerly combined with him once again joined the Māgrays. Finding that they were hostile, Kājī Chak came out of the city and along with a large group left for the Indian mountains[84] to pass the winter there.[85] With the advent of spring, he requested the Sulṭān[86] for full reinforcements.

In the same spring, Malik Regī Chak set out for Jammu via Bānihāl with the purpose of marrying the daughter of Rājā of Jammu. Malik Kājī Chak took advantage of this and with the manpower he had received [from the Ghakkars] entered into Kashmir. The Māgrays, combined a large group of Malik Regī Chak's men, the nobles of Chādūra and Doona [*sic*] with their own soldiers, and garrisoned in the town of Sopor. Malik Kājī Chak camped at the village Kesu to give them a fight. A month later, Malik Regī Chak returned from Jammu, entered the city [of Srinagar] and rose in opposition to Malik Kājī Chak.

Now Malik Kājī Chak found that he had been sandwiched between two formidable enemies – numerous troops of the Māgrays and Kashmiri chiefs on one side, and Malik Regī Chak on the other – and as both of them were ready to crush him, he thought it prudent to consult with Ibrāhīm Khān, Malik Daulat, his nobles and his sons. Their opinion was that he should proceed to deal with Regī Chak, and that Malik Ibrāhīm Khān accompanied by Malik Daulat and a group of his nobles should offer resistance to the Māgrays. Malik Kājī

83. Zenu / Zeti?

84. Ghakkar mountains. See *TḤK*, p. 244.

85. *Ibid.*

86. Identified as Ādam Khān Ghakkar. See *TḤK*, p. 244n.

Chak asked Ibrāhīm Khān as to what strategy he had [drawn] in case he was forced to fight a battle with the outnumbering troops of the Māgrays. To this he replied that since he was fully convinced of his bravery, he would wield his sword over the heads of his enemies in such a manner that their heads would roll on the ground.

[*verses*]

Battle for the city

Greatly delighted and encouraged by the reply of Ibrāhīm Khān, Malik Kājī Chak went ahead with his plan; and, shortly after evening prayers, he came out to deal with Regī Chak, leaving the result of his venture to God. By nightfall, Regī Chak came to know that Malik Kājī Chak had moved his whole force against him. He drew away from ʻĪdgāh to the locality of ʻAlāu'd-Dīn Pora for a fight. By about afternoon [of the next day], Malik Kājī Chak entered the city by Nowshehr route. On reaching near ʻAlāu'd-Dīn Pora he deployed a strong contingent of his troops under commanders like Dervīsh Thakkur, Malik [illegible] (illeg.) and Khwāja Ibrāhīm on the Gānkhan passage to stop the advance of Malik Regī Chak. Himself he headed towards Kalāshpora with another strong contingent and took up a position in the *khānqāh* of Kajdarār (Gojehwār ?]. He sent his son Muḥammad Chak and his soldiers to engage Ragī Chak, who had demolished the Kalāshpora bund, rendering the passage impassable. Malik Kājī Chak despatched Ḥamza Nāyak [*sic*] and Nājī Nāyak from the Maisumeh [*sic*] route. At first Malik Regī Chak proceeded to confront them, but when people spread the rumour that Sayyid Ibrāhīm Khān, Malik Daulat Chak and Zetu Chak were on their way to the city, which they planned to enter from their side, he did not think it proper to go ahead with his plan of attacking them and, therefore, retraced his steps.

During the time he was crossing and re-crossing, the troops of Malik Regī Chak and the Jammu soldiers stationed at the Gānkhan passage had been badly mauled. Malik Kājī Chak's foot-soldiers had pressed them hard so as to demoralise them and to force them to take to their heels. The troops of Kājī Chak were followed by cavalrymen who reached near the *khānqāh* of Sayyid 'Alī Hamadānī. When Malik Regī Chak heard the names of Ibrāhīm Khān, Malik Daulat Chak, and Zetu Chak, he chose to withdraw. In the neighbourhood of the *khānqāh*, he had an encounter with Dervīsh Thakkur and killed him. Near the gate of the *khānqāh*, he also smote Khwāja Ibrāhīm to death. The rest of his enemies dispersed and hid themselves in the nearby lanes and private houses. Thus Regī Chak came closer to the Gānkhan passage. His enquiries revealed to him that Malik Kājī Chak was heading towards Kalāshpora. Thereupon, he retraced his steps and made for Kalāshpora. On reaching the site where the bund had been demolished, he found that Muḥammad Chak, son of Malik Kājī Chak, had taken up position there. He threatened him and made him go back, so that he did not become a victim of his adversary's sword. News was brought to Malik Kājī Chak that Regī was heading towards the same approach; he mounted his horse and moved on to Kalāshpora mosque and waited in the compound of Nūnī Ganāī mosque for his enemy. On reaching the site of the broken bund, he learnt that Ḥamza Nāyak was approaching from Monjehdār [locality]. Thus the earlier information about Ibrāhīm Khān and Malik Daulat proved to be false. He then thought it advisable to face them and turning back adopted the same path. Face to face with them, Malik Ḥamza Nāyak fled to a private house, but Malik Nājī Nāyak was captured and brought before him. Regī Chak reproached him severely, and let him go. Himself he took the Phāk route and fled to Lār. But Malik Kājī Chak struck and crushed him and then moved towards Kinsu [*sic*]. He spent the night at Barthana grounds.

Kājī returns to Sopor

At Sopor, the Māgrays learnt of Malik Kājī Chak's movement. Early in the morning they repaired the bridges a little below Sopor which they had destroyed, and crossed the river to fight against Sayyid Ibrāhīm Khān, Malik Daulat Chak and Ghāzī Khān. The numerical strength of the troops of Baihaqī Sayyids and Chaks was small in comparison with that of the Māgrays. Some of the army commanders suggested [to Sayyid Ibrāhīm Khān] to destroy the bridges and move away to let the water separate them [from the enemy]. Ibrāhīm Khān and Daulat Chak were too brave to accept this ignominious suggestion. They argued that their retreat would result in defeat and dismemberment of their own troops. Hence they decided to fight with full courage and bravery and stood with rock-like firmness on the battlefield. Like roaring lions, Malik Kājī Chak's soldiers fell upon their adversaries, "When God wills, the lesser in number shall overpower the larger in number," so goes the saying, and they emerged victorious. In this battle, Malik Mas'ūd Chak, the brother of Malik Regī Chak, was slain by Sayyid Ya'qūb Baihaqī, son of Mīr Sayyid Muḥammad. The rest of the Māgray group suffered defeat and fled towards India. The Sayyids of Baihaq made such desperate and severe attacks on their enemies in the course of this battle as would elicit eloquent praise from the bravest of all times. This event occurred in A.H. 945 (A.D. 1538), corresponding to the 14th year of Kashmiri calendar.

Kājī Chak's administration

After this victory, the domain of Kashmir was divided into three parts: Ismā'īl Shāh and Kājī Chak received one share each and the third went to Mīrzā Sayyid Ibrāhīm Khān. For nearly two and a half years, Malik Kājī Chak was the undisputed sovereign authority and administrative head of this land. This was the time when Islamic religion and the customs of this faith reached the heights of glory. In fact, it was he who virtually issued royal commands in this country, because Ismā'īl Shāh was his son-in-law and he remained only a titular king; his authority was limited to the striking of coins and reading of *khutba* in his name. Malik Kājī Chak held absolute power during those times.

Most of the tribal chiefs and clan leaders who were seditious and bred strife, or revolted against him, would be thrown into prison, but none of them was sentenced to death. After some time, he would grant them pardon and re-confer upon them their *jāgīrs*. Though he did sense that they had malicious designs against his life, his large-heartedness reduced these to insignificance, and he never ordered any one of them to be put to the sword. His sons and descendants, who today boast of their independent anti autocratic rule, are in truth reaping the fruits of his generosity and benevolence, whether they know it or not.

Mīrzā Ḥaidar again

Let it not remain unrevealed that consequent upon their defeat at Kinsu [*sic*] the Māgrays fled to the India mountains where Malik Regī Chak joined them after some time. Humāyūn Pādshāh was defeated at Agra around the same time, and he withdrew to Lahore. Sher Shāh had ascended the throne of India. Malik Abdāl and Malik Regī Chak sent their sons/descendants to [the court at] Lahore. Through the help of Khwāja Ḥājjī, they managed to secure the support of Mīrzā Ḥaidar who at that time was in the service of Humāyūn in India, and they came to Kashmir.[87] Leading

87. Ḥasan writes that through Mīrzā Ḥaidar and Khwāja Ḥājjī Bānday they conveyed to Humāyūn Pādshāh the details regarding the (*Contd.*)

their troops, Malik Kājī Chak and Sayyid Ibrāhīm Khān proceeded along the Hirpur route to make an exit without any fighting.

On 21 Rajab, A.H. 947 (21 October 1540), corresponding to the 16th year of Kashmiri calendar, the Māgrays, assisted by the Mughal troops,[88] entered Kashmir via Tsereh-Ḥār. Malik Kājī Chak continued his march along Hirpur route together with his sons, troops and equippage.[89] Mīrzā Ḥaidar extended remarkable courtesy to Kashmiri nobles. The domain was divided into three parts; one was given to Mīrzā Ḥaidar, the second to Abdāl Māgray along with administrative authority and ministry, and the third to Malik Regī Chak.

This arrangement continued till the end of winter. In early spring, on the new year's day of Kashmiris', Abdāl Māgray – in accordance with the Qur'ānic saying that all that has life must taste of death – passed to the everlasting world. Mīrzā Ḥaidar elevated Malik Ḥusain Māgray, Malik Abdāl Māgray's eldest son, to his late father's office and *jāgīr* without diminishing it.

---

domination of the followers of Shams Araki and propagation of Shia' faith in Kashmir and submitted a. copy of *Ahwat* written by Shams Araki. They requested for reform (*iṣlāh*) in religion and also for troops. *TḤK*, p. 248. Malik Ḥaidar writes that Malik Abdāl Māgray and Malik Regī Chak brought Mīrzā Ḥaidar Kāshghari from the court of Humāyūn. *TMḤ*, MS f. 52^{b}.

88. Ḥasan writes that Mīrzā Hindāl and other nobles advised Humāyūn against deciding to proceed to Kashmir. However, on the instance of the Kashmiri nobles and of his own wish, Mīrzā Ḥaidar took leave of Humāyūn and with a contingent of four hundred troops proceeded to help the Māgrays. See *TḤK*, p. 249 and Mīrzā Ḥaidar's *Tārīkh-i-Rashīdī*, p. 479.
89. The author makes no allusion to any fighting between the troops of Kājī Chak and Mīrzā Ḥaidar. Perhaps it is because Malik Ḥaidar says, "he had no strength for resistance." See *TMḤ*, MS f. 52^{b} and *TḤK*, p. 249.

Kājī meets Sher Shāh

From the Indian mountains, Malik Kājī Chak went to Sher Shāh for assistance.[90] The latter showed him full courtesy and due regard and saw the scars and wounds all over his body. He made him remove his head gear, and saw the marks of healing wounds on his head and asked him whether all those wounds had been sustained by him in a single battle or in many (in Kashmir). Malik Kājī Chak told him that the wounds had been sustained in not one but many battles. Sher Shāh, thereupon, caressed him profusely and conferred upon him the title of Khān-i-Khānān. He left it to his choice to call for as much of assistance as he desired.

Trusting the promises and the letters of agreement which had come to him from Kashmiri nobles, Kājī Chak brought along with him Ḥusain Sherwānī and Lāl Khān[91] from among the nobles of Sher Shāh's court and also a handful of his troops.[92] He made his entry into Kashmir through Hirpur when the passes opened [after winter]. Mīrzā Ḥaidar sent Khwāja Ḥājjī and Ibrāhīm Khān to Regī Chak at ـسـ (illeg.) and persuaded him with conciliatory words to join him. He agreed to do so and Mīrzā Ḥaidar left his family, womenfolk and children at Andarkol [*sic*].[93]

Kājī Chak defeated

The two armies took their respective positions at Wothnār. Intermittent skirmishes and sporadic fighting between them

---

90. Ḥasan says that Kājī Chak gave him his niece, the daughter of Sulṭān Muḥammad Shāh, in marriage, but there is no mention of this either in the history of Malik Ḥaidar or of Mīrzā Ḥaidar Dughlat. See *TḤK*, p. 250.
91. Ḥasan says that it was Ādīl Khān. *TḤK*, p. 250.
92. It is five thousand soldiers in Ḥasan. *TḤK*, p 250.
93. Should be Andarkot, the well-known fort of Hindū period in the village of the same name at the site of ancient Jayāpur. See *Rājat.*, iv. 506-11n.

continued for nearly a month, after which fighting had to be suspended owing to heavy rains and floods. Both the armies withdrew from the scene of operations. Malik Kājī Chak camped at Gīrdār [*sic*] and Malik Regī Chak and Mīrzā Ḥaidar at Kohtār (Kothār ?). A royal battle was fought near Wahthore.[94] Mullā Ḥusain Khatīb has recorded the year of this battle in the chronogram *fatḥ-e muqarrar* (Repeat victory) which corresponds to the year 49.[95] Malik Nowroz was slain and Kājī Chak's army suffered defeat and disaster. Malik Kājī Chak, Mīr Sayyid Ibrāhīm Khān, Malik Daulat Chak and a number of their army commanders fled to India by the Hirpur route.

Mīrzā Ḥaidar visits Zadibal

After the victory was won by Mīrzā Ḥaidar, Malik Regī Chak took leave of him and left for Kāmarāj for rest and relaxation. Had he chosen to assume administrative authority and be the minister, Mīrzā Ḥaidar would have complied with his orders and agreed to his policies. He would not have disregarded his wishes. Mīrzā Ḥaidar's obedience and submissiveness to Regī Chak may well be estimated from the following anecdote.

Shāh Sayyid Aḥmad Majzūb paid a visit to the domain of Kashmir. Regī Chak declared that since Shāh Aḥmad Noor Bakhshī had arrived in Zadibal rest house, he would like to pay him a visit. He asked for the opinion of Malik Ḥaidar who readily agreed with him, adding that he himself would like to accompany him. He then suggested that since it was the mid-hour of the day and they would be obliged to stay with the saint for some time, the warm weather could prove oppressive for him; and that, therefore, it would be advisable

94. Zalsu in *TMḤ*, MS f. 53[a].

95. Malik Ḥaidar writes that in this battle Malik Muḥammad Nājī Chādūra shot an arrow at Mīrzā Ḥaidar's horse which wounded the animal seriously and Mīrzā Ḥaidar had to abandon it and take another horse. See *TMḤ*, MS f. 53[a].

to choose late afternoon hour for this visit. Till then they could retire to their respective places for an afternoon siesta. Malik Regī Chak returned to his house to have rest and sleep and did not wake up before the late afternoon praying hour. But Mīrzā Ḥaidar offered the late afternoon prayer and sent somebody to Malik Regī Chak bidding him to get ready for meeting Shāh Sayyid Aḥmad Noor Bakhshī. Regī Chak woke up and began offering prayers. But before he could finish, Mīrzā Ḥaidar rode into his house. Then they both proceeded to Zadibal. On reaching near the tomb of Amīr Shamsu'd-Dīn Muḥammad Araki, Mīrzā Ḥaidar entered the mausoleum (*rowza*) with perfect humility and submission. First, he stood on the footsteps of the grave, offered prayers for the dead, and then facing towards *qibla*, sat in mausoleum and called for a reciter to read out portions from the Qur'ān. He summoned one Khwāja Ismā'īl who had come from India after having acquired grace and elegance in the art of recitation. Mīrzā Ḥaidar sat close to the grave of Amīr Shamsu'd-Dīn Araki and read out the chapter *āyatu'l-kursī*. It was followed by a second prayer for the departed one; and finally, with humility and modesty, he left the tomb. All the people known or unknown to him, who observed the deportment of Mīrzā Ḥaidar, expressed their surprise and said that the faithful and the followers of this place should learn the manner and procedures of veneration and courtesy from him. This was followed by a meeting with Shāh Aḥmad in the upper story of the *khānqāh*. In the course of his conversation with Shāh Aḥmad, Mīrzā Ḥaidar expressed his strong belief and faith in the noble order of Noor Bakhshiyyeh [sect]. Then, in his address to the *sufis* of Zadibal, he offered them pieces of advice. Malik Regī Chak was annoyed at this and told him angrily that they had not come there for offering sermons. Malik Ḥaidar noticed his displeasure and put an abrupt end to his sermon, and shifted to some other topic. Then, bidding good bye to the Shāh, he walked the whole distance of the compound up to the outgoing flight of stairs by retracing his steps backward without showing his back to the saint (as a mark of extreme respect). Then he came down the stairs, went round the interior and the exterior of the *khānqāh*, had a look at the stony floor of its compound and praised Amīr Shams Araki for his great deeds.[96] (See *Tohfatu'l Ahbab*, Tr. K.N. Pandit)

Malik Ḥaidar did all this just to please Malik Regī Chak. In fact, in his heart he bore malice and enmity against that order (Noor Bakhshiyyeh), of which he gave a proof when the opportunity came.

Regī Chak escapes

On finding that Regī Chak paid scant or no attention to his commands and accorded no respect to his authority, he (Ḥaidar) began to search for ways and means of destroying him in the following year. He aligned Malik 'Idī Raina and Ḥusain Māgray with himself and, through the good offices of Khwāja Ḥājjī, fostered an accord with them.[97] Then he proceeded towards Kāmarāj with the aim of capturing Malik Regī Chak, who, however, fled to India via the Karnāv route. Settling temporarily at Poonch, he established and strengthened bonds of cooperation and amity with Malik Kājī Chak. Malik Ḥaidar plundered and destroyed Regī Chak's buildings and mansions in Kāmarāj and then returned to Andarkol [*sic*] in the city.

Shaykh Dāniyāl

While Mīrzā Ḥaidar was conducting operations in Kāmarāj, Shaykh Dāniyāl,[98] on learning about the arrival of Shāh

96. This story does not figure in the histories of Ḥasan and Malik Ḥaidar Chādūra.
97. Mīrzā Ḥaidar succeeded in winning the support of Malik Muḥammad Najī through the latter's relative named 'Idī Raina, See *TMḤ*, MS f. 53^{b}.
98. The son of Mīr Shamsu'd-Dīn Araki. *TḤK*, p. 255.

Sayyid Aḥmad Noor Bakhshī [in Kashmir], moved from Tibet to Kashmir. On arriving in the village Karaj[99] [*sic*] he learnt of Regī Chak's disaster. Per necessity, he halted at Drang where he left his equipment and proceeded towards Mīrzā Ḥaidar's camp. He came to the camp of Malik 'Īdī Raina who received him with respect and honour, The Malik avoiding committing any lapse in extending support and favour to the Shaykh, but at last, he withdrew his support. When Malik Ḥaidar found that 'Idī Raina no more supported him, he ventured to take the step which led to the Shaykh's martyrdom.[100]

It has already been said that Regī Chak had suffered a defeat and had withdrawn to Poonch where, in the following year,[101] he joined hands with Kājī Chak and entered into Kashmir via Havel, encamping in Goori Marg range.[102] Mīrzā Ḥaidar took with him a contingent of Mughal and Kashmiri soldiers and encircled them. After some time, the Turkish soldiers made a night-assault on them in which Malik Kājī Chak, Regī Chak and Mīr Sayyid Ibrāhīm again

99. It could not even be Kāmarāj because Kāmarāj was a *pargana* and not a village.

100. There are conflicting versions about Shaykh Dāniyāl's movement from Tibet to Kashmir. Malik Ḥaidar says that initially he had fled to Tibet because he feared Ḥaidar. Later Ḥaidar gave him a promise and brought him to this place. But soon after arriving in Kashmir, Ḥaidar went back on his word and he was put to the sword. Ḥasan's version is that Dāniyāl propagated his faith in Askardū. Mīrzā Ḥaidar brought him to this place after reproaching him severely and put him in prison for one year. Later, on the strength of a few witnesses, Dāniyāl was charged with cursing the companions of the Prophet (*sabh-i ṣuhābah-i-Kabīr bar ū thābit kard*). Qāḍī Ibrāhīm and Qāḍī 'Abdul Ghaffūr issued a decree against him and he was put to the sword. See *TMḤ*, MS f. 54[a] and *TḤK*, p. 255.

101. A.H. 951 (A.D. 1544) in *TḤK*, p. 252.

102. Present-day Gulmarg.

suffered a defeat and were forced to retreat towards the Indian mountains.

After the Goori Marg victory, Mīrzā Ḥaidar strengthened his bonds of unity with Malik 'Idī Raina and Ḥusain Māgray. In spite of Mīrzā Ḥaidar's managing to capture power and authority of government, Nāzuk Shāh continued to be the titular king. For some time, coins – dinār – continued to be struck in his name; Mīrzā Ḥaidar could not strike the coins in his name.

Kājī Chak dies

In the year A.H. 951 (A.D. 1544), 23rd of Jumāda al-Ukhrā, Malik Kājī Chak died of fever at a place near Dana Kala (Gala) in India.[103] The date of his death was found in the phrase *faut-e sardār*. With the passing away of this intrepid commander, who, in truth, may be called the king of the clan of Chaks, disunity and confusion spread in his tribe and community.

Mīrzā Ḥaidar now let loose oppression which sprang from his fanaticism. He did not conceal his enmity towards the lovers of the house of Prophet and the adherents of 'Alī, the saint of God (*walīu'llāh*). His rabid fanaticism and deep-seated malice touched such proportions that he issued an order to destroy the holy *khānqāh* of Mīr Shamsu'd-Dīn Araki and started killing Muslims and the faithful.[104] On the 8th of Dhu'l-Ḥijja, A.H. 955 (A.D. 1548), Ḥazrat Rishī[105] was martyred.

---

103. Thana in Rajouri in *TḤK*, p. 252.
104. The details about the plunder and persecution of Shias, destruction of their houses, burning of the khānqāh and desecration of the grave of Mīr Shamsu'd-Dīn Irāqī, see *TḤK*, p. 254.
105. Shanglī Rishī, a disciple of Bābā Alī Najjār. Another notable person executed was Ṣūfī Dāwūd. Another person named Mīr Alī was expelled from Kashmir. See *TMḤ*, MS f. 54[a].

Shaykh Dāniyāl's execution

In A.H. 956 (A.D. 1549), he (Mīrzā Ḥaidar) left for Tibet where he arrested Shaykh Dāniyāl and brought him back as his captive; for nearly a year, he was enchained in prison and subjected to physical torture. A sum of one thousand five hundred gold coins (*ashrafīs*) was also exacted from him. In order to put an end to the reproaches and accusations of 'Abdu'r-Rashīd Khān, he (Mīrzā Ḥaidar) decided to put an end to his (Dāniyāl's) life. He summoned Shaykh Fatḥu'llah to his presence and told him to fabricate false witnesses and the proofs against Shaykh Dāniyāl. That god-unfearing (*Khudā nā tars*) fellow made strenuous efforts and bribed for this purpose some corrupt and wicked people, whose decrees in matters of religion were hardly tenable and whose moral dispensations were hardly popular. Some of the persons were induced to depose that he announced *rafz* (abandoning of faith), and showed disrespect to men of faith. Some other vouched for the honesty and irreproachable conduct of the witnesses. Thus under the decrees of the Qāḍīs of the time, namely Qāḍī Ḥabīb, Qāḍī Ibrāhīm, and Qāḍī Abdu'l-Ghaffūr, he was martyred on 24th of Ṣafar, A.H. 957 (A.D. 1550). Some of his associates found the date of this event in the phrase *dasht-i Kerbalā*. In the darkness of the night, a devotee of the innocent martyr hid his severed head at some unknown place and, on the next day, another devotee, removed his body in a boat and buried it at some other place. After the murder of Mīrzā Ḥaidar, the severed head and body of Shaykh Dāniyāl were put together and re-buried in the shrine of Amīr Shamsu'd-Dīn Muḥammad Araki.[106] It is strange that Mīrzā Ḥaidar should have considered it in the interest of the state to put him to death. During the days when his death sentence was under consideration, Mullā 'Abdullah made an attempt to dissuade Mīrzā Ḥaidar from committing such an act, but Ḥaidar told

106. See note 100 *supra*.

him that the beheading of the Shaykh was justified in the interests of the state and its integrity and for the security of his government. He further told him that accusations and defamation levelled by Rashīd Khān against him could be silenced only by putting him to death.

Muḥammad Kot besieged

In truth, the murder of that innocent man was the cause of the downfall of Mīrzā Ḥaidar and the destruction of his regime.[107] Shortly afterwards, there sprang in his mind a desire to send a contingent of Mughal troops to Muḥammad Kot.[108] For this purpose, Qarā Bahādur Mīrzā[109] was given a contingent of about one thousand Mughal and Kashmiri soldiers[110] and by the end of the month of Ramaḍān in the aforesaid year, he marched towards Muḥammad Kot via Baramulla.[111] Malik 'Idī Raina joined hands with Nāzuk Shāh and Khwāja Ḥājjī (Bānday), and managed to win the cooperation of the brothers and followers of Ḥusain Māgray; the strategy was to find a narrow and steep passage where he would lie in ambush, and strike at the Mughal troops and

---

107. Ḥasan writes that the execution of Dāniyāl by Mīrzā Ḥaidar created a sense of insecurity among the people and Shias, in particular, became more active in opposing him. See *TḤK*, p. 255. Malik Ḥaidar records the story of one Bābā 'Alī to prove Mīrzā Ḥaidar's partiality. He says that such acts incurred him the hatred of Kashmiri commanders. They began to conspire to put him to death. See *TMḤ*, MS f. 54^b.

108. In the district of Poonch between the towns of Poonch and Kotli See *Gazetteer*, p. 267.

109. A nephew of Mīrzā Ḥaidar. See *TḤK*, p. 256.

110. Ḥasan's break up of the soldiers is 1000 Mughals and 1500 Kashmiris. *TḤK*, p. 256.

111. Ḥasan writes that almost everybody induced him to undertake this campaign. Malik Ḥaidar writes that he sent 'Idī Raina towards the Indian mountains. See *TḤK*, p. 256 and *TMḤ*, MS f. 54^b.

destroy them.[112] On reaching Muḥammad Kot, they found that its passes and difficult paths were highly suited to their purpose. On the 13th of Shawwāl, in the aforesaid year,[113] all the Kashmiri commanders and their rank and file took positions atop the mountain heights. Some of the princes were provided with additional reinforcements from the local highlanders and were deputed to seal the passes leading to the valley.

Kashmiris strike

In the early hours of one particular morning, groups of fearless warriors and veterans of battlefields swooped upon the Mughal soldiers and made a fierce attack, and both sides got engaged in fighting. The warriors on either side exhibited feats of remarkable bravery, especially in the use of arrows and muskets (*tufak*).[114] The Mughal soldiers continued their strike and displayed their bravery in fighting the Kashmiris but were compelled to flee towards Bahrel.[115] This marked the beginning of the end of Mughal rule in Kashmir. For nearly one *farsakh* (three miles), the Kashmiris chased the fleeing Mughal soldiers, inflicting heavy casualties upon them. Kashmiri commanders gave up the chase after a distance of one *farsakh* but Keecham Khān, along with his highland soldiers (Khahān/Khaśās), pursued the Mughals right up to Bahrel, hoping that he would be able to capture horses and other equipment of the fleeing Mughals.

---

112. When Mīrzā Ḥaidar was informed about it, he retorted by saying that the Mughals in no way lagged behind the Kashmiris in intrigues and fomenting trouble. The news of the betrayal was conveyed to him by Ḥasan Māgray through his brother Alī Māgray. See *TḤK*, p. 256.
113. A.H. 957/A.D. 1550.
114. *Tufang* in Persian means a musket.
115. See *TḤK*, p. 257.

Qarā Bahādur defeated

On reaching Bahrel, the fleeing Mughal troops sought refuge in its fort, which Keecham Khān along with the Khahis[116] found it difficult to besiege; hence he conveyed to 'Idī Raina and the Kashmiri nobles that four to five hundred fully armed Mughal warriors had reached Bahrel and had arrived at their destination in safety. If they ('Idī Raina and his troops) headed towards Poonch, the Mughal soldiers would be left with no alternative but to take the road to Kashmir and rejoin Mīrzā Ḥaidar.

Malik 'Idī Raina was about to leave Muḥammad Kot for Poonch when this news was brought to him. Thus the entire Kashmir army felt perturbed and discomfited by the thought that should that group [of the Mughals] succeeded in rejoining Mīrzā Ḥaidar, the prospect would be too disturbing for them. However, they took a decision as a result of which Shams Malik and Nājī Malik. Muḥammad Khān and Ḥusain Māgray and the sons of Khwāja Ḥājjī, each with his respective contingent, agreed to proceed to Bahral.[117] Malik 'Idī Raina, along with other commanders and troops, headed towards Poonch. The fort at Bahral in which the Mughal soldiers had taken refuge was besieged. Finding that the Kashmiri army, assisted by the Khahis, had swollen in number, the Mughal commanders, namely, Qarā Bahādur, Quṭb Alī Kokā and Muḥammad Nazar became disheartened and decided to initiate negotiations with the Kashmiris, but some of their commanders like Sayyid Mīrzā, Mīrzā Alī Kokā, Daulat Kokā, Quṭb Alī Dīwāna and others did not agree to this. They argued that for many years the Kashmiris

116. See *Rājat.*, vii, 1271 and 1278. Ḥasan calls them Ghakhars. See *TḤK*, p. 258.

117. 'Idī Raina deputed five hundred soldiers under the command of Shams Chak and Nājī Malik to besiege the fort. However Ḥasan does not comment on the strategy adopted by Kashmiri commanders to trap the Mughal troops. See *TḤK*, p. 257.

had been drawing up plans of annihilating them and had now united to achieve this purpose. Since they were determined to spill their blood, their conciliatory talk would not make them kind towards them. They proposed that those of the Mughal soldiers who had been gifted with bravery, might accompany them on their way to the land of Ghakkars, and those who were timid and cowardly might choose to go with Qarā Bahādur. Next morning, Qarā Bahādur took a group of Mughal soldiers with him to contact the Kashmiris to enter into negotiations with them. They had just reached the camp of Kashmiri army when the hosts of Khahis and Kashmiri foot-soldiers fell upon them, plundered their equipment and possessions and started killing them.

While the Mughal troops [of Qarā Bahādur] were under an attack, Sayyid Mīrzā took with him a group of soldiers, came out of the fort and brandishing their swords marched towards the land of Ghakkars. While the other Mughal contingent was being routed [by the Kashmiris], they fled about a mile away and the Kashmiris were not able to pursue them. No doubt a body of highlanders (Khuhis) was sent in their pursuit, but it could reach nowhere close to them. The result was that the group succeeded in arriving in safety at Ādam Sulṭān from where it dispersed [in different directions].

Kashmiri troops slew some of the Mughal soldiers, took others as prisoners, and headed towards Poonch. On joining the troops of Malik 'Idī Raina, the commanders held consultations, whereupon it was agreed that three persons among the captives, namely Qarā Bahādur, Quṭb 'Alī Kokā and Muḥammad Nazar be detained. They amputated the hands of the rest of the Mughal soldiers who numbered about sixty. As a result of this action, some of these soldiers succumbed to wounds at Poonch and some others got scattered in the adjoining areas.

Malik 'Idī Raina proceeded to Kashmir via the Hirpur route and managed to seek the goodwill and cooperation of Mīr Sayyid Ibrāhīm Khān and Ghāzī Khān. He despatched messengers to Malik Daulat Chak entreating him to come over from Nowshehr. Himself he entered the valley from Hirpur. A day later, Malik Daulat Chak also arrived. [In this way] very large number of Kashmiri soldiers gathered to initiate deliberations about finding the ways and means of forcing entry into the city.

Mīrzā Ḥaidar killed

Mīrzā Ḥaidar also held consultations with his advisers and aids at that time. A Mughal contingent was left behind at Andarkol (Andarkot) to guard his womenfolk.[118] With a force of about a thousand horsemen, besides a number of Kashmiri soldiers, he proceeded to face the Kashmiri army. Let it not remain unknown that, since the wheel of destiny had started moving against Mīrzā Ḥaidar and the stars promised no favour to him, his troops, in whatever part of Kashmir they were, suffered severe reverses and were routed. Mullā Qāsim and Mullā Bāqī were among his senior and high-ranking commanders who had been holding Tibet under their control. At a time when winter was at its peak, the people of Tibet rose unitedly to put Mullā Qāsim and a large number of his troops to the sword.[119] Mullā Bāqī fled to Kashmir and joined Mīrzā Ḥaidar when the latter was about to leave Andarkol. The news of the revolt of the

118. Ḥasan writes that while Ḥaidar camped at Zāldagar, Fatḥ Shāh, with a strong force of three thousand soldiers proceeded to Andarkot where he set Mīrzā Ḥaidar's house on fire. As a retaliatory measure Mīrzā Ḥaidar's supporters burnt Sulṭān Zainu'l-'Ābidīn's buildings in Sopor. The houses of 'Idī Raina and Nowroz Chak were also set on fire in the city. However, Mīrzā Ḥaidar did not approve of such acts. See *THK*, p. 258.

119. Many of his associates were put to the sword along with him. *THK*, p. 259.

Tibetans was in no way less than an insult added to injury. Mullā 'Abdullah Samarqandī, another prominent person of a high rank and a Mughal noble of Mīrzā Ḥaidar, who had been assigned the task of capturing Pakhli lands also met with defeat. On learning about the reverses that befell the Mughals at Muḥammad Kot, he lost heart, and withdrew towards Kashmir. On reaching Baramulla, he fell in the hands of a few ungodly[120] men and was murdered. Mīrzā Ḥaidar reached the city and learnt of his death, which added to his grief:

[*verses*]

Despite these depressing reverses and disconcerting debacles, Mīrzā Ḥaidar was steadily drawing nearer and nearer to a battle with the Kashmiris. He encamped at the village of Wāhthore.[121] Kashmiri army also came closer to Mīrzā Ḥaidar's troops; with its headquarters at Khāmpore,[122] it clung to the stronghold of Mahnor.[123] Mīrzā Ḥaidar held consultations with such of his commanders and seniors as were of proven ability and judgement regarding military tactics in fighting Kashmiris. Their considered opinion was to launch a night-assault to take the enemy by surprise.[124] On the very night the Kashmiri troops made a halt in the fort, Mīrzā Ḥaidar picked a well-equipped body of seven to eight hundred soldiers for this purpose. They made a forward dash till they reached the foot of the fort and then halted for a while. Not more than thirty horsemen, including Mīrzā Ḥaidar, ascended the hill and, even out of this handful of Mughal troops, only seven or eight could stand by the side of Mīrzā Ḥaidar, who, without loss of time, engaged

120. *Khudā nā tars* in the text.
121. Zāldagar in *TḤK*, p. 258.
122. See *Rājat.*, i, 168n.
123. Probably present Mahanor.
124. Mīrzā Ḥaidar halted at Ompora. See *TMḤ*, MS f. 55[a].

himself in close fighting and killing. As God willed it, the same night – 8th of Ḍhu'l-Qa'da., A.H. 957 (A.D. 1550), Mīrzā Ḥaidar sustained a fatal blow of lance from Kamāl Doonī and was killed.[125] The entire Mughal contingent fled towards Andarkol.

Ḥabib Khān's incursion

Mīrzā Ḥaidar held the reins of the government of Kashmir for ten years. After his disappearance from the scene, Malik 'Idī Raina assumed power in the same year and installed Nāzuk Shāh on the throne as the Sulṭān of Kashmir at Qaṣr-i-Sulṭān. However, it was practically he who ruled the country. During his times Ḥabīb Khān Niyāzī, in alignment with his brave brethren, emerged from the mountains of Jammu with the intention of conquering Kashmir.[126] Malik

---

125. Historians have given contradictory statements about Mīrzā Ḥaidar's end. He was struck by an arrow: killed by an accident; murdered by a butcher with an axe. See *TḤK*, p. 260 and *TMḤ*, MS f. 55^{b}. Ḥasan also writes that Daulat Chak, Ghāzī Chak and others wanted to throw the dead body of Mīrzā Ḥaidar to dogs, but Sayyid Muḥammad Baihaqī, Ḥusain Māgray, and some more people of Sunni faith lifted the dead body five days after he was murdered and buried it in the Mazār-i-Salāṭin on the left side of the grave of Sulṭān Zainu'l-'Ābidīn.

    The chronogram inscribed on the tombstone is as this:

    Shah-i Gūrkān Mīrzā Ḥaidar ākhir
    be mulk-i shahādat zadeh kūs-i shāhī
    qazā-e ilāhī chunīn būd tārīkh
    shudeh bahr-i waslash qazā-i ilāhī

    Malik Ḥaidar writes that in spite of the misdeeds of Mīrzā Ḥaidar, the Kashmiri commanders magnanimously handed over his family members to Qārā Bahādur and gave them a courteous send-off to Kāshghar; See *TMḤ*, MS f. 55^{b}.

126. Ḥasan says that he was deputed by Salīm Shāh with a strong force to conquer Kashmir. *TḤK*, p. 263. The name given in *Tabaqāt-i-Akbarī* is Islam Shāh, p. 620.

Daulat Chak received this information and forthwith assembled his commanders and Khwāja Ḥājjī and marched towards Banihal to resist him. But both Malik 'Idī Raina and Ḥussain Māgray deliberately slackened their pace. Malik Daulat wasted no time and, moving at full speed, took position at the top of Hākarniku [*sic*]. They could see bonfires in each other's camps.

Malik Daulat Chak deployed his troops on two sides to force a battle on the enemy. Next day, from morning till the commencement of afternoon prayers, fierce fighting took place between them. Although in bravery and valour [the forces of Niyāzī] had no parallel in the entire kingdom of India, yet, under the dictates of destiny, they gave up all hope of their survival. Even though they were but a handful of people, they fought against an overwhelming majority of nearly ten thousand Kashmiri troops, including their highland allies from early morning till the afternoon. At last they were unnerved by the wounds inflicted on them by a relentless shower of arrows and musket shots in the battle. Except two of their men, all of them were slain. Kashmiri commanders carried to Malik Daulat Chak the severed heads of Ḥabīb Khān, Sa'eed Khān, and Shahbāz Khān.[127] In return, Daulat Chak sent these to Salīm Shāh in India. When a letter and report were to be drafted and sent to Salīm Shāh, he (Daulat Chak) did not take Shams Chak and Nājī Malik into confidence, who had been his associates before they joined Malik 'Idī Raina. Their earlier jealousy and malice were intensified by this. The clan of the Chaks became haughty and tyrannical by this victory and they now aspired to gain control over the kingdom of Kashmir. On entering the valley, they held a conference with Malik 'Idī Raina, in the *pargana* of Vernāg. Ḥusain Māgray had not yet arrived on the scene when Malik Raina

127. Among the slain was Āzam Humāyūn, the wife of Haibat Khān Niyāzī. *Tabaqāt-i-Akbarī*, p. 620.

came down and began to draw plans for destroying the Chaks.

'Idī defeated

He, thereupon, combined with himself the militant people of Kupwāra, the Māgrays, the Baihaqī Sayyids, and all the people who were men of substance and influence. In the month of Ramaḍān, A.H. 958 (A.D. 1551), he launched his scheme of destroying the Chak power. One night Shams Malik, Nājī Malik and Khwāja Ḥājjī, in alliance with Bahrām Chak and Yūsuf Chak,[128] took with themselves a group of the members of their clan and destroyed the bridges in the city. Malik Daulat Chak and Ghāzī Khān offered resistance and succeeded in capturing Mīr Sayyid Ibrāhīm Khān and Ḥusain Māgray. The rest of the group escaped to join Malik 'Idī Raina. After a few days, Fatḥ Malik, Nasi [*sic*] Malik and Yūsuf Chak combined to confront Daulat Chak. A day later, Malik Daulat crossed the lake and headed towards them. Malik 'Idī Raina was defeated[129] and fled from the battlefield. He hid himself in the Shumeh Nāg[130] jungle where he was taken ill and later brought to the city. He died a few days later.

Assessment of Mīrzā Ḥaidar

Behold the perfidy of the treacherous world that the ungodly Mīrzā Ḥaidar should have, under the pretext of expediency, let the onus of Shaykh Dāniyāl's murder[131] fall on him, given bribes to false witnesses, made Mullā Fatḥu'llah to commit perjury and martyred Shaykh Dāniyāl. Wilfully, he made himself responsible for shedding the

128. The Chaks of Kupwāra professed Sunnī faith. See *TḤK*, p. 265.
129. Ḥasan exaggeratingly computes the number of the dead in thousands. *TḤK*, p. 266.
130. In *pargana* Votar. *TḤK*, p. 266.
131. For the story of Shiekh Dāniyāl see note 100 *supra*.

blood of that respected and innocent man so that the material world and its comforts might endure with him. After the martyrdom of Shaykh Dāniyāl, he did not survive for more than nine months. Similarly, Malik 'Idī Raina strovs to spill the blood of the Mughals with the sole intention of holding sway over the kingdom of Kashmir for some time, but he did not survive for more than a year, after the death of the Mīrzā:

[*verses*]

In short, after Malik 'Idī Raina, Malik Daulat Chak became the governor and administrative head of this country in the year A.H. 958 (A.D. 1551). He was kind to Mīr Sayyid Ibrāhīm Khān: he set him free, and in order to strengthen his own position as head of the government, he entered into a matrimonial alliance with him.

Daulat Chak's achievements

During the period of his administration, this noble Malik did certain things such as the construction of two holy shrines which shall certainly win him good name in this world and salvation in the next. One of these is that in spite of sharing the realm of Kashmir with 'Idī Raina, he allowed the bier of Shaykh Dāniyāl to be brought into the city. As it reached near the city, word was sent around in advance so that the faithful and the devout came out to receive it. At this time, Malik Daulat happened to be at 'Īdgāh with Malik Idī Raina and Ghāzī Khān On learning about the news of the bier, Malik 'Idī Raina got up and left for his house in disgust. Fearing the opposition and enmity of Malik 'Idī Raina, Ghāzī Khān rose in opposition to Malik Daulat and left for his residence. Malik Daulat Chak summoned all his courage and came out of the 'Īdgāh to proceed to the site where the coffin had been lowered. He took a boat and was rowed down the river in the city to receive the bier. The dead body [of Shaykh Dāniyāl] was buried in the graveyard of his illustrious father;[132] the place became a shrine for the devotees and the faithful.

Another work of Daulat Chak worth mentioning is that he rebuilt the *khānqāh* of Amīr Shamsu'd-Dīn Muḥammad Araki which Mīrzā Ḥaidar Gorkān had fully destroyed because of his bigotry. By completing the reconstruction of the holy shrine in A.H. 959 (A.D. 1551/52), he helped in its restoration to prosperity. Out of the old endowments he earmarked a few villages for the maintenance of the children and descendants of Shamsu'd-Dīn Araki. He gave stipends and scholarships to the attendants and devout inmates of the shrine. Thus that holy *khānqāh* resumed once again its previous prosperity and was frequented by the 'People of Forty,' (*arba'īn*).[133] It was also marked by a revival of Islamic laws and fundamental modes of worship by the believers and by the chanting of special Friday prayers and holding of congregations and all other formalities of 'repetitive prayers.' On account of Mīrzā Ḥaidar's total rejection of Noor Bakhshiyyeh and Hamadāniyyeh orders, he effaced their traces in the length and breadth of this country. For eight years, none of the citizens or aliens in this land could even bring to his lips the name of these orders. Owing to his fierce bigotry, people could not even speak of the faith they professed. He forbade the inhabitants of this land to profess the *Shāfi'ī*

132. Ḥasan writes that after the execution of Shaykh Dāniyāl, his dead body was buried at a place called Shoonsh Mar. The popular legend is that Shoonsh Mar existed somewhere near present Chādūra. Later on the body was buried in the graveyard of Mīr Shams Araki. See *TḤK*, p. 267.

133. Fortieth day after the martyrdom of Imām Ḥusain, observed by the Shia' community. To make the devotees recite from the scripture for forty days without break and ending with the fortieth day of Imām Ḥusain's martyrdom is called *ba arba'in nishāndan*.

faith. He issued orders to all the subjects in the state to adopt Ḥanafī faith and proclaimed that all the religions and beliefs other than that of Ḥanafī faith be discarded and done away with.

Another laudable achievement of Daulat Chak was to revive the Hamadānī[134] order and to give it a firm footing. He extended support and help to Bābā Ḥasan to build a *khānqāh* and a house for the devotees who would retire therein during lent. He made untiring efforts to patronize and propagate Hamadāniyyeh order. He brought together the surviving dervishes and *sūfīs* of this order living in different parts of the land, and made them recite prayers for forty days (*arba'īn*). He revived the customs and practices of the Hamadāniyyeh order and the Noor Bakhshiyyeh sect. He issued a writ throughout this land that all citizens and aliens were free to profess any faith they wished and that no one could either dictate or obstruct others in this matter.

Bābā Ḥasan had visited many attractive places, and selected Ḥasan Ābād for his burial and for raising a tomb. The fortunate Malik bought lands and gardens in the aforesaid locality by making cash payment out of his private funds to their owners.[135] The coffin of Ḥazrat Bābā was brought to the locality and he was buried there. Malik Daulat issued orders for the repair and development of those places. The grounds were levelled and the site beautified to make it attractive and endearing to pilgrims and lovers of the faith. He ordered the construction of a spacious and lofty *khānqāh*. Each of the sons of Ḥazrat Bābā undertook the

134. The sūfī/dervish order of which Mīr Sayyid 'Alī Hamadānī was the founder.

135. Ḥasan writes that developed as well as undeveloped lands around the locality were forcibly taken away from their owners and given as a gift to Ḥasan Bābā. This contradicts the statement of the chronicler. See *TḤK*, p. 268.

construction of houses and dwelling places at Ḥasan Ābād where the descendants, relatives, and the kinsmen of the Bābā took up their residence. This was another laudable achievement of Malik Daulat Chak.

Owing to the threats and intimidations from Mīrzā Ḥaidar and the fears he aroused, none of the inhabitants of this land had the courage even to mention the names of the Innocent Imāms. The *mullās* of this land had misled and misguided them to such an extent that people never took the names of the Twelve Imāms.[136] The *mullās* had told them that it was a sin and sacrilege to do so. The citizens and the aliens in this land were ignorant of the names and the story of the Innocent Imāms, and the members of the lofty house of the Prophet to such an appalling extent that once when Ḥusain Shāh enquired of Qāḍī Ḥabīb in an assembly the names of Imāms, he could name the Commander of the Faithful (Alī), Imām Ḥasan, Imām Ḥusain and then he knew of no other name except that of Imām Ja'far-i Ṣādiq. He knew nothing of their lives and history, and of their exalted status. The entire assembly was taken aback by his ignorance and indifference.

During the period of his government, Malik Daulat Chak issued an order that the homily (*khuṭbā*) in the name of the Twelve Imāms be read in the Jāmi' mosque.[137] In this way this practice, observed during the life-time of Amīr Shamsu'd-Dīn Araki, was revived and followed in the Jāmi' mosque prayers and elsewhere. People began to ask for the history of the Innocent Imāms. It is fervently hoped that the rewards for such noble deeds and actions will become the instruments of salvation for that man of excellent qualities.

136. Ḥasan writes that Daulat Chak oppressed the Hindus and the people of Sunni faith and forced them to give up their religion. *THK*, p. 268.

137. It is corroborated by Ḥasan. See *THK*, p. 268.

Ismā'īl Shāh

It may also be mentioned that up to the time of the government of Daulat Chak, Sulṭān Nāzuk Shāh continued to be the king of this country in accordance with the prevailing practice of kingship and Sultanate. But during the times of the said Malik he was deposed and forced to go to the Indian mountains. In his place, Ismā'īl Shāh was installed on the throne.

Malik Daulat Chak's government did not last beyond four years during which he and Ghāzī Khān came into conflict with each other several times. However, they resolved their differences through conciliation. After four years, some of his uncles and near or distant relatives joined hands to cause estrangement between Malik Daulat Chak and Ghāzī Khān. They instigated Ḥusain Malik, the brother of Daulat Chak, to capture him on the first of the month of Dhu'l-Ḥijja, A.H. 962 (A.D. 1554) on the lake of Phāk.[138] When once Malik Daulat Chak went for a shikar, he learnt about the ill-intentions of his rivals;[139] he left the boat and went up the Phāk mountains. Ghāzī Khān despatched his troops to all parts of the domain in search of him and finally captured him.[140] The group of people responsible for

138. Probably Mānasbal lake.

139. The immediate reason for differences between Daulat Chak and his rivals was that through deceit and cunning Daulat Chak contrived his marriage with the second wife of Kājī Chak, who also happened to be the mother of Ghāzī Khān, Ḥusain Khān and Alī Khān. This infuriated Ghāzī Khān and others. *TḤK*, p. 269.

140. He was captured by a shepherd who recognized him because of his immense corpulence. Malik Ḥaidar has recorded two interesting stories about Daulat Chak's physical strength. When he went to Sher Shāh Sūrī for help, he demonstrated to him that he could stop an elephant from moving by holding it by its tail. Another story is that during the construction of a house, a log of

(*Contd.*)

creating disorder in the state dinned into the ear of Ḥusain Chak that Ghāzī Khān was disposed to let, Malik Daulat live safely. Two days later, he was misled into gouging out the eyes of Malik Daulat Chak. How tragic that such a good-natured person should have been tortured in a manner that he was virtually put on the road to death!

[Subsequent to this event] Sayyid Ibrāhīm Khān was deprived of his servants and establishment and his son Mīr Sayyid Mubārak Khān was installed in his position.

---

wood, twenty yards in length and a yard thick slipped from the hands of the labourers who were hauling it. The Malik held the big log with only one hand and placed the other on the earth to support himself. Under the weight of the log, his hand deepened up to the forearm into the earth. See *TMḤ*, MS f. 57^{b}.

Chapter VI
Chak Rulers

Ghāzī Shāh

Ghāzī Khān became the ruler of this domain in the aforesaid year (A.D. 1554). In early spring the same group of his near and distant people whose mission was only to perpetrate mischief, disorder and bloodshed, once again entered into an alliance to put an end to the lives of Ghāzī Khān and Malik Ḥusain and to become the masters of this land.. But they were not destined to succeed in their mission and Ghāzī Khān learnt of their intentions. He summoned Nuṣrat Khān, Yūsuf Chak, son of Regī Chak, and Shankar Malik to his presence, and told them that he had learnt of [their] conspiracy. He spoke to them in soft tone so that their kinsmen would not unite with them. He detained them at his house for the night. Next morning, Nuṣrat Chak's brethren and their associates destroyed the bridges in the city, took defensive positions in a certain quarter [of the city], and rose in opposition against him. Ghāzī Khān came out to meet them. He crossed the river by boats and inflicted a crushing defeat upon them. Nuṣrat Chak's brothers and some of their accomplices were slain in the battle and he himself was taken prisoner. A short while later, Yūsuf Chak, the son of Regī Chak, was captured and enchained in prison.

Some time later, a group of people, comprising Shankar Chak, Bahrām Chak and others raised a band of their soldiers and offered stubborn resistance to Ghāzī Khān in the town of Soipor (Sopor). Ghāzī Khān struck hard at them and put them to rout. Bahrām Chak was brought as a captive from Khuihāma and was beheaded. Although an attempt was made to gouge out the eyes of Yūsuf Chak, yet, by God's supreme will, his eyes remained intact.[1] After some days he escaped from the prison and went to India. His brother, Ibrāhīm Chak was also put to the sword. In combination with his brothers, Malik Ḥusain Chak and Alī Chak, he (Ghāzī Khān) converted the domain of Kashmir into a veritable fortress.

Mughal menace

During his rule, Ghāzī Khān demonstrated qualities of courage and manliness in crushing the army of the Mughals which had been joined by a section of Kashmiri soldiers and had attacked him. Stories of his bravery and extraordinary heroism spread in the domain of India. Here is one of these.

Shāh Abu'l-Ma'ālī[2] aspired to conquer India and, therefore, adopted a policy of confrontation with Jalālu'd-Dīn Akbar and Bairam Khān. A large number of Kashmiri nobles aligned themselves with him and brought him into Kashmir via the Baramulla route[3] to head towards the city (Srinagar). A large number of Kashmiris, in small and large groups, joined the army of Abu'l-Ma'ālī. Ghāzī Khān had with him only two of his brothers, his sons and a handful of kinsmen. Nuṣrat Chak was brought on the battlefield in chains. At this time, Ghāzī Khān adopted a soft conciliatory attitude towards Mīr Sayyid Ibrāhīm Khān. He also

1. Ḥasan does not confirm that he did not become blind. See *TḤK*, p. 274.
2. According to Ḥasan he was a Sayyid from Kāshghar and an adopted son of Humāyūn. See *TḤK*, p. 274.
3. Ḥasan's version is that it was through cunning that he succeeded in bringing him to the town of Pattan along with his troops. See *TḤK*, p. 275.

established matrimonial relations with him.[4] Thus, after appeasing Mīr Sayyid Ibrāhīm Khān, he proceeded to meet his foe. A confrontation between the two armies took place at Hānjiverah.[5] Ghāzī Khān demonstrated remarkable bravery and overpowered and destroyed the enemy. In this battle, Nasi Chak and Ḥusī Chak, the sons of Zaiti Chak, and a considerable number of Kashmiri warriors fell on the battlefield; the Mughals also suffered numerous casualties.[6] The slaying of a large number of Mughal soldiers bred a feeling of fear in their hearts which remained there for many years. Shams Raina, the son of 'Idī Raina, was captured in a forest and put to the sword.[7] Thus commenced the period of Ghāzī Khān's independent and autocratic government over Kashmir; be distributed presents to his soldiers.

Second encounter

Some years later, Khwāja Ḥajjī, Nājī Malik and Nuṣrat Chak united together, took Qarā Bahādur and a contingent of Mughal soldiers with them, and entered Kashmir via the Nowshehr route.[8] Ghāzī Khān, accompanied by his brothers, Mīr Sayyid Ibrāhīm Khān and their troops proceeded to face them via the Hirpur route. His troops occupied the posts over the mountains from Bahrām Gala to Soel [*sic*]. At this time Fatḥ Chak and Lohar Chak were in the mountains of Poonch. They held consultations with their advisers and did not go over to the Mughal troops but joined Ghāzī Khān.

4. Ghāzī Khān's daughter was given in marriage to Ibrāhīm's nephew *Ibid*.
5. About three kilometres from Pattan on road to Srinagar.
6. Malik Ḥaidar computes the number of the slain at four thousand *TMḤ*, MS f. 57^{b}.
7. Ḥasan says that Shams Raina was captured because he had helped the Mughals in leaving Kashmir. See *TḤK*, p. 276.
8. Qarā Bahādur had five to six thousand troops with him and about two to three thousand Kashmiri soldiers also joined him. *TMḤ*, MS f. 59^{b}.

Nuṣrat Chak also happened to be in India at that time.[9] He sent a message to Ghāzī Khān informing him of his intention of joining him[10] and not the Mughals. This discouraged the Mughal army. Not feeling itself strong enough to proceed further, it decided to halt at Rajouri under these circumstances. Ghāzī Khān attacked them and a big battle followed. The Mughal army consisted of brave and dauntless soldiers like Kūchak Bahādur and several others. From dawn to early afternoon, there was heavy fighting in which many people on both sides were slain. In late afternoon the Mughals suffered a defeat and they lost a large number of their warriors on the battlefield. With great difficulty, their commanders managed to escape to India. Victorious Ghāzī Khān and his brothers entered Kashmir along with their troops.[11]

These two wars with the Mughals are among the notable events in Ghāzī Khān's career. Otherwise his record is inglorious. In acts of cruelty and oppression, in causing bloodshed and in gouging out eyes of his enemies, in inflicting physical tortures and in chopping off the limbs of human beings and in killing near and distant ones, no one has ever known or heard of a tyrant like him. It must also be mentioned that during the days of Ghāzī Khān, as long as Sulṭān Ismā'īl Shāh lived, he was a Sulṭān only in name, living in the palaces of the former Sulṭān(s). After his death, Ghāzī Khān installed his nephew Ḥabīb Shāh on the throne in his place. Finding that Ḥabīb Shāh was not

9. In the outskirts of Lahore. *TḤK*, p. 278.

10. Ghāzī Khān stationed his troops at Lohar Kot. *TMḤ*, MS f. 59[b].

11. Ghāzī Khān had promised to pay the Doombs one gold coin as a prize for each severed Mughal head. The Doombs performed the duties of sentries or border scouts. In fact it was they who put the Mughals to rout and Kashmiri regular troops were not deployed. See *TMḤ*, MS f. 60[a]. They brought seven thousand severed heads of Mughal soldiers to Ghāzī Khān. See *TNK*, MS f. 64.

even worth the name of the office to which he had been elevated, Ghāzī Khān aspired to adopt this title, ascend the throne, and assume the status of an independent ruler.[12] Consequently he held consultations with his counsellors and advisers and formally ascended the throne in the year A.H. 960 (A.D. 1552).

It was Ghāzī Khān who first established a kingship for the tribe of Chaks. Two hundred and eight years after Sulṭān Shamsu'd-Dīn, the kingdom of Kashmir passed from the hands of his descendants into those of the descendants of Lankar Chak.

Ḥusain Shāh

Ghāzī Khān reigned for a period of nine years. After he was inflicted with leprosy which made him blind, he abdicated in favour of his blood brother, Ḥusain Shāh. But some of the courtiers and nobles made him to repent over his decision of abdicating the throne so much so that he thought of taking back the reins of power from him.[13] This resulted in a quarrel between the two; Ḥusain Shāh aligned some of the nobles with himself and took by force the reins of the state. Ghāzī Chak was deposed and interned in his house.

At the beginning of his reign, Ḥusain Shāh adopted a just and benevolent policy towards his subjects so much so that aliens and natives of this land considered him

12. The story of Ḥabīb Khān's deposition is described by Malik Ḥaidar like this. Once he behaved in his court in such a manner that the nobles present at that occasion were put to great embarrassment. 'Alī Khān, the younger brother of Ghāzī Khān, took it as an offence and declared that Ḥabīb Khān was misfit as a Sulṭān. He lifted the crown from his head and put it on the head of Ghāzī Khān and made him sit on the throne. See *TMḤ*, MS f. 58[b].
13. Malik Ḥaidar makes no mention of Ghāzī Khān's attempting to change his previous decision.

Nowsherwān the Just[14] in comparison to the tyrant Ghāzī Khān. On finding him a benign and just ruler, some of the poets [of the time] produced a chronogram of his accession to the throne as *Khusraw-i-'Ādīl* (the Just King).

Fatḥ Khwāja's revolt

Some time later, those of the miscreants who had been responsible for creating enmity and discord between Ghāzī Shāh and Malik Daulat and had escaped reprisals at the hands of the former, joined hands to work towards the decline and fall of Ḥusain Shāh. However, Ḥusain Shāh came to know their nefarious designs and reprimanded some of them. He ordered that the eyes of Aḥamad Khān, son of Ghāzī Shāh, and Muḥammad Khān, son of Abdāl Māgray, be gouged out. A short while after owing to the provocations of some wicked persons whose habit was to foment trouble, Fatḥ Khwāja,[15] a protege of Ḥusain Shāh and titled Khān Zamān, was made to fear Ḥusain Shāh. Hence out of fear to his life, he aligned with himself some Kashmiri chiefs, like

14. Nowsherwān-i-'Ādil, the famous Sāsānian king of Iran, who reigned in the 6/7 century. But Ḥasan writes that in his zeal for propagating Shia' faith and custom, he oppressed the Sunnis and the Ḥindus. Although he showed regard to the *'ulemā* of Ḥanafi school in their service to religion, it is also a fact that he engineered the killing of a number of men of Sunni faith. See *TḤK*, p. 283.
15. Malik Ḥaidar says that he was a grocer but received favours from Ḥusain Khān and was given the title Khān Zamān by him. He aligned some of the commanders with himself and tried to stage a revolt. See *TMḤ*, MS f. 61^{b}. It appears that soon after Ḥusain Shāh's accession to the throne, there started a rivalry for power between his Chief Vizir Malik Muḥammad Nājī and Fatḥ Khwāja (Khān Zamān). This Khān Zamān and Bahādur Khān were the associates of the 'lord of the border' (*marzbān*). See *TḤK*, p. 281. *Marzbān* (*Marz* = border + *bān* = keeper, appears to be the Persian equivalent of Sanskrit *dvārnāyaka* or *dvārpati* (Lord of the Gate). Regarding his title and functions, see *Rājat.*, v, 214 *et seq.*

Fatḥ Malik, sons of Zaitī Malik, Shams Dūnī,[16] Ḥaidar Khān, son of Ibrāhīm Khān, and others, and waited for a suitable opportunity to kill some of his opponents.[17] It came his way on a day when Ḥusain Shāh had gone on shikar[18] and Khān Zamān and his opponents were in the secretariat.[19] Khān Zamān took time by the forelock and made a sudden attack on them. [The followers of Ḥusain Shāh] found themselves trapped in the royal house. Fatḥ Chak and Bahādur Khān opened several passages and entered the mansion of Ḥusain Shāh. But it did not please God Almighty to crown them with success and both were slain on the spot. Khān Zamān and Shams Dūnī suffered reverses and tried to flee, but their pursuers captured and brought them back. Ḥusain Shāh ordered amputation of their limbs. Now Mabārez Khān assumed authority, though, not much later, his religious bigotry made him to invent excuses to get rid of Ḥusain Shāh.[20] The Sulṭān came to know of his foul intentions, and therefore, got him arrested and his hands and feet were cut off. Lohar Malik also met with a similar fate, and Nuṣrat Chak, who had already been under arrest, was deprived of his eyesight by a royal command on the same day. This group which had acted treacherously with Ghāzī Khān in arresting and blinding Malik Daulat Chak, met with the same fate which they had meted out to others. So did it please God Almighty and thus was proved the axiom "as you sow, so shall you reap."

After some time, Looli Malik was dismissed as Chief Vizir and divested of his authority. He was succeeded by Alī

16. Shams Dubi in *TḤK*, p. 281.
17. The author does not mention the name of Muḥammad Nājī as an opponent of Khān Zamān.
18. At a place called Wothnār. See *TḤK*, p. 281.
19. *Dāru'l-Amāreh.*
20. The inference is that Mabārez Khān did not subscribe to Shia' faith.

Kokā. On account of his sectarian bigotry.[21] he was not disposed favourably towards the beneficiaries of the Shia' faith (*muhibbān*) and the aliens.[22]

Yūsuf Inder's episode

During his times, there lived a person popularly known as Yūsuf Inder[23] who once happened to meet Qāḍī Ḥabīb on a roadside. The Qāḍī was notorious for his malice towards the members of the house of the Prophet: he hurled abuses on the adherents of *Rāfiḍī* faith and spat at Yūsuf Mīr Inder, who retaliated by meting out the same treatment to him, though somewhat recklessly. The Qāḍī lashed him with his whip on his head. Since Yūsuf Mīr Inder happened to be a soldier by profession, his (soldier's) pride was touched and, drawing his sword, he inflicted one or two wounds upon the Qāḍī. Wounded and bleeding, the Qāḍī fell down from his horse and Yūsuf Mīr Inder ran away. 'Alī Kokā, the bigot that he was, sent many people in search of him so that he was caught and brought back. 'Alī Kokā and Datī,[24] thereupon, conspired to obtain permission from Ḥusain Shāh to the effect that the judgement of the Qāḍīs and the dispensers of Muḥammadan religious law be enforced in regard to this matter. They got this when Ḥusain Shāh was under the effect of drink and narcotics.[25] 'Alī Kokā and Datī Kokā plotted to call in Qāḍī Mūsā, Mullā Petcheh [*sic*] Ganāī and Mullā Yūsuf Almās and elicit from them a unanimous

---

21. He professed Sunni faith. See *TḤK*, p. 282.
22. The two words in the text are *muḥibbān* and *mawāliyān*. Perhaps the allusion is to the followers of the Imāms and of 'Alī.
23. Yūsuf Muno in *Wāqa'āt-i-Kashmir*, p. 91. Ḥasan writes that this Yūsuf Inder was in the entourage of Mīrzā Muqīm, the Shia'. See *TḤK*, p. 283.
24. They were Shias. See *TḤK*, p. 284.
25. Ḥasan contradicts this and writes that the orders of the Sulṭān were obtained when he was holding the public court (*Dīwān-i-'Āmm*). See *TḤK*, p. 284.

decree condemning Inder to death. Extreme brutality which resulted from this bigoted action was reflected in his execution.[26] The flesh of his body was cut into pieces which people carried as a gift for their womenfolk, and many people drank his blood as *sherbet.*

This execution engineered by 'Alī Kokā and Datī Kokā with the connivance of the Qāḍīs and jurisconsults brought to surface the hidden calamity. The blood of a large number of Muslims was spilt and many people on either side lost their lives.[27] Ḥusain Shāh was unaware of these happenings.

Shortly after the execution of that poor man (Yūsuf Inder), a group of Sunni divines sought a meeting with Qāḍī Zen and Mullā Rezā, son of Mullā Salmān Muftī, in which they offered to enter into a debate with the party of the *mullās* who claimed to have issued the decree of Yūsuf Mīr Inder's execution in conformity with the provisions of Islamic religion. They argued that no religion justified his execution and that in issuing a decree sentencing him to death the Qāḍīs and the theologians had only been prompted by malice and bigotry. The sentence, they claimed, was unwarranted and uncalled-for.

Qāḍī Zen and Mullā Rezā then undertook the mission of calling at the private lodgings of the nobles, courtiers, and distinguished persons of Ḥusain Shāh's court one by one and placed before them the case of Mīr Inder. These people brought the matter also to the notice of Ḥusain Shāh.

Akbar's envoy to Kashmir

While the issue continued to be a subject of hot discussion, Mīrzā Muqīm arrived in these lands as the envoy of Jalālu'd-Dīn Akbar Bādshāh. Ḥusain Shāh had a son, Ibrāhīm Khān by name, who had unparalleled physical

26. Ḥasan says that he was killed by a mob. *Ibid.*
27. It apparently seems to be a Sunni-Shia' riot.

beauty and charm; he had also attained excellence in the skills of archery, horsemanship and soldiery. He died because of some incurable disease.[28] Ḥusain Shāh was told that he had to pay the heavy price of his son's life for the bloodshed of innocent Yūsuf Mīr. In fact, Ḥusain Shāh repented over Yūsuf's killing and directed that the issue which was being debated by the *mullās*, be left to the judgement of Mīrzā Muqīm, the messenger and envoy of Jalālu'd-Dīn Akbar Bādshāh. He would preside over the meeting of the *mullās* in which they would debate the issue. Among the persons present were Mullā Petcheh Ganāī and Mullā Almās, the two *mullās* who were signatories to the decree of Yūsuf Mīr's execution. The rest of the Qāḍī hid themselves. Qāḍī Zen and Mullā Rezā put questions to Petcheh Ganāī and Mullā Yūsuf Almās in the presence of Mīrzā Muqīm and a large number of learned and scholarly men, dignitaries, theologians and the elite of the city. They asked them the authority – book and religion – on the basis of which they had issued a verdict of Yūsuf Mīr's execution. Their argument was that he had not inflicted more than two or three wounds by his sword upon Qāḍī Ḥabīb and although he did not die of those wounds and would not have died, they had issued the decree of his execution. They were told that if they had issued the said verdict in accordance with the postulates of the Ḥanafī sect, the books of the sect were available there, and if they had done it in accordance with the postulates of Shāfi'ī faith, their books, too, were at hand. It was now for them to cite the relevant authority and the source that justified the death penalty on the innocent victim. They were further told that in the Islamic community and in the religion of the Prophet and among the jurisconsults (*mujtahids*) throughout the length and breadth of the Islamic world retribution for each wound inflicted and injury caused had been set forth in the

28. Probably small-pox. See *TḤK*, p. 284.

books of each pedagogue and also in the handbook of each theologian. They were asked to explain as to under the sanction of which sect did they put that defenceless man into the hands of his executioners.

Both of them found themselves unable to furnish any reply, but pointed out that they had only carried out the orders of Ḥusain Shāh. They stated that 'Alī Kokā had openly told them of Ḥusain Shāh's intention of putting an end to Yūsuf Mīr Inder's life for political reasons and had insisted upon them to issue a decree to the effect. In this way, they contended, it was the King who got him executed for political reasons and they were not to be held responsible for the act.

But Ḥusain Shāh made a solemn declaration that he, for one, had absolutely no intention of putting Yūsuf to death and that he had left the case to the judgement and dispensation of the Qāḍīs and the learned men of religion so that nobody would make an attempt to kill him.

Retribution

When this statement of Ḥusain Shāh was announced in the assembly, both the *mullās* were struck dumb and had nothing to say. The *'ulemā* of *sunnat* and *jamā'at* present in the assembly unanimously agreed to issue a decree in conformity with the creed of Imām Shāfi'ī.

It is said that the ruler of this domain, the sitting Qāḍī and the executed person, all professed the creed of Imām Shāfi'ī. The *mullās* of *sunnat* and the *jamā'at* were shown the letters with royal signets and they declared the decree as sound. The decree pronounced that both the *mullās* on account of having issued false judgement and unjustifiable order [of execution] regarding the shedding of an innocent person's blood, should suffer retribution Endorsing the aforesaid decree Qāḍī Abdu'l-Ghaffūr of Ḥanafī faith and

Qāḍī Zenu'd-Dīn of Shāfi'ī faith announced the verdict of retribution.[29] On the basis of this verdict of the Qāḍīs and the learned men of theology, Ḥusain Shāh permitted the handing over of the two *mullās* to the next of kin of the late Yūsuf Mīr, who completed the retribution. The rest of the *mullās* emigrated to parts of India and Lahore. Some of them, however, succeeded in resuming their original offices, but only after the intercession for and advocacy of some of the nobles, governors and their former patrons. 'Alī Kokā, and Datī Kokā, the main accomplices in the conspiracy, not still satisfied with enormous bloodshed caused by them, kept lying low and waited for a suitable opportunity when they could forment trouble once again.

Envoy returns

After some time, Ḥusain Shāh attended to the arrangements concerning the gifts to be sent to Jalālu'd-Dīn Akbar Bādshāh. He then permitted Mīrzā Muqīm to return along with Ya'qūb Mīr as his (Ḥusain Shāh's) envoy.[30] 'Alī Kokā and Datī Kokā, seizing the opportunity, sought the permission of Ḥusain Shāh to send Khwāja Ḥājjī Gānī, a

29. The descendants of Yūsuf stated that as he was practising swordsmanship outside the mosque, he inadvertently struck a blow which wounded the Qāḍī in his hand. Ḥasan further writes that on the particular day on which the two *muftīs* were ordered to be beheaded, most of the people of the city [*sic*] had gone on an excursion to the Dal lake. The city had almost become empty and Ḥusain Shāh seized the opportunity of getting them executed. *THK*, p. 286. The executioner was Fatḥ Khān Chak. See Ferishta, *History*, p. 364.
30. Ḥasan writes that after the martyrdom of those two elderly persons, Muqīm Khān hastened his departure from Kashmir. By agreeing to comply with royal orders, Ḥusain Chak 'threw round his neck the collar of servility,' and along with many excellent presents, sent his daughter through Muqīm Khān for Akbar to marry. *THK*, p. 286.

prominent and trusted man of theirs, with the party of Mīrzā Muqīm and Ya'qūb Mīr under the pretext that he would look to the needs of the party on its way and also give them presents at Lahore. But close at their heels, they sent a party of wicked persons of this country, with despatches and gifts to (*Mullā*) 'Abdulla Shaykh 'Abdu'n-Nabī, and a number of Qāḍī's and *mullās* – all of whom were rabid bigots. They also entreated and implored them to give false witness and to leave no stone unturned in getting rid of them[31] (Mīrzā Muqīm and Ya'qūb Mīr).

Muqīm's fate

Mullā 'Abdullah headed a delegation of *mullās* to Agra, the purpose being the one already mentioned. He sought a meeting with Jalālu'd-Dīn Akbar and having briefed the false witnesses, got Mīrzā Muqīm and Mīrzā Ya'qūb executed. The flames of disturbance and turmoil [following this event] leapt so high that Mīr Sayyid Ṣibī [*sic*], in spite of being a true descendant of the line of Ḥusainī Sayyids, was engulfed in it and martyred.[32]

Mullās punished

At last when, because of his mature understanding, Jalālu'd-Dīn Bādshāh could see through the subversive activities of Mullā 'Abdullah and the disruptive role of the other *mullās*, he ordered their expulsion from the kingdom of India. Some of them were ordered to be beheaded. Mullā 'Abdullah was banished to Gujerat and all the

31. From this and the preceding sentence it appears that Khwāja Ḥājjī's mission was to mould the opinion of some prominent men of religion, such as Mullā 'Abdullah and Shaykh *'Abdu'n-Nabī* and others so that the matter could be brought to the notice of Akbar.
32. It may be inferred from these sentences that after the execution of Mīr Muqīm and Ya'qūb Mīr, Shia'-Sunni riots erupted there.

trouble-mongers and miscreants were exiled. In this way the Indian lands and Gujerat were totally freed from the malevolence of the miscreants and malefactors. The country was restored to prosperity and plenty through the dispensation of justice and by initiating works of public welfare. People and communities of different faiths and professions; of different religions; worshippers of idols and followers of Islamic faith and its teachings; people of all ranks, high and low, lived cordially and even extended cooperation and support to one another. No one would become a cause of hindrance to the other nor would anyone have the courage and audacity to object to or assail the religion and faith of others.[33]

'Alī Shāh revolts

'Alī Kokā and Datī did not rest satisfied with (this) trouble and disturbances they had caused. After some time, Ḥusain Shāh suffered a stroke of paralysis. Through craftiness and cunning, 'Alī and Datī Kokā made Ḥusain Shāh agree to detain and put in chains his brother 'Alī Shāh, his virtuous son Yūsuf and also his close and intimate associate, the warrior Sayyid Mubārak Khān. They planned to install one of the children of Ḥusain Shāh on the throne so that they would share between themselves the government and authority of the domain of Kashmir with the consent of Nājī Malik.

Some courtiers of Ḥusain Shāh informed 'Alī Shāh about this; fearing their cunning, he moved between Marāj and Kāmarāj under the pretext of shikar and sight-seeing. A few days later, on the advice and promptings of Mīrān Sayyid Mubārak Khān, he left the city under the pretext of shikar and encamped in the town of Sopor. As a matter of political

33. Malik Ḥaidar makes no mention of Yūsuf Mīr Inder's episode and its aftermath and Ḥasan makes no mention of Akbar's reprisals on *mullās*.

expediency, however, Mīrān Sayyid Mubārak himself negotiated an accord with 'Alī' Khān, Ibeh Shāh and Lūlī Malik Lavand. Then he sent Muḥammad Bhat to take them out [of the city]. Taking leave of Ḥusain Shāh, he himself headed towards Sopor. But 'Alī Kokā, got wind of it and deputed a couple of his trusted men to seek 'Alī Khān and bring him to his lodging where he waited to imprison him. 'Alī Khān left his house and showed great courage in heading towards Sopor. 'Alī Kokā's men brought back the news to him of 'Alī Khān's move towards Sopor upon which he sent a large number of troops in his pursuit. 'Alī Khān and his companions were overtaken, but his brother Daulat Chak, with a handful of his people, offered resistance and by sheer toughness of spirit succeeded in repulsing them. In this encounter a fair number of people on either side including Daulat Chak sustained wounds. 'Alī Khān succeeded in reaching Sopor along with his men. On the same day, Ibeh Shāh ran away from shikar and came to 'Alī Shāh. After a few days; Abdāl Khān, who was in the mountains of Poonch, learnt of these developments and wasted no time in joining 'Alī Shāh. Lūlī Malik also escaped from the city along with his sons and associates via the Shihābu'd-Dīn Pora route and established contact with 'Alī Shāh. When 'Alī Shāh's troops increased in number, he left Sopor and marched to the city. That day he halted at the village of Fatḥ Yārī.

On the other side, after holding consultations among themselves, 'Alī Kokā, Datī and Nājī Malik agreed to make a night assault on 'Alī Shāh, hoping that taking him by surprise would yield the desired result. The aforesaid Datī Kokā lost no time in conveying the news of this strategy to 'Alī Shāh at the village of Fatḥ Yārī. He summoned Dā'ūd Bhat Paloo [*sic*], an employee of Mīrzā Sayyid Mubārak Khān, and told him about it:

[*verses*]

Along with his troops, Dā'ūd Bhat waited for the enemy at Hānjīvereh. The enemy made a night-assault on the army of 'Alī Shāh and he forthwith sent this information to 'Alī Shāh [who was in the rear] and engaged himself in a fierce battle with his opponents. Many warriors were wounded on either side. Ḥusain Shāh's troops could make no headway; they succeeded only in killing a few of Sayyid Mubārak Khān's soldiers with their arrows and then announced a retreat to rejoin their army:

[*verses*]

Early in the morning, 'Alī Shāh made Sayyid Mubārak Khān the commander of his troops and turned towards the city, halting at the village of Zenakot.

'Alī Kokā subdued

On the other side, Nājī Malik, 'Alī Kokā and some prominent people of this land made an assessment of the fighting that had taken place recently, and came to the conclusion that if the whole lot of their choicest soldiers could not cope just with Dā'ūd Bhat, how could they expect them to be able to fight and subdue the veteran commanders and stalwarts of 'Alī Shāh's army. Thinking over this situation, they conceded that none but 'Alī Shāh deserved to be the rightful successor to the throne. After careful consideration and taking a practical view of the situation, they sent the royal crown and the fly-whisker (*quṭās*) to 'Alī Shāh through Bābā Khalīlu'llah the "exponent of divine light and the fountain of divine secrets." Apprehending possible disruption in the army, and also oppressed by their own doubts, the sons of Nājī Malik and Daulat Khān and some of the army commanders of this land defected to Sayyid Mubārak Khān and sought refuge in his house.

'Alī Shāh

In A.H. 978 (A.D. 1570), Ḥusain Shāh was deposed[34] and 'Alī Shāh succeeded him to the throne. He had already won over Sayyid Mubārak Khān to his side during the times of Ghāzī Shāh and, through promises and an understanding with him, he worked towards the strengthening and consolidation of his position as ruler. To fulfil his promises and also with a view to consolidating his position soon after succeeding to the throne, he left the entire administrative authority of the state in the hands of the aforesaid Sayyid and, besides, gave his daughter in marriage to his son Shāh Abu'l-Ma'ālī. Thus 'Alī Shāh stood steadfast, by his commitments and promises.

As already mentioned, the sons of Nājī Malik and Daulat Khān and others had sought refuge in the house of Mīrān Sayyid Mubārak Khān. Although 'Alī Shāh nursed sinister malice against them, yet in deference to the wishes of Mīrān Sayyid Mubārak Khān, he desisted from causing any embarrassment to the Sayyid. On the contrary, he extended his favours to him. In order to substantiate this, the writer feels prompted to recount a few stories to show in what high esteem 'Alī Shāh held the Sayyid.

In the beginning of his ('Alī Shāh's) reign, all the kith and kin of Ḥusain Shāh conspired with the counsellors and advisers of 'Alī Shāh to gouge out the eyes of Ḥusain Shāh and imprison him. The aforesaid Sayyid Mubārak Khān came to know of their intentions. He implored 'Alī Shāh to be kind to Ḥusain Shāh and to abandon that idea. He conceded that during Ḥusain Shāh's rule over the lands of Kashmir, there had been a decline in its prosperity, and although even with much strenuous effort it would not be

34. Both Malik Ḥaidar and Ḥasan write that he spent his remaining days of life at Zenapore. *TMḤ*, MS f. 62[a] and *TḤK*, p. 288.

possible to restore it to its prosperity, yet he should take pity on him.

[*verses*]

'Alī Shāh acts discreetly

This considered and welcome opinion was liked by 'Alī Shāh, with the result that he refrained from gouging out his eyes and putting him in prison. Not only that, he even began to show compassion for Ḥusain Shāh, a gesture which gave him a new lease of life. He was allowed to retain such of his treasures as were already in his possession and also the staff he had in his employ, and was permitted to take up his dwelling at Zenapore.

[*verses*]

After a lapse of a year and some days. Ḥusain Shāh died in the aforesaid village.

[*verses*]

The cruel spheres do not let honest souls enjoy even a moment of rest in this desolate abode. This example of 'Alī Shāh's magnanimity and the administrative prudence of Sayyid Mubārak Khān shall be remembered in this country down to the day of judgement.

Here is another anecdote in this context. Two years after the occurrence of the event mentioned above, 'Alī Khān, the son of Nawroz Chak, made pledges and promises to the nobles of his clan to stage opposition to 'Alī Shāh and wrest for themselves the governorship and revenue authority of this country. But the government authorities came to know of their intention, which they conveyed to 'Alī Shāh. They told him that "thousands of eyes of the opponents continued to be wide awake day and night in support of 'Alī Khān." The matter was thus put before him in an exaggerated manner because they wanted 'Alī Shāh to issue an order of

'Alī Khān's execution. The above-named Sayyid came to know of it. Through soft and subtle methods, he at once undertook to dissuade the Sulṭān from issuing such an order. 'Alī Khān was relieved of his ministry and sent back to his native place in Kāmarāj.

But 'Alī Khān was not a person to rest contented. Ungratefully forgetting 'Alī Shāh's kindness and Sayyid Mubārak Khān's intercession in his behalf, he escaped to Lahore in search of help from Ḥasan Qulī Khān. The miscreants in 'Alī Shāh's kingdom seized this opportunity of throwing their lot with the rebel 'Alī Khān. The story of the rebels was related to 'Alī Shāh in the presence of Sayyid Mubārak Khān; and news came in the meanwhile from the city of Lahore that 'Alī Khān had not been able to get along with Ḥasan Qulī Khān[35] on account of the latter's arrogance and, consequently, had left his services. He was reported to have fled to Muḥammad Kot mountains. Thereupon 'Alī Shāh's troops marched on to Muḥammad kot, besieged him and brought him as a captive before 'Alī Shāh.

[*verses*]

For some time he remained interned in the house of the landlord of Chatr (Jatr ?). A year and some months later, the above-mentioned Sayyid pleaded on his behalf with 'Alī Shāh and succeeded in making him to forget his spite against 'Alī Khān. He got him released from prison-chains and a hundred *dinārs*[36] of pure gold were gifted away to him.

[*verses*]

Thus did the above-mentioned Sayyid graciously answer the prayer of the supplicants as long as he had the power and authority of the government in his hands.

---

35. Ḥusain Quli Khān Turkmān was the governor of Panjab. See *TḤK*, p. 291n.
36. For *dinār* see *Rājat.*, Vol. II, p. 308 *et seq.*

Yet another story runs like this. Ibeh Shāh, the son of Ghāzī Shāh, often aspired to gain power and authority of this country. He would, therefore, criticise and find fault with Yūsuf Shāh. When Yūsuf Shāh came to know of this, he walked straight into his chamber, held him by his shirt collar, and had him killed by the stroke of a sword of his attendant. Then he set out for Sopor followed by most of the nobles of this land. This marked the signs of disintegration in 'Alī Shāh's rule.

Abdāl Khān told Sayyid Mubārak Khān that he had assured Ibeh Shāh by swearing in the name of God that he would plead his case before 'Alī Shāh, and see that he remained unhurt. Ibeh Shāh had trusted him to the time of his murder, but as things were, his life was put to an end.

[*verses*]

Abdāl Khān overemphasized the incident and 'Alī Shāh provided him with troops to exterminate the unruly elements. 'Alī Shāh warned him not to break his promise, as otherwise he would come to harm.

The above-mentioned Mubārak Khān, without paying much heed to 'Alī Shāh, told Abdāl Khān that "by faithful adherence to your pledges and by your life-giving breath, you cannot revive [Ibeh Shāh] to life. Hence, whatever good you had intended for him, better offer that to his heirs." In the course of these happenings, the above-mentioned Sayyid wrote an admonishing letter to Yūsuf Shāh on receipt of which he abandoned his intention of fighting his adversaries and returned to the city. This sort of explosive situation could certainly not have been brought under control by an indiscriminate use of brute forcc and bloodshed by the recalcitrant warriors of this land. It was a single stroke of an auspicious pen that averted an impending calamity of great magnitude and put 'Alī Shāh in grateful obligation to Sayyid Mubārak Khān.

[*verses*]

There is one more story of 'Alī Shāh's magnanimity and Sayyid Mubārak Khān's intercession with him. Chroniclers and historians have mentioned that during the reign of 'Alī Shāh, Shams Dooni and Muḥammad Marāj, two of the nobles of this land, entered into collusion with some chieftains of Kashmir, with the intention of fomenting trouble and discord in 'Alī Shāh's kingdom. Their activities were regularly reported by authorities to the staff officers at the royal court. When 'Alī Shāh was apprised of this, he forthwith despatched a select armed contingent to apprehend the miscreants and insurgents. But the latter received advance information of this and sought refuge in the house of Sayyid Mubārak Khān. This was also brought to the notice of 'Alī Shāh. In order to show due regard to the Sayyid, which would result in the strengthening and consolidation of his rule, 'Alī Shāh condescended to pardon their misdeeds. However, Yūsuf Shāh, after ascending the throne, did not agree to Sayyid Mubārak's such intercessions and his support [to the people] in the manner in which 'Alī Shāh did. The result was that it led to such a chaos and confusion as could not be set right to this day. God willing, the details of those events will be recorded at their proper place.

Mīr Badlā

The above-mentioned Sayyid was a follower of Mīr Badlā Rizvī, a person of spiritual and temporal eminence, who died in the early hours of Friday at the time for offering *namāz*. It was under the influence of his association and teachings that Sayyid Mubārak regularly attended the congregational prayers and visited the graves and tombs of saints and dervishes whose lone attachment is with God. Further notice of him shall be recorded in this book:

[*verses*]

'Alī Shāh's character

'Alī Shāh abolished all brutal punishments like gouging out of eyes, wanton killings, and amputation of limbs of human beings, which had been in vogue during the days of earlier Sulṭāns. Instead, he provided even-handed justice to his subjects and was compassionate towards them. He lost no Opportunity in being equitable and kind to them. He extended his patronage to all sections and groups of nobles and officials, in order to help them regain their previous positions. His reign lasted nine years.[37] In his public dealings he strictly adhered to godliness; performed duties and obligations; refrained from what was forbidden and vile; observed the mandates of the Prophet of Islam by conforming to what was allowed and disallowed in his religion.[38]

[*verses*]

His death

During his reign, 'Alī Shāh regularly played the game of polo (*chowgān*) on the Īdgāh maidān on mornings and late afternoons. It so happened that Bābā Khalīlu'llah, who had the power of knowing the unknown, insistently solicited Alī Shāh to stop participating in future in the game of polo. But as God willed it, in the year A.H. 986 (A.D. 1578), the angel of death suddenly brought him the message there on the very polo-ground where his nobles and his whole retinue were attending upon him. In order to hit the ball, the king bent his body which pressed his belly against the pommel

37. He ascended the throne in A.H. 978/A.D. 1570.

38. Ḥasan records that he used to present himself before Shaykh Makhdūm Ḥamza (Sulṭānu'l-Arifīn, d. A.D. 1566) and the saint Hardi Bābā Rishī. Three couplets from an encomium called *qaside lāmiyyeh* composed by the famous poet and saint Bābā Dā'ūd-Khākī in praise of 'Alī Shāh have been included by Ḥasan in his history. See *TḤK*, pp. 288-89.

and ripped open his intestines. His heart began to sink and he forthwith retired to his palace, where he reached in the early hours of the morning, and then died.

[*verses*]

Abdāl vs Yūsuf Shāh

When Abdāl Khān learnt of the death of his brother 'Alī Shāh, he galvanized his troops into action to capture kingship and government of this country. In order to achieve this objective, he decided to fight Yūsuf Khān with full might and main in the locality of Nowhatta. When Yūsuf Khān came to know of these developments, he held consultations with the commanders and counsellors of his late father[39] to drive out this menace. But nobody could provide a remedy for this and the two adversaries, like pawns being manoeuvred on a chess-board, found themselves locked in a stalemate. This situation was reported to Sayyid Mubārak Khān. He activated a group of soldiers and his sons and proceeded towards the palace of 'Alī Shāh. Simultaneously he deliberated with Yūsuf Khān over the possibility of reconciliation with Abdāl Khān and, outlining the conditions of an accord, he sent word to Abdāl Khān through Bābā Khalīlu'llah, one of the Kashmiri Shaykhs.[40] Abdāl Khān had not forgotten that, in spite of his intervention, Ibeh Shāh had been tragically murdered by Yūsuf Khān and, therefore, he did not trust his word and deed. Consequently, he considered Bābā Khalīlu'llah's entreaties and admonitions no more than an exercise in futility. The result was that their mutual jealousy and acrimony deepened and they appeared to be on the verge of

39. The dead body of Sulṭān 'Alī Shāh was temporarily buried in the compound of Jāmi' Masjid. See *TḤK*, p. 294.

40. Sayyid Mubārak Khān had tried to resolve the deadlock through the mediation of Muḥammad Chak, Bābā Khalīl and some more nobles, but the effort yielded no result. See *TḤK*, p. 294.

fighting each other. In short, Bābā Khalīlu'llah failed in his mission of preventing the impending disorder. But once again at the behest of Yūsuf Khān, Sayyid Mubārak Khān proceeded to meet Abdāl Khān in person along with Bābā Khalīlu'llah and Muḥammad Bhat. He brought home to him the facts that "the royal robes fitted well on the body of no man other than Yūsuf Shāh, for he was the heir to 'Alī Shāh in letter and spirit and that 'Alī Shāh had always shown his singular favour and affection for him." The Sayyid told him that Yūsuf's authority had an edge over his (Abdāl's) command; he also told him to desist from taking any precipitate action, and take the counsel of well-meaning friends as something highly helpful in the situation in which he was placed. He emphasised to him the need for re-establishing cooperation and goodwill with Yūsuf Shāh and of ceasing hostilities. The Sayyid invited his whole-hearted attention to these counsels and warned him that if he did not pay heed to his advice, he would have to face dire consequences.

[*verses*]

Sayyid Mubārak's role

Abdāl Khān was in no mood to heed the advice of the above-mentioned Sayyid, and then followed what was inevitable. Abdāl did not act with wisdom and far-sightedness, and Sayyid Mubārak Khān returned to Yūsuf Shāh.[41] Having noticed Abdāl Khān's intransigence and

---

41. Malik Ḥaidar gives a different version of the struggle for power between Yūsuf Khān and Abdāl Khān. When the news of Yūsuf Khān's taking over the reins of the government reached his uncle Abdāl Khān, everybody suggested to him that he (Abdāl) should put up resistance. But he did not agree to do so and said that Yūsuf Khān was like his child, and in his old age he did not have the physical strength to bear the strain of fighting. He said that he

(*Contd.*)

obstinacy, some prominent persons of the land spoke of him critically, and wanted to induce Sayyid Mubārak Khān to an open confrontation with him. They insisted that he should take quick action. But wise people gifted with far-sightedness, clear and piercing intelligence, first try for peace, which is a good beginning. As long as issues can be settled amicably through negotiations and peaceful means, they desist from the use of brute force and do not take recourse to active fighting.

[*verses*]

The decisive battle

Sayyid Mubārak Khān was infuriated by Abdāl's attitude. He insisted on him to adopt the path of peace and friendship, but again he turned it down, which added to his animosity [towards him].

[*verses*]

Sayyid Mubārak Khān was infuriated by Abdāl's attitude. He forthwith undertook to see that Yūsuf Shāh assumed the royal robes. He put the crown on his head after the manner of powerful kings; drew the fly-whisker (*quṭās*) on his head,

---

was prepared to accept him as the new ruler. He then sent a few persons to Yūsuf Khān directing them to join the funeral procession of the late Sulṭān. He even prepared himself to join it. But his eldest son Ḥabīb Khān dissuaded him from doing so. It was then resolved that they should draft an agreement and then proceed to the house of Yūsuf Khān. When the news of the contemplated agreement reached Yūsuf Khān, he did make promises and commitments to them. But malicious people played mischief and Yūsuf Khān deferred giving funeral to his dead father. On the same day, he initiated fighting with Abdāl Khān. In the battle which was fought in the locality of Nowhatta, Abdāl Khān was slain by Sayyid Mubārak. *TMḤ*, MS ff. 64[b]-65[a]. For more details see *Tabaqāt-i-Akbari*, p. 629 and *Tārīkh-i-Firishta*, Vol. II, p. 365.

and unfolded the royal parasol over his head. At the same time, he made a firm resolve to fight Abdāl Khān and, in vindication of this pledge, he recruited a brigade of local warriors, and placed them under the command of Muḥammad Khān, son of Ḥusī Chak, to serve as vanguard to Yūsuf's army. Himself, he commanded a contingent of crack soldiers, including his sons, and took the central position in the formation of troops. He marched towards Abdāl Khān's camp to the beat of war drums.

[*verses*]

After putting Yūsuf Shāh's troops in their proper position, he put them behind his own for support and strength. But before Yūsuf's contingents could join him, Muḥammad Khān, leading Yūsuf's force, came under enemy attack. Shams Chak, son of Daulat Chak, Mīr Muḥammad, son of 'Idī Raina, Mīr Ḥasan, son of Nājī Malik, and the rest of their group launched a fierce attack on his (Muḥammad Khān's) troops and mauled them, after which they turned towards the Sayyid's troops.

Abdāl defeated

The first to make a gallant counter-attack on them were Sayyid Jalāl Khān and Sayyid Abu'l-Ma'ālī, the two sons of the aforesaid Sayyid Mubārak Khān. In the fierce battle that followed both sides exhibited feats of extraordinary valour. Nuṣrat Chak son of Shams Chak, was slain by Jalāl Khān on the battlefield,

[*verses*]

Shāh Abu'l-Ma'ālī made a swift attack on Shams Chak, who, after sustaining wounds on his hands, rejoined his troops. Mullā Muḥammad Amīn found the date of this event in the chronogram *awwalan Shāh bar sar-i ṣaf zad.*[42]

---

42. A.H. 987/A.D. 1579.

Abdāl Khān saw the signs of disruption and disorder in his army, but continued to offer tough resistance to Sayyid Mubārak. In the course of fighting he received a wound from an arrow shot at him by Abu'l-Ma'ālī. Then he came in confrontation with Sayyid Ḥusain Khān who lost no time in wielding his sword and killing him.

[*verses*]

On finding his father slain, Ḥabīb Khān left the battlefield, but Sayyid Jalālu'd-Dīn, riding a swift horse, gave him a hot pursuit in the hope of inflicting a wound on him. The fleeing Ḥabīb Khān turned round and shot an arrow at him, which, after piercing his coat of mail, went deep into his heart. He died instantaneously on his horse.

The clan of the Baihaqī Sayyids displayed such remarkable feats of heroism in this battle as the war veterans of this land eulogised them and their ancestors in very eloquent words.

[*verses*]

Yūsuf Shāh had not, so far, arrived on the scene. Beating the drums of victory, the victorious Sayyid Mubārak Khān marched off the field and joined him half way. They heartily exchanged felicitations on their success and thanked God for upholding unity among friends.

[*verses*]

Abdāl's dead body

The Sayyid then proceeded to his private quarters and Yūsuf Shāh to the battlefield, where he saw the dead body of Abdāl Khān lying in a pool of blood. Nobody was permitted to give it a burial. Yūsuf Shāh then retired to his palace.

At this time Qāḍī Mūsā dispensed justice in the country in accordance with the Islamic law. Without seeking the permission of Yūsuf Shāh, but working with the sole purpose of pleasing God, he courageously went to the battlefield and removed the dead body of Abdāl Khān from dust and blood to the graveyard of his ancestors. Since it happened to be a day of sporadic fighting and skirmishes, he did not get time to carry out the task of burying the dead. Early next morning, Sayyid Mubārak Khān got the dead body of his son, who had been slain on the previous day, buried with full rites in the burial ground of his ancestors. Then he rejoined Yūsuf Shāh for deliberations over state affairs. Yūsuf Shāh, too, carried the dead body of his father, the late ʻAlī Shāh, to his ancestral burial ground.

Chapter VII

Yūsuf Shāh Chak: Accession and Dethronement

Sayyid Mubārak retires

Yūsuf Shāh formally ascended the throne in the year A.H. 986 (A.D. 1578):

[*verses*]

With his accession, the office of the Chief Vizir passed on to Muḥammad Bhat. Sayyid Mubārak Khān now found himself preoccupied by thoughts of the transience of human life and the need for humility on the part of man. Holding his sons by their hands, he brought them to Yūsuf Shāh in the presence of the elders of this land, and said to him: "All the three sons of mine solemnly declare their allegiance to you and promise to fulfil all the pre-requisites of faithful subordination to you." He reiterated that he had decided to spend the rest of his life in seclusion and retirement, meditating all the time. He said, "It is too well-known that for a long time I have been seized by this desire but the late 'Alī Shāh always dissuaded me from taking a step in that direction and, in deference to his wishes, this could not, in fact, materialize." Yūsuf Shāh heard these words and nodded in agreement, At this, Mīrān Sayyid Mubārak felt; overjoyed. But he did not cease to pay occasional visits to Yūsuf Shāh.

Abdāl's revolt

During the reign of Yūsuf Shāh, when Muḥammad Bhat had been in office for a little over two months, Abdāl Bhat, a rival to the high office of the Chief Vizir, finding himself disappointed, adapted a hostile attitude towards Yūsuf Shāh. He tried to align with himself disgruntled sections of the people of the land; and, through guile and craft, secured their assistance for realizing his plans. Finding that Sayyid Mubārak Khān rarely went to Yūsuf Shāh, he concluded that it was an indication of some great confusion in the country.[1] By using false and sinister words, he frightened most of the people like 'Alī Khān, son of Nawroz Chak, and Shams Chak, son of Nājī Chak. In spite of the fact that they were near relatives of Yūsuf, he managed to align them with himself.

Abdāl Bhat chose a certain night for raising the banner of revolt, and destroyed the bridges over the river in the city, and on the 16th of Rabī'u'th-Thānī, A.H. 986 (A.D. 1578), he sought shelter in the house of Mīrān Sayyid Mubārak Khān. Showing profound regards and respect to him, he told him submissively that the Sayyid should not disappoint the supplicants by refusing to grant their request. They declared that bad times had forced them to seek redress of their grievances at the doors of the benign and generous Sayyid.

[*verses*]

The situation caused the Sayyid embarrassment; for a moment he could not decide what course of action he should adopt. But, in conformity with his previous attitude of dissuading 'Alī Shāh from inflicting brutal punishments,

1. The relationship between Yūsuf Shāh and Sayyid Mubārak Shāh is somewhat intriguing. At the time of Yūsuf Shāh's accession to the throne of Kashmir, the Sayyid affirms his and his sons' loyalty to (*Contd.*)

he undertook to intercede for this group also and forthwith rode to meet Yūsuf Shāh.[2] But on his way he was told that this group, out of dread and fear of Yūsuf's soldiers, had hewed down the bridges over the river in the city and had, thus, precipitated trouble for Yūsuf Shāh. As the crossing of the river was rendered impossible by the hewed and destroyed bridges, the Sayyid was forced to retrace his steps. He came to the Īdgāh mosque and summoned Bābā Khalīlu'llah to his presence to entrust him the mission of intercession for this group with Yūsuf Chak. Through him, he sent a verbal message to Yūsuf Shāh, entreating him to follow the policy of his father in upholding his (Sayyid's) intercession for the repenting insurgents. He expressed his faith in Yūsuf's laudable qualities of character and recommended that he overlook the acts of omission and commission of people, both high and low, of this land. He advised him to patronize them and thus work for the return of peace and tranquillity in the kingdom. But, despite Bābā Khalīl's forceful, persuasive and eloquent representation of their case with the intention of diffusing the tense situation, the counsellors and advisers of the Sulṭān did not pay heed to his words. On the contrary, they said that the culprits be brought before Yūsuf Shāh with their hands and feet put in fetters. They further threatened that anybody promising support to them or showing a partisan attitude towards them would only land himself in the throes of death and destruction.

---

him. After some time, however, the Sayyid, who had nearly given up his earthly ambitions, becomes instrumental in dislodging him from the throne. Therefore the nature of the relationship between them needs a thorough investigation.

2. Ḥasan says that the Sayyid declined to intervene directly in the matter because he considered it harmful to his own interests. Instead, he sent Bābā Khalīl to Yūsuf Shāh to persuade him to take recourse to reconciliation with the insurgents. See *THK*, p. 299.

Sayyid Mubārak confronts

Bābā Khalīlu'llah was disappointed for having failed in carrying out the mission entrusted to him by Sayyid Mubārak Khān. He was directed to go back, and close at his heels was despatched Muḥammad Khān, son of Ḥusī Chak, an acknowledged veteran of Yūsuf's army, for fighting Sayyid Mubārak Khān; His troops repaired the bridges over the river in the city near the *langar* of Bābā Bulbul; and crossing the river along with his troops and the ancillary staff, Yūsuf Shāh reached the Īdgāh maidān to fight Sayyid Mubārak Khān. It now became clear to the Sayyid that they [Yūsuf and his advisers] had abandoned the path of peace and compromise and had taken recourse to confrontation and fighting. Hence, without losing time, he came out with his small force to fight the large army of Yūsuf Shāh. But, before the actual fighting, he, once again, as on previous occasions, offered to negotiate and intercede on behalf of that (Abdāl's) group. But Yūsuf Shāh's commanders did not listen to him. They thought it an easy task to wipe out a handful of their Opponents by making use of arrows, musket fire, and fire-missiles; thus they thought of strengthening and consolidating the position of Yūsuf Shāh.

As against this, the aforesaid Sayyid, proud of his inherent traits of bravery and manliness, got involved in a fight with a large number of his opponents. Historians have given an account of this battle in prose as well as in verse.

[*verses*]

Battle at Īdgāh

Being very close to each other the two armies found it impracticable to use arrows and lances. Consequently, they used their swords and daggers and got locked up in a hand to hand fight. In the course of fighting, Muḥammad Khān, a peerless warrior of this land, fell from his horse, but quickly got back into the saddle and continued to fight bravely and was slain.

[*verses*]

In the battle, Malik Mīr Qāsim, the youthful son of Nājī Malik, fought gallantly but was slain. 'Alī Malik, an accomplice of Abdāl Bhat and the cause of turmoil and destruction of Yūsuf Shāh's regime, received a blow from the sword of Mīr Muḥammad, son of Nājī Malik, which sliced off one of his nostrils and he fell down from his horse.

[*verses*]

At the instance of Lohar Chak, son of Shankar Chak, he got a second cut on the same wound which caused his death after a few days. Another recognized Kashmiri warrior, Ibrāhīm Ganāī, was slain on the battlefield by a stroke from the sword of Sayyid Ḥusain Khān. Most of the soldiers of Yūsuf's army sustained many deep wounds at the hands of the sons of the above-mentioned Sayyid. At last, finding themselves hard-pressed, they retreated by crossing the Nawākadal bridge and then rejoined Yūsuf Shāh at Zāldagar maidān. Some of his soldiers joined Mīrān Sayyid Mubārak Khān's camp and the opponents of Yūsuf Shāh. It led to a large scale disorder and disruption in Yūsuf Shāh's domain.

[*verses*]

Yūsuf's tactics

On account of these developments, Yūsuf Shāh reproached his counsellors and advisers, accusing them of their short-sightedness and poor intelligence. He stressed that if they had heeded to the recommendations of Mīrān Sayyid Mubārak Khān and acted upon them as they did in the past, they would not have seen this day of defeat and misery.

[*verses*]

Perceiving that Yūsuf Shāh had been overtaken by defeat and dejection, his opponents went to Mīrān Sayyid Mubārak Khān and suggested to him that he should forthwith move towards Yūsuf Shāh and deny him a chance of withdrawing from the battlefield unhurt so that he does not become a cause of further chaos and confusion.

[*verses*]

For the good of the land this was sound advice but being a devotedly God-fearing man, he turned it down, and told them: "Only dogs fight over wretched morsels; it does not behove friends to fight over material possessions."

Mullā Ḥasan's negotiations

The Sayyid thus turned down the suggestion of chasing Yūsuf Shāh, saying that they had not to forget that he was the descendant of 'Alī Shāh. Yūsuf Shāh came to know of it and, because of his helplessness, adopted an attitude of friendship and conciliation. He deputed Mullā Ḥasan Aswad, the tutor of the late 'Alī Shāh, on a mission to apprise Sayyid Mubārak Khān of the circumstances which had led to the present crisis. Mullā Ḥasan, in turn, communicated to the Sayyid all that Yūsuf had desired of him to report regarding the condoning of his past acts of omission. The Sayyid listened to the Mullā with full attention and told him that unlike in the past nobody was prepared to take his counsel then; and the result was chaos and disorder of great magnitude. If the ugly exchange of insults and counter-insults had not taken place, he would have called on Yūsuf Shāh that very moment, revealed the facts to him, and reinstalled him on the throne. But as the disturbances were on the increase, it would be advisable that the aforesaid Shāh retired to some mountain place in Kashmir, the climate of which would suit him. He should live there for sometime with all his treasures and equipage. God willing, he would be recalled after some time, and re-installed on the throne of his kingdom.

Yūsuf dethroned

It may be recalled that, on account of a breakdown in the administration during the days of Yūsuf Shāh,[3] Ḥaidar Chak moved in from Kāmarāj and entered the services of Mīrān Sayyid Mubārak Khān after the above-mentioned battle was over. In the course of deliberations between the Sayyid and Yūsuf's envoy, named Mullā Ḥasan, Ḥaidar Chak addressed the Mullā in uncivil words. Taking cue from the Sayyid, the Mullā reacted with harsh words, saying that the illustrious king had a hundred thousand footmen like him to run errands and it hardly behoved a man of his diminutive stature to speak contemptuously of him.

[*verses*]

Mīrān Sayyid Mubārak Khān ignored them, and sent Bābā Khalīlu'llah, Mīrān Sayyid Barkhordār, and Mullā Ḥasan to Yūsuf Shāh to convey to him permission to leave. Yūsuf Shāh sent his royal belongings to the house of 'Alī Khān, son of Nawroz Chak,[4] through the brave and capable Nājī Malik; he proceeded to the mountains of Nāyaks,[5] a site for which he had a liking.

---

3. Malik Ḥaidar also alludes to a breakdown in the administration of the state during the first term of Yūsuf Shāh's reign, which lasted forty days. See *TMḤ*, MS f. 65[b].
4. Ḥasan says that he sent his crown to Sayyid Mubārak Khān through Bābā Khalīlu'llah. *TḤK*, p. 300. According to Malik Ḥaidar, it was sent through Malik Muḥammad Nājī. *TMḤ*, MS f. 66[b]. In another MS of Malik Ḥaidar's history, it is recorded that the crown and the royal parasol were sent to the Sayyid through Malik Muḥammad Nājī and Qāḍī Mūsā. *TMḤ*, MS(A), f. 68.
5. Malik Ḥaidar says that he went to the Indian mountains. *TMḤ*, MS f. 66[b].

The stalemate

This course of action was hardly agreeable to Yūsuf's opponents, and the efforts of Mīrān Sayyid Mubārak Khān to re-establish law and order in the state earned him nothing but their malice. All of them together with 'Alī Khān and Abdāl Bhat retired with pomp from the locality of Īdgāh to their respective places. Showing due courtesy to them the Sayyid retired to his place.

Mubārak declines crown

Mīrān Sayyid was too self-abnegating to be tempted by worldly things and, as such, the throne of this land remained unoccupied for some time for want of an incumbent. Alī Khān, the eldest of brothers, saw that Mīrān Sayyid Mubārak Khān did not covet worldly possessions and, therefore, resolved to seize the authority of this land for himself. He felt encouraged by the support of his brothers and associates and felt haughty by the riches left by Yūsuf Shāh in his trust. For three successive days he remained confined to his house and did not call on Mīrān Sayyid Mubārak. The counsellors, the secretaries and the sons of Mīrān Sayyid came to him (Mīrān Sayyid) one by one and talked to him about the nature of the situation that prevailed. They told him that even a single minute of kingship was a boon and that royal robes befitted the body of none but he.

[*verses*]

They declared that he was the finest of the clan of noble Sayyids and the most illustrious of the elderly persons of that house. The Sayyid declined to oblige and told them that he was not interested and if they wanted him to be their friend he should be left alone. He further told them that they could entrust this important responsibility to anyone they liked.

[*verses*]

After saying these words, he came out of his private chamber and sat in the audience-hall.[6] He then distributed the crown and the royal parasol which had been artistically decorated and studded with precious jewels among his soldiers and spiritualists.[7] In this way, he caused searing pain to people with material ambitions.

[*verses*]

Mubārak assumes power

In the year A.H. 988 (A.D. 1580), the reins of authority of this realm passed into the hands of that illustrious Sayyid. But he detested and, therefore, denied himself the display of pomp and glory. He freed the minds of the people of this land from fear of oppression and tyranny and opened the doors of equitable justice and compassion for one and all.[8] Years after this event, Kashmiri nobles and commanders received encouragement from Yūsuf Shāh,[9] and developed rancour and malice against Mubārak Shāh. They joined

6. Ḥasan writes that about an hour after he was crowned he retired to his private room, lifted the crown from his head, placed it in front of him and said, "Oh my inauspicious self, verily this royal crown is of no worth. Do not be proud because on the day of death, the head will lay on vile dust. The crown, which may be worn for a few days only, is in truth a burden." *TḤK*, p. 301.
7. Ḥasan states that the Sayyid put on ordinary clothes and began attending to the affairs of the state. *TḤK*, p. 301.
8. Ḥasan says that he abolished oppressive and tyrannical practices which had become rampant during the reign of the Chaks. *Ibid.*
9. This statement is not corroborated either by Ḥasan or by Malik Ḥaidar. In fact, the latter writes that it was not Yūsuf Shāh who encouraged them, but they who made overtures to him. The reason was that during his short reign of fifteen days the Sayyid treated the commanders badly and was tyrannical even to the common people. In this way the author's statement that he was just and compassionate to wards people is repudiated by him. This too, calls for further investigation. See *TMḤ*, MS f. 67[a].

hands and on the second Sha'bān of the aforesaid year[10] recalled Yūsuf Shāh from the mountains.

Yūsuf returns

Yūsuf was brought to Barthal ranges.[11] and was joined by a large number of soldiers, villagers, horsemen, footmen and highlanders. On the other side, Mīrān Sayyid Mubārak Shāh also started necessary preparations to keep his troops in readiness and moved on to the village Sast[12] [*sic*] wherefrom he sent a message to Yūsuf Shāh.[13] It said that since life was uncertain, he was sure that a mutual dialogue would be in the interests of peace and would lead to a solution to the crisis. "Let all fears be given up to help the beginning of a dialogue," it said. The message was conveyed to Yūsuf Shāh through one Dā'ūd Mīr. Yūsuf Shāh trusted the words of Sayyid Mubārak Shāh and despatched two of his sons, Mīrzā Ya'qūb and Mīrzā Ibrāhīm, to him along with Dā'ūd Mīr and Mullā Ḥasan Aswad. He was also inclined to hold a meeting with him.

Meanwhile, Abdāl Bhat learnt about these negotiations. He sent word to Yūsuf Shāh and his commanders imploring them not to trust Sayyid Mubārak Khān and not to be duped into a meeting with him. He also added that [Abdāl Bhat and his party] had rectified their past lapses on their own and would henceforth strive their every nerve to achieve whatever aims and objectives he had. At last through flattery and cunning, he (Abdāl) succeeded in aligning with himself

---

10. A.H. 988/A.D. 1580.
11. In the *pargana* of Vesu in *TMḤ*, MS f. 67[a].
12. Sindh in *TḤK*, p. 302.
13. A written message was sent which began with this Persian couplet:

    Shahā faqr-o fanā az mā wa mulk-o azz-o jāh az tū
    kih dunyā rā wofāī nīst khwāh az mā wa khwāh az tū.

    TḤK, p. 302.

a majority of nobles, commanders and soldiers of the realm of Kashmir and thus imagined himself to have been elevated to some superior position. In this way started the rivalry and ill-will between them.[14]

The clash

Abdāl Bhat's words eventually destroyed Yūsuf Shāh's power of right thinking. His counsellors and advisers showed contemptuous indifference to Dā'ūd Mīr, the emissary, and spoke to him harshly:

[*verses*]

The emissary informed Mīrān Sayyid Muḥammad how badly he had been treated and what harsh and uncivil words were spoken to him [by the advisers of Yūsuf Shāh]. He further told him that they thought of nothing but fighting him. The aforesaid Sayyid, infused with a sense of valour and heroism, so pre-eminently needed in a warrior, set up a royal pageant and swiftly crossed mountains and plains with such facility as if he was moving through gardens, and engaged himself in fighting with his adversary. In this battle some enemy warriors of considerable renown like Gedā Beg Turkmān and Bolar Khān Afghān[15] were slain on the battlefield.

[*verses*]

Shanki Mīr Chādūra and others were taken prisoner and brought before the Sayyid with their hands and feet in

14. The contents of the letter which have been put in the form of verse in the present text have also been used by Ḥasan in his history, with some variations. Ḥasan has only three verses as against eight in the present text, and even in those three there are two or three variations. Since the verses are a part of a message which must have been recorded earlier, it seems likely that the source for both the historians is the same.

15. Bolar Khān Tīmūr in *TḤK*, p. 303.

chains. All the houses of Nājī Raina in the village of Barthal were set on fire and got reduced to ashes.

Yūsuf Shāh, preferring death to a dishonourable life, took position on the steep mountain summit of Bartal along with a handful of his associates.[16]

[*verses*]

Mubārak relents

Sayyid Mīrān was moved by this, and out of compassion, he adapted a patronizing attitude towards Yūsuf Shāh's staff. He put a stop to the attempts of his soldiers and commanders to take revenge against Yūsuf Shāh. On aforesaid day, along with his soldiers, he entered the city triumphantly. It almost looked like a pageant.

'Alī Khān, son of Nawroz Chak, held himself back for sometime in the countryside on the pretext of shikar and did not join Yūsuf Shāh. He explained his conduct to Sayyid Mubārak and returned to the city.

[*verses*]

Before doing so, he divulged to Abdāl Bhat all that had transpired between him and Yūsuf Shāh and also the words of love and friendship which he had spoken to him out of expediency. Although Abdāl was revolted by his words, he gave no expression to his feelings and kept it a secret.

During this time, Mīrān Sayyid Mubārak Shāh was taken ill. Abdāl Bhat looked upon the Sayyid's temporary illness as a serious set-back to his plans. Forthwith he came to see him and persuaded him to imprison 'Alī Khān for some time because, according to him, 'Alī Khān had once again taken

---

16. According to Malik Ḥaidar a group of soldiers who had hitherto committed themselves to Yūsuf Khān, betrayed him, which forced him to return to the Indian mountains without hazarding a battle with his opponents. *TMḤ*, MS f. 67[a].

to subversive activities. He also told him that it was necessary because of his failing health. Abdāl Bhat pleaded that 'Alī Khān could be set free after the disturbances had subsided and he was restored to health.

'Alī Khān trapped

Having discussed the proposed course of action with the advisers of Sayyid Mubārak so as to get it ratified by him, he went to 'Alī Khān and through deceit and cunning sent him to the presence of Sayyid Mubārak with pomp and show. Himself he returned to his lodging with the hope that on seeing the physical infirmity of the Sayyid, 'Alī Khān might be tempted to rise in revolt against him. 'Alī Khān dismounted from his horse and proceeded towards Mīrān Sayyid. Dā'ūd Mīr Piloo (Biloo ?), one of the veteran warriors of the Sayyid, took him by hand and led him straight to the prison-house. Most of his military officers and commanders, like Shams Dooni and Daulat Khān, became confused and sought refuge in the house of Mīrān Sayyid Ḥusain Khān. Shams Chak, 'Alam Sher Khān and others came as supplicants to the house of Mīrān Sayyid Shāh Abu'l-Ma'ālī and offered to keep themselves at his disposal.

Abdāl's trick

Abdāl Bhat combined in himself the twin qualities of shrewdness and villainy. He told Lohar Chak and the top leaders of the tribe of Chaks that in that matter Mīrān Sayyid had acted independently and had never sought his advice. He cautioned them that a similar treatment could be meted out to them as well. This caused serious anxiety among the advisers and counsellors of Yūsuf Shāh, with the result that each of them took steps to ensure his own safety. They sent letters to Yūsuf Shāh in which they apparently appealed for unity with him, but these in fact carried the seeds of discord.

They promised to him that even at the cost of their lives, they would try to achieve and fulfil whatever objective was set before them. They assured him that they would make a public announcement of the relevant facts when the time was ripe. At that time he was to move to the city swiftly without hesitation.

On the 15th of Sha'bān in the aforesaid year, Abdāl Bhat gave out the false story that Yūsuf Shāh had entered into the city. This rumour spread among the commoners as well as the soldiers. He got a soldier attired in royal robes and decorated with other regal appendages so that he looked like Yūsuf Shāh. An imposing pavilion was also set up and the imposter was brought to take the royal seat. The soldiers and the civilians believed that Yūsuf Shāh had returned to the city.[17] At the same time they also came to know of the physical infirmity of the Sayyid. Hence many people joined Abdāl Bhat in groups.

Mubārak reacts

Mīrān Sayyid learnt about the situation and, early in the morning, despite his physical infirmity, moved on to Īdgāh maidān along with his troops and battle equipment to fight his opponents. He despatched the garrulous and sweet-tongued Muḥammad Padar as his messenger to Abdāl Bhat, conveying to him that it behoved the valiant to display whatever feats of valour they laid claim to on the battlefield. He had come on the Īdgāh maidān to challenge him. Like a good warrior he should trust his words, cross the river in the city, and move his horsemen to the Īdgāh maidān. Alternatively, he should give him a gentleman's promise to let his soldiers cross the river and take up their position at Zāldagar. They would prove their strength on the battlefield

17. The strange story of the imposter does not figure either in Ḥasan or in Malik Ḥaidar.

and whomsoever God blesses with victory, shall occupy the seat of governance of this realm.

The message touched the sense of honour of Kashmiri commanders who resolved to give a tough fight to the Sayyid; and, consequently, moved on to the river bank. Apart from possessing considerable experience in fighting, Abdāl Bhat was as wise as he was brave. Many a time had he been a witness to the bravery of the aforesaid Sayyid on the battlefield and, besides, had also heard stories of his dauntless courage. Therefore, in the context of the impending situation, he held consultations with his field commanders and issued strict instructions to them not to move from their positions. He cautioned them that a fight with that group would affect them adversely and nobody could save his life unless he fled from the battlefield.

[*verses*]

"It is only prudent that our numerical strength should not make us complacent nor should we feel overconfident about our bravery. It would be sheer stupidity to decide upon a fight for revenge without taking cognizance of the realities of the situation. Certainly, duplicity and craft shall have to be employed to deal with the situation," he observed.[18]

[*verses*]

Abdāl's cunning

After taking stock of things, Abdāl Bhat thought of resorting to guile to further his objective, although he was not very sure whether his villainy would succeed. He immediately summoned to his presence. Bābā Khalīlu'llah, in whose

18. Ḥasan criticizes him for his reluctance to have a straight fight with the Sayyid. See *TḤK*, p. 305.

august presence he sent a messenger to Yūsuf Shāh with a letter stating that the nobles and commanders of Kashmir had concluded a solemn agreement and resolved to act upon one another's friendly advice according to which they meant to offer to him the power and authority of the government of this land. As such he was to make no delay in coming. A verbal message was also sent to him which conveyed 'Alī Khān's agreement to what they had stated in their letter. At that time 'Alī Khān was a prisoner in the hands of the representatives of Mīrān Sayyid Mubārak Shāh.

[*verses*]

Abdāl Bhat drew the plans in the presence of Bābā Khalīlu'llah and Mīrān Sayyid Barkhordār. He employed whatever craft he could and sent a message to Mīrān Sayyid Mubārak at Īdgāh: "Sayyid Mubārak Khān should not consider today's event as a mere happening. Since 'Alī Khān has been detained by your agents without reason, the people have become apprehensive. They destroyed the bridges over the river in the city to secure themselves against danger. In fact, this group requests your protection and does not want to confront you."

[*verses*]

An action which was inherently dangerous did not take place and a calamity which could have caused chaos had been averted. The message ran further: "Inglorious is the person who rakes up trouble and disorder or takes recourse to fighting and hostility when a possibility of solving the issue through peaceful means and negotiations is not lacking. It has been our considered opinion that Yūsuf Shāh should be recalled and a conference be held with your officials at the *khānqāh* of Bābā Khalīlu'llah in honest faith with a view to laying down necessary conditions of agreement. Yūsuf Shāh should be re-installed on his throne and all the chiefs and commanders should be allowed to resume authority and control over their respective frontiers and divisions as per the practice in the past. In this way chaos and disorder shall be stamped out and order restored. You may come to the *khānqāh* of Bābā Khalīl along with 'Alī Khān to put seal on the proposed agreement."

Mīr Sayyid trapped

The aforesaid Sayyid acted upon their suggestion and got 'Alī Khān's fetters removed. 'Alī Khān consulted his son Yūsuf Khān about Abdāl Bhat's action. His opinion was that it would not be practicable to implement the suggestion unless Mīrān Sayyid was restored to his health and strength. He said that if they visited the camp of the enemy in his state of physical infirmity, they might be taken captives. His opinion was that prudence demanded that since the sons and counsellors of Mīrān Sayyid were disturbed by his physical weakness and that there was virtually no dispute or cause for dispute between them ['Alī Khān and his son], rather as the Sayyids were sorry for their faults, they should not take the risk of going to the camp of the enemy and allow themselves to be overpowered by them.

[*verses*]

Trusting the friendly overtures of Abdāl Bhat and not paying heed to the right suggestion of his son and not thoroughly considering these words to be of an interested person, 'Alī Khān left the battlefield and walked the distance from Īdgāh and arrived at the *khānqāh* of Bābā Khalīlu'llah. The aforesaid Sayyid, too, dismounted from his horse and, because of his weak health, reclined against the wall of the *khānqāh*. His sons and soldiers saw that crowds of people had begun to assemble around them. Hence they dispersed and retired to safe place. Only two of his sons, namely Mīrān Sayyid Shāh Abu'l-Ma'ālī and Ibrāhīm Khān, kept him company.

Delegation under Ḥaidar Chak

Most of his (Sayyid Mubārak Khān's) kinsmen and near ones, confused and embarrassed as they were, joined Yūsuf Shāh at the village called Pantehchuk.[19] Thus the plan of Abdāl Bhat succeeded:

[*verses*]

He immediately sent Ḥaidar Chak along with a team of seniors to Sayyid Mubārak Khān. They found that the lion of the battlefields had lost his power and strength on account of his illness, and had now taken to meditation and telling of beads. 'Alī Khān was granted permission to return to his house. To Mīrān Sayyid Mubārak Khān he showed due courtesy and regard and sat with him in the boat that brought him to his lodging. But there is a saying that what is ordained cannot be changed:

[*verses*]

That very moment 'Alī Khān, along with his son, was dragged out of his house, brought to the house of Lohar Chak, and finally put in chains. His son Yūsuf Khān, on witnessing the turn of events, could have said after the poet:

> (On my dear, much did I entreat ye not to go to a place where ye be caught. Ye did go and then happened what I had feared.)[20]

After this event Abdāl Bhat felt sorry for having acted unfairly and for having broken his promise. He sent his son to Yūsuf Khān post-haste to tell him that the situation was such that his coming would bring harm to him and could

---

19. Between the present-day Batwāra and Pampore near Srinagar.

20. *guftam ay dil maraw ānjā kih giriftār shawī*
'āgebat rafti-o ham guft-i manat pīsh āmad

even aggravate the situation further. He advised him to turn back:

[*verses*]

This news forced Yūsuf Shāh to think, but for a while he was overtaken by confusion. At last he returned to his old place.[21] There he spent a few days and then established liaison with the cousins of Mīrān Sayyid Mubārak Shāh and proceeded to the court of Akbar Pādshāh at Agra to seek assistance.

Lohar Chak

In the aforesaid year,[22] Abdāl Bhat, with the support and consent of the commanders of this land, installed Lohar Chak, son of Shankar Chak, on the throne of Kashmir. But in effect, he concentrated all power in his own hands and reduced Lohar Chak to the position of a nominal king. Except for reading the homily (*khuṭba*) and the striking of coins in his name, Lohar Chak had no authority whatsoever.

Some of the notable persons of this land, such as Ḥabīb Khān, son of Abdāl Khān, who loved Yūsuf Shāh's company, broke away from Mīrān Sayyid Mubārak Shāh and joined hands with Abdāl Bhat.[23] But this shift of loyalty caused them much anxiety, because Abdāl Bhat dealt with them in an arbitrary and autocratic manner. He either put them in prison or held out threats to them, but did not take the extreme step of liquidating them or putting them to the sword. In fact, later on, he was not really unfavourably disposed towards them.

---

21. Ḥasan writes that Yūsuf Khān reached Pattan at that time. See *THK*, p. 306. But the actual place where he had camped has not been mentioned.
22. A.H. 988/A.D. 1580.
23. Malik Ḥaidar says that they were fed up with the bad temperament of Sayyid Mubārak Khān. *TMḤ*, MS 67[a].

For one year, he (Abdāl Bhat) ruled over the people of this land in a manner already mentioned.[24] In course of time most of the people of this land, including soldiers and horsemen, ran away to join Yūsuf Shāh whenever an opportunity came their way. These, for instance, included men like Shams Chak and 'Alam Sher Khān.

Akbar and Yūsuf Shāh

A year after the assumption of reins of kingship, Akbar showed royal favour to Yūsuf Shāh by offering him two mistresses.[25] He entrusted the mission of conquering Kashmir to Mīrzā Yūsuf Khān and Rājā Mān Singh.[26] The victorious imperial army reached the capital city of Lahore. Yūsuf Shāh, along with his troops, proceeded towards Bahlool Pore to know about the commanders of that land and also to meet his sons.[27] These reports were brought to Abdāl Bhat and his commanders who lost no time in despatching their secret messengers with letters to Yūsuf Shāh, the contents of which were couched in soft words. They wrote to him that he should be careful about the

24. Historians have recorded that Lohar Chak meted out just and kind treatment to the people. There was a good harvest during his reign and paddy was available at cheap rates. See *TMḤ*, MS f. 67[b], and *TḤK*, pp. 306-7.
25. According to Ḥasan, Yūsuf Shāh stayed at the Imperial Court for eleven months. *TḤK*, p. 307.
26. For details about their mission see *Ma'āthiru'l-Umarā*, Vol. III, pp. 314-21.
27. From Malik Ḥaidar's *Tārīkh* it appears that Yūsuf Shāh was given very small military help by Akbar. Muḥammad Bhat the former Chief Vizir of Yūsuf Shāh proceeded to Lahore leaving behind at Bahlool Pora about a thousand soldiers (MS f. 68[a]). In Lahore and some other parts of Panjab, he managed to raise a force of about four thousand soldiers. He also raised a huge loan from the business community of Lahore. See *TḤK*, p. 309. Also see *Wāqa'āt-i-Kashmir*, Muḥammad Āzam Dedemari, p. 95.

developments which had taken place and know that the imperial troops might behave in a different manner after they had occupied the land.

[*verses*]

[In his letter Abdāl Bhat told him to trust his words and promises and not hold him responsible for whatever faults there were in the past. He suggested to him that he should leave the imperial troops and return to this country without entertaining any fears.[28]

[*verses*]

Yūsuf deserts

Ensnared by false promises and trusting the deceptive overtures of that group of people, Yūsuf Shāh turned towards Rajouri mountain range from Bahlool Pora.[29] He left his family and children in the fort at Parot [*sic*] and himself descended on the village Verinag situated at the foot of Kashmir mountains.

The news of Yūsuf Shāh's escape was received by Akbar with disapproval. He felt displeased and criticised Rājā Mān Singh and Yūsuf Khān. Yūsuf Shāh stationed himself at Verinag and in this way Abdāl Bhat created trouble for himself. In order to ensure security and safety of Hirpur pass, Yūsuf Khān, son of Ḥusain Shāh sent a contingent of troops with commanders such as Ḥusain Khān, son of Ibeh Shāh, and others. But this group of soldiers took advantage of the opportunity and joined Yūsuf Shāh at the aforesaid village. Mīr Ḥasan Chādūru (Chādūra) and Shams Dooni also joined Yūsuf Shāh along with their troops.

---

28. For more details about Abdāl Bhat's communication to Yūsuf Shāh, see *TḤK*, pp. 308-9.

29. Rai Bahādur, the *Zamīndār* of Rajouri, joined hands with Yūsuf Khān and he made Rai the foremost commander of his army. See *TMḤ*, MS f. 68[a].

Everyday footmen and horsemen of this land ran away and joined Yūsuf Shāh's army, whenever they got an opportunity to do so.

Abdāl Bhat broke his pledges and promises and made preparations for a confrontation with Yūsuf Shāh and sealed all paths through which his troops could have forced their entry into the Valley:

[*verses*]

From Abdāl Bhat's actions Yūsuf Shāh could follow that he (Abdāl) would try to seek the support of Mīrān Sayyid Mubārak Shāh for himself through flattery and guile. He, therefore, sent a secret messenger with a letter to Mīrān Sayyid Mubārak Shāh reminding him that Abdāl Bhat was trying to make overtures to him for no purpose other than that of soliciting his support to strengthen his own position and for his selfish interests. As such, he requested him to oblige him (Yūsuf Shāh) by not extending his support to Abdāl Bhat. Yūsuf Shāh conveyed to him that he had left the fruition of his enterprise to God Almighty and the blessings of the respected Sayyid. He was sure that any adventure undertaken by Abdāl Bhat without the tactical advice of the Sayyid was bound to fail.

[*verses*]

Yūsuf Shāh strikes

The message from Yūsuf Shāh fully confirmed Mīrān Sayyid's own assessment of the situation and he found himself disposed to agree with him. Thus sings the bard:[30]

> A heart finds its way to a reciprocating heart under the dome of the sky. Love begets love and enmity begets enmity.

30. *dil rā ba dil rahīst darin gonbad-e spehr*
az sū-i kineh kineh-o az sū-i mehr mehr.

Thus Mīrān Sayyid responded to the message of Yūsuf Shāh. Expressing his approval of Yūsuf Shāh's onward march [to the city], he bade farewell to his messenger. Mīrān Sayyid's encouraging reply brought joy and exultation to Yūsuf Shāh. Without loss of time, he mounted his horse and, making a dash from the aforesaid village, took the Tsereh-Ḥār route, struck a devastating blow to the pass-holders of Abdāl Bhat, and forced his entry into the town of Kashmir [Sopor].[31] Lohar Chak's troops had been stationed at Sopor with the purpose of ensuring the security of those areas. But with God's help, Yūsuf Shāh broke their might and occupied the town of Sopor and its surrounding areas. He stationed himself at that place and sent word to Abdāl Bhat through a messenger that, relying on his promises and letters, he had left the imperial troops and encamped at Sopor. If Abdāl was true to his word, he should immediately proceed to meet him and submit to him so that with his cooperation, he would march on to occupy the seat of kingship.

[*verses*]

Abdāl's overtures

To this message Abdāl Bhat reacted with cool-headed diplomacy of giving false assurances to the messenger and bidding him return to his master. For the purpose of strengthening Lohar Shāh's regime, Abdāl Bhat released Mīrān Sayyid Mubārak Shāh and 'Alī Khān from prison and tried to win them over by soft words. Although this action increased the prestige of Mīrān Sayyid Mubārak Shāh, yet, fully conscious of the fact that the glib-tongued Abdāl Bhat's words were nonsense, he preferred to remain

31. *baldah-e Kashmir* means the town of Kashmir or Sopor as against *shahr-i Kashmir* meaning the city of Kashmir or Srinagar.

tight-lipped and sought to engage himself in meditation in the prayer-house to the last day of his life.

[*verses*]

Mīrān Sayyid Mubārak prayed and meditated devotedly and this shall receive further notice shortly.

Ya'qūb trapped

'Alī Khān, acting in concert with Lohar Shāh and Abdāl Bhat, raised the banner of opposition against Yūsuf Shāh to further his interests. In this way they determined to destroy Yūsuf Shāh.

[*verses*]

They also incited Ya'qūb Shāh, the son of Yūsuf Shāh, to adopt a bellicose stance towards his father and force an armed confrontation with him. On finding that 'Alī Khān, Mīrzā Ya'qūb and others had united to rise against Yūsuf Shāh, Abdāl Bhat regretted the promises and commitments he had made for him. He then marched out of the city and headed towards Sopor where he finally took position on the bank of the river. For some days, they were engaged in sporadic fighting, shooting a casual arrow or firing a stray musket. What prevented the sides from a major conflict was the river and their inability to cross it. After holding consultations of tactical nature with 'Alī Khān, Abdāl Bhat placed a force of two thousand strong and well-equipped horsemen under the command of Ḥaidar Chak to proceed via Kiyamah[32] [*sic*] route for engaging Yūsuf Shāh's troops. On the same day, he deployed his brother, 'Alī Bhat, on the adventure of crossing the river at Sopor and, in this way, he played the role of a fox and lion.[33] Through Bābā Khalīl he advised Yūsuf Shāh purporting that "this humble servant

32. Khuīhāma in *TḤK*, p. 310.

33. Allusion is to *Kalileh wa Dimneh.*

had been the beneficiary of 'Alī Shāh, and it was his magnanimity which had elevated him from the dust. It, therefore, was incumbent upon him not to conceal from him whatever nefarious designs or plans were being drawn to create anarchy and confusion in the state. He meant to report that some of the nobles and commanders of his army conspired to desert him when the fighting would be in full swing and join the ranks of Lohar Shāh's troops. Lohar Shāh had drawn a plan to cross the river in the early hours of the morning along with the entire body of his soldiers and camp followers and give him a tough fight. Again, Ḥaidar Chak, as the head of two thousand troops, all armed to the teeth, had already taken position at the village Buyeh Sangari[34] and he was poised to launch an attack from the rear. So he was warned in strict confidence that that very night he should hasten towards Poonch, failing which, he would only help his enemy to become their prisoner.[35]

[*verses*]

To these veiled threats and intimidation, conveyed through Bābā Khalīlu'llah, Yūsuf Shāh sent a versified reply:[36]

[*verses*]

---

34. Present Bābā Shakūru'd-Dīn hill-top between Khuīhāma and Sopor where Rājā Prahlād had built the Prateśwara temple. It was called Bosangeri. The other name of the hillock given in Kashmirian histories is Sherehkot. See *TḤK*, p. 34.
35. Malik Ḥaidar does not give this story; instead he says it was Shams Dooni, one of his commanders, who suggested to him that since he had a smaller number of troops at his disposal, he should retire to Poonch via Gurimarg (Gulmarg) route, but the suggestion was turned down by Malik Muḥammad Ḥasan. See *TMḤ*, MS f. 68^b.
36. This versified reply figures in the history of Ḥasan also, confirming the earlier guess that the two historians had a common source. See *TḤK*, p. 311.

Abdāl Bhat received this reply but, emboldened by superior numerical strength of his troops in comparison to those of Yūsuf, he made a cool and calculated assessment and chose to send no reply. Permitting Bābā Khalīlu'llah to return to the city, he kept himself in readiness for a battle with Yūsuf Shāh:

[*verses*]

The battle

In the early hours of the following morning, Yūsuf Shāh cleared his way a little downwards the town of Sopor,[37] and, riding a swift horse crossed over to the other bank. He deployed his troops in accordance with the plan he had drawn in advance. A contingent of foot soldiers was deployed on the right flank and some of his fire-spitting machines on the left. With this arrangement, he made an advance to meet his adversary. Lohar Shāh was informed of this tactical move of Yūsuf's troops. Consequently, he placed Abdāl Bhat in charge of the vanguard of his grand army and made a direct onslaught on the enemy. The two warring armies stood with an eye-ball to eye-ball stance, and it was Abdāl Bhat who struck first. With a single stroke of his dragon-piercing lance, Yūsuf Shāh relieved Abdāl Bhat of his life.

[*verses*]

The date of his death on the battlefield has been recorded in the chronogram *nāgahān shīr darīdeh dimnak.* Then followed the lightening attacks from Yūsuf Shāh and his veteran commanders like Yūsuf Khān, son of Ḥusain Shāh, Ḥusain Khān, son of Ibeh Shāh, Shams Chak, son of Daulat Chak, Mīr Ḥasan, son of Nājī Malik, 'Alam Sher Khān,

37. He crossed the river near Delina shortly after midnight under candlelight. See *THK*, p. 312.

Shams Dooni, Sayyid Saif Khān Baihaqī and his brothers, each of whom had won the rightful title of the battle hero. Unable to withstand their attacks, Lohar Shāh abandoned the royal parasol on the battlefield and fled for his life.

[*verses*]

Ḥabīb Khān, son of Abdāl Khān, whom Abdāl Bhat had, prior to Yūsuf Shāh's attack, thrown into the prison and was found on the battlefield groaning under heavy and painful chains, was released.

By sheer bravery and courage, Yūsuf Shāh proceeded triumphantly towards the city. His advance caused confusion in the ranks of Ḥaidar Chak's army, and soldiers began to desert him. Ḥaidar Chak was also forced to flee virtually barefoot, along with a handful of his followers, through Tsereh-Ḥār pass.

Chapter VIII

The Rise and Fall of Yūsuf Shāh Chak

Muḥammad Bhat's ministry

Yūsuf Shāh ascended the throne for the second time[1] in A.H. 988 (A.D. 1580), entrusting Muḥammad Bhat with the power and position of the Chief Vizir of his domain. This Muḥammad Bhat was a sagacious and clear-headed man, an excellent conversationalist and was gifted with a sweet and persuasive tongue; he could enliven his companions with his brilliant wit and devastating repartees. He was bounteous towards the poor and the destitute:

[*verses*]

---

1. Ḥasan writes that people of all ranks and positions in the city of Srinagar came out to receive Yūsuf Shāh at Barthana. Mullā Muḥammad Amin Mustaghni found this apt verse of Hāfiz by way of an augury:

   Yūsuf-e gumgashteh bāz āyad ba kan ān gham makhor
   kulbeh-e ehzān shavad rūzī gulistān gham ma khor

   Speaking about the second tenure of Yūsuf Shāh's regime, Ḥasan writes that he strove very hard to eradicate corrupt practices [in matters of religion] (*bid'at*) which had taken root in earlier days. He paid visits to the graves of the saints and derived benefit from the company of the elderly Shaykhs. Once he visited Bābā Hardi Reshi barefooted. *TḤK*, p. 315. Commenting on the same subject, Malik Ḥaidar writes that unjust taxes imposed on some sections of people, were abolished by him. Corvee (*begār*) exacted from people by forcing them to proceed on journey without receiving remuneration was also abolished. Taxes on fruit-bearing trees and on craftsmen were also abolished. See *TMḤ*, MS f. 72[b].

[At this time] five thousand soldiers, who had fled the battlefield at Sopor and had sought refuge in the city of Kashmir [Srinagar], were still at large and had not surrendered to Yūsuf Shāh. Muḥammad Mīr put it wittily saying that perhaps five thousand absconding cavalrymen could still invite them to a battle-feast. Yūsuf Shāh replied by saying that he was God's grace for the virtuous and the pure, but God's scourge for the wicked and the seditious. He declared that he combined in himself wrath and compassion, poison and elixir.

[*verses*]

Lohar's failure

Wise men say that the affairs of the world hinge on statesmanship: it functions as a provost marshal in this material world. For want of statesmanship, important affairs of the world can end disastrously. If disciplinary laws are non-existent, affairs of this world will end in disaster. Without censure and without necessary reprimand, there will be disruption in the world. No country can exist without a proper system of justice; and yet it will not look like one without statesmanship.[2] Muḥammad Bhat said that prudence demanded that spies be pressed into service to seek the fleeing soldiers from their houses or wherever they were hiding and to bring them to book. Secret agents were sent to several places. Lohar Shāh was found hiding in the basement of the house of Qāḍī, and Muḥammad Khān was found in the house Mīrān Sayyid Barkhordār. Both were brought to the presence of Yūsuf Shāh.

Opponents crushed

Ḥusī Chak had always boasted of his bravery and valour on the battlefield, and people in these lands begun to give

2. This theme has been borrowed from Jāmī's *Lawāyeh*.

credence to his boastful words. But he was so badly mauled by Yūsuf Shāh on the battlefield that he could not even manage his escape either to India or to Tibet, though he had sufficient time at his disposal. He abandoned his horse and hid himself in the barn of Chamshi Mamosa [*sic*]. Ḥusī Bhat, the brother of Muḥammad Bhat, found him and brought him to the presence of Yūsuf Shāh. Finding that he (Ḥusī Chak) was unable to answer him because of his nervousness. Yūsuf Shāh was reminded of this verse:

> A complete man is one who speaks not, but acts,
> One who speaks and acts is but half a man.
>
> He who speaks not and acts not is but a woman,
> And half the woman is one who Speaks but does not act.

Petseh Ganāī, a ring leader of the trouble-mongers of this land, had sought refuge in the house of Yūsuf Khān, son of Ḥusain Shāh. He was dragged out and brought before Yūsuf Shāh who interrogated him. Driven by his innate vulgarity, this person, who lacked sense, made indiscreet and vain utterances in the presence of Yūsuf Shāh. But the latter exhibited self-control, and did not take any retaliatory action to censure him. One by one, the remaining troops and villagers, who were among the fleeing group, were brought out from their hiding places to Yūsuf's presence. They were brought together and he addressed them in person. He enumerated their failings one after another, as thus:

> "First, by taking recourse to animosity and defiance, you totally ignored the path of peace and conciliation and made no secret of your disloyalty to me. You deserted me and joined hands with Mīrān Sayyid Mubārak Shāh with the sole purpose of raising the banner of revolt. You involved the Sayyid in your treason. Secondly, that elderly Sayyid had bestowed benefactions upon you, but you proved ungrateful to him by indulging in acts of subterfuge and sabotage. You recalled me

from the village of Bartal but subsequently went back on your commitment, putting me in an embarrassing situation. Then you aligned yourselves with Lohar Shāh and connived at his accession to the throne. Thirdly, when I sought the help of the imperial army to re-conquer Kashmir, you sent me flattering letters holding out solemn promises that henceforth you would neither back out nor defy nor disregard my authority. Relying on these promises, I left the imperial army and came to this domain. But then, feigning ignorance, you forgot the promises you had made. Not only that, you arrayed troops against me. Fourthly, my father was kind and generous to you. From the depths of lowliness he lifted you to the heights of manliness, and I, in my own turn, extended the same liberal treatment to you. In fact, I added something to enhance your prestige. But you proved your ingratitude by instigating rebellion against me. You have, thus, wilfully transgressed the tenets of the religion of Muḥammad and flouted the conventions of the Ḥanafī sect, and, not acted in accordance with the Qur'ānic commands – be obedient to God, to the Prophet and to those who command authority over you.[3] You pressed yourselves into the company of rebels. Therefore, killing you and depriving you of your property will be in conformity with the sanctions of religion."

On hearing these words of Yūsuf Shāh, Abdāl Bhat almost lost his speech. Yūsuf Shāh got the eyes of Lohar Shāh, his brother Muḥammad Khān and Ḥusī Chak[4] gouged out and they were, thus, deprived of their eyesight: Petseh Ganāī, Fatḥ Khān Jand [*sic*] and Ḥusain Kokeh were punished by amputation of their limbs. Yūsuf Lund, Alī Khān Sirigāma [*sic*] and 'Alī Bhat, the brother of Abdāl Bhat, were ordered to pay a certain amount of money as indemnity usually imposed on prisoners of war. 'Alī Khān, Nawroz

3. *aṭiu'llah wa aṭiu'rrasūl wa ulu'l amr minkum.*
4. Ḥusī Chak was captured in the *pargana* of Bengil, and Muḥammad Khān in Baramulla by a *thānedār*. *TMḤ*, MS f. 71^{b}.

Chak and his son Yūsuf Khān, were spared their lives, but were put in prison. The rest of the soldiers and the villagers were pardoned and were reinstated in their *jāgīrs* as of old.

Conciliation with Mīrān Sayyid

After dealing with the situation in a manner described above, Yūsuf Shāh decided to call on Mīrān Sayyid Mubārak. In order to strengthen his regime, he concluded matrimonial alliance with "that house by giving his daughter in marriage to Mīrān Sayyid's grandson. After this, he ruled without any worry and anxiety. There was a revival of his cordial and affectionate relations with Mīrān Sayyid's house and frequent visits to the Sayyid's house strengthened these bonds. He also occasionally invited Mīrān Sayyid to his palace.

Yūsuf's personality

Yūsuf Shāh was gifted with a beautiful and graceful body and disposition. He was well versed in music and Hindi, Kashmiri and Persian poetry; His compositions were popular with the lovers of music; His Hindi, Kashmiri and Persian verses were well-known in Hindustan and Kashmir and often quoted by the erudite and the poets. Of his Persian compositions, we quote one verse in this chronicle.[5] He spent most of his time in physical and sensuous enjoyments; he amused himself with sport, gave himself up to the tune of the lute and dulcimer after the true spirit of the verse:[6]

> Enjoy yourself because in just a twinkling of the eye.
> The autumn is about to arrive and the spring about to go.

---

5. *dil-e pur dard-i man jānā basān-e ghuncheh pur khūn ast / chih berahmī na pursīdī kih aḥwāl-e dilat chūn ast*
6. *ba avsh kūsh kih tā chesm mizanī barham*
Khazānat mī rasad-o nawbahār mī guzarad

Uprising suppressed

Some of the prominent nobles of this land, Shamsi Chak, 'Alam Sher Khān, Sayyid Saif Khān and Muḥammad Lung found that Yūsuf Shāh, on account of his excessive carelessness, had been grossly neglecting state affairs. As such, they firmly resolved to create disorder in the state afresh. On knowing this, Yūsuf Shāh got all the four persons arrested and imprisoned. The event brought this verse to his lips:[7]

> 'I am seized of the serious thought of how to extend my patronage to him, but he is seized of the thought of uprooting me.'

Sometime later, Saif Khān and Muḥammad Lung were released, but Shamsi Chak and 'Alam Sher Khān continued to languish in prison. Ḥabīb Khān was filled with fear and apprehension and he broke his promises and commitments, and fled to Udreseh mountains from where he began to foment trouble.[8] After two or three months, Ḥaidar Chak, who returned from India,[9] joined him. Shamsi Chak, with the abetment of Ḥaidar Malik, a blood relation of his, led a revolt against Yūsuf Shāh in the fort of Bulūr which was situated on the borders of Kāmarāj. Yūsuf Shāh's troops laid a siege to the fort and overpowered him by sheer numerical strength. Shamsi was captured and brought before him. Although he was related to the children of Yūsuf Shāh, and on that basis pleaded with him for his acquittal, his pleadings

7. *man dar andesheh kih chūn sāyeh kunam bar sar-i ū*
   ū dar ān gham kih chisān mikanad az bonyādam
8. To Panjab in *TḤK*, p. 315.
9. After Yūsuf Shāh's victory at Sopor, Ḥaidar Chak escaped to Tibet. Later he appeared in Kishtwar and often fought against the local *thānedārs*. After four years of wandering, he went to the Indian plains and appealed to Rājā Ram Singh of Lahore for assistance. The Rājā showed him respect and consideration and granted him a *jāgīr* in Nowshehr. See *TMḤ*, MS f. 72[b].

were of no avail because he was the ring-leader of the group of seditionists. "To expect faithfulness from a king is like expecting fruit from a cypress tree."

Ḥaidar Chak's uprising

However, some time later, Yūsuf Khān, son of 'Alī Khān and Nawroz Chak, who have already figured in the pages of this chronicle, escaped from the house of Lohar [*sic*], where they had been interned, and joined the forces of Ḥabīb Khān. A large number of the sons of nobles of this land assembled and deliberated over the ways and means of destroying the authority of Yūsuf Shāh. They approached the governor of Greater Tibet for assistance. The governor named Bamaldi, a man of commanding personality, was sovereign and powerful, with innumerable troops under his command. He placed four to five thousand soldiers at their disposal and for their assistance; all fully equipped with such arms and equipment as are required in a battle.

Yūsuf Shāh came to know of the troops and materials given by the ruler of Tibet [to the Kashmiri nobles]. Consequently, he also sent his troops as well as private combatants of this land, all equipped with necessary arms, to face them. Ḥabīb Khān, Ḥaidar Chak, and Yūsuf Khan got the news that Yūsuf Shāh's columns were advancing. It caused them great confusion. Their forces were torn by internal conflicts and mutual jealousy. This disturbing situation disheartened the reinforcing columns from Tibet who decided upon retracing their steps without getting involved in a battle.

Ḥaidar Chak was defeated and he fled towards Kāthwār (Kishtwār) but Ḥabīb Khān's routes of escape were blocked and he was forced to turn towards the city where he hid himself, and even in that state, he continued his disruptive activities.

[*verses*]

After several days of search and enquiry, about ten rebellious nobles were captured around the village of Sonwār and brought before Yūsuf Shāh. Yūsuf Khān, son of 'Alī Khān, was captured along with his brothers in the *pargana* of Bring. Yūsuf Shāh punished them so that the disorder created by them was remedied:

[*verses*]

Ḥabīb Khān's eyes were gouged out and Yūsuf Khān, son of 'Alī Khān, and his brothers were punished with amputation of limbs, 'Alī Khān, son of Nawroz Chak, was a pious and God-loving man, alive to the duties and obligations of the material and spiritual world. When he lost his eyes in the manner mentioned above – a matter of divine ordination – he stood up the next moment to offer prayers in thankfulness to God the Needless, uttering the quatrain:

[*verses*]

Muḥammad Bhat's conduct

Thereafter, the office of the Chief Vizir of Yūsuf Shāh remained with Muḥammad Bhat. He was obsessed with his enmity towards Shamsi Dooni, and time and again instigated Yūsuf Shāh to seek revenge against him on one pretext or the other. But, because of Yūsuf Shāh's innate good disposition, he did not listen to his interested words and did not take any vindictive step against Shams Dooni. The disgruntled Muḥammad Bhat thus became malicious towards Yūsuf Shāh, and eventually, joined hands with Yūsuf Khān, son of Ḥusain Shāh. They worked in collusion to find an opportunity to put an end to his life. But it did not materialize because of their inability to make the sons of Mīrān Sayyid Mubārak Shāh agree to this. Under these circumstances, Yūsuf Khān grew apprehensive and, along with some of his soldiers, fled in the darkness of the night to Udrasah[10] mountains. Leading his troops, Yūsuf Shāh, along with the sons of Mīrān Sayyid, gave him a hot pursuit right up to the above-mentioned mountains. During their pursuit, there was an encounter between them in which Ḥusī Bhat, the brother of the above-mentioned Muḥammad Bhat, was wounded and his troops were overpowered. They were forced to withdraw to the summits of the mountains, where they were surrounded by Yūsuf Shāh. Muḥammad Mīr [*sic*] was taken prisoner. Some of his soldiers sustained wounds, but managed to join Ḥaidar Chak. Others got scattered over those areas in a miserable plight. Ḥaidar Chak felt strengthened on account of an increase in his troops.

Ya'qūb's defiance

After these events, Mīrzā Ya'qūb, being immature and also having come under the vicious influence of a group of miscreants, felt dissatisfied in the service of his illustrious father. With the connivance of Ibeh Khān, son of Abdāl Khān, he escaped to Kāthwāl mountains. After a few days, Yūsuf Shāh despatched one Mullā Ḥasan Aswad as his emissary to his son. Using mild and persuasive words and tact, he exhorted Ya'qūb to return to his father and show him due respect:

[*verses*]

Ḥaidar Chak escapes

Frightened of Yūsuf Shāh's wrath, Ibeh Khān went to Ḥaidar Chak. After this event, Shamsi Chak, who had been imprisoned when Yūsuf Shāh ascended the throne, contrived his escape and joined Ḥaidar Chak at Kāthwāl. Finding that Yūsuf Shāh's position had become vulnerable, the trouble-mongers took to subversive disorderly acts wherever they

10. Present Vutrus. See *Rajat.*, vii. 1254; Vol. II, p. 467.

could. In order to prevent people from establishing rapport with Ḥaidar Chak and also for reasons of security, Yūsuf Shāh deputed Sher ʻAlī Bhat and Nājī Raina to encamp at Kenal [*sic*] (Konehbal ?). But these commanders abandoned themselves to negligence, forgot the enemy and whiled away a few days at that place. Ḥaidar Chak found that they were completely negligent and, taking advantage of the opportunity, brought his troops out of Kāthwāl and moving with great speed, launched a night-assault on them:

[*verses*]

Sher ʻAlī Bhat and his soldiers displayed feats of valour, but he was slain by Shamsi Chak; Nājī Raina was captured by Ḥaidar Chak and brought to the village of Daksum. Most of the troops of Yūsuf Shāh joined Ḥaidar Chak.

Ḥaidar Chak defeated

Under these circumstances, Yūsuf Shāh was compelled to come out of the city. The vanguard of his army got engaged in a battle with Ḥaidar Chak, Shamsi Chak, Ibeh Khān and others at the aforesaid village. But since his opponents had established strongholds in the narrow mountain gorges, many of Yūsuf Shāh's soldiers were wounded and, as such, forced to retrace their steps and rejoin the main body of the force advancing from the rear. But the sons of Mīrān Sayyid Mubārak Shāh, namely Shāh Abu'l-Maʻālī, Ibrāhīm Khān and others, held on to their positions extending support to Mīrzā Yaʻqūb so that he did not join the fleeing troops and returned to his father. Holding on fast to their position, their fifteen or sixteen warriors fought heroically against a large number of their opponents. Some of the fleeing soldiers carried baseless and disturbing rumours about Mīrzā Yaʻqūb and the sons of Mīrān Sayyid to Yūsuf Shāh which distressed and disheartened him so much that he suspended his advance for a few days and ordered a halt to his troops and camp followers. But then Mīrān Sayyid Ḥusain Khān, the son of Mīrān Sayyid Mubārak Khān, prompted him to resume the onward march; and he reached the battlefield. Before Yūsuf Shāh's arrival, Ḥaidar Chak and his troops had come out of narrow mountain gorges, and a fierce battle took place between him and the sons of Sayyid Mīrān. Like an immovable mountain, the valiant Sayyids stuck to their positions and did not budge even an inch from there.

[*verses*]

As God willed it, Ḥaidar Chak found himself in a depressing situation, dismounted from his horse and ran away to hide himself in a mountain gorge. The Sayyids raised high the banner of their victory and chased the fleeing enemy whose soldiers fell victims to their lashing swords.

Meanwhile, Yūsuf Shāh arrived with his army on the actual scene of the battle and witnessed the gallantry and bravery of the Sayyids. He eulogised Mīrān Sayyid Abu'l-Ma'ālī in loud terms. On the recommendation of the aforesaid Sayyid, he honoured most of his soldiers with befitting rewards and robes of honour. Then he returned to the capital of Kashmir.

Sometime later, Shamsi Chak, Ibeh Khān and others felt pangs of conscience in Ḥaidar Chak's company and, therefore, tried to establish links with Yūsuf Shāh to renew their old bonds of friendship.

[*verses*]

Mughals appear

Ḥaidar Chak, Yūsuf Lūnd, and 'Alī Khān Surigāma descended from the Kāthwāl mountains and headed towards the capital city of Lahore where they joined the services of Rājā Man Singh.

It has already been recorded in the pages of this chronicle that, on account of Yūsuf Shāh's violations of his pledges and his dilatory tactics in connection with his services to. Rājā Mān Singh, the Rājā had become displeased with him. This situation was further aggravated because his opponents joined Rājā Mān Singh.[11] The only person with whom he shared the 'secret'[12] and in whom he confided was Khwāja Qāsim, son of Khwāja Ḥaidar and a grandson of Khwāja Ḥājjī. He told him that "it was far removed from prudence and wisdom to feel secure against a cunning enemy."

[*verses*]

He, therefore, did not want that Ḥaidar Chak should get a chance of going to Rājā Mān Singh and further his aims.

Yūsuf's overtures

Khwāja Qāsim appreciated Yūsuf Shāh's approach. With exquisite presents and choicest gifts for the Rājā and his senior commanders, and accompanied by Khwāja Ghanī Kābulī, he [Qāsim] presented himself before the Rājā at Lahore. He waited until a suitable opportunity came his way to speak to the Rājā and his senior officers in a manner which maligned Ḥaidar Chak. The bard sings: "Listen not to the selfish; should you do so, you will only repent."[13]

11. Rājā Mān Singh was displeased with Yūsuf Shāh for leaving his court without seeking formal permission from him See *TḤK*, p. 318.
12. The chronicler does not tell us anything about the secret understanding that was between Yūsuf Shāh and Mān Singh; there is a definite hint to the effect that there must have been some agreement between the two which Yūsuf Shāh appears to have violated. This points to a guess that perhaps the chronicler is deliberately withholding some information. By and large, he adopts the method of telling us about such secret deals and compacts, but never spells the terms of agreement.
13. *kih gar kār bandi pashīmān shavī*
kih gar kār bandi pashīmān shavī

Not being convinced that Khwāja Qāsim was not acting without some interest, the Rājā did not listen to his account. Instead, his effort of maligning Ḥaidar Chak only strengthened his (Mān Singh's) favourable opinion of Ḥaidar Chak.[14] Having been convinced that he could make no headway and that his mission had met with utter failure, Khwāja Qāsim sought the permission of Rājā Mān Singh to leave his court.

Ya'qūb assesses situation

Khwāja Qāsim reported the words of Mān Singh to Yūsuf Shāh but with distortions and suggesting that his words could be taken as an indirect expression of support. Thereupon, Yūsuf Shāh conferred the title of Mīrzā upon him and invested him with the authority of administering this domain.[15]

[*verses*]

Mīrzā Ya'qūb, the son of Yūsuf, Shāh, was a man gifted with wisdom, sagacity, prudence, and understanding. He found that this man (Qāsim) crossed the limits of discretion in handling the affairs of the state and took recourse to flattering Yūsuf Shāh and giving him false reports to further his selfish interests. He marked that Qāsim did not speak what was in the interests of the state. Therefore Ya'qūb protested against Mīrzā Qāsim's assertions and even reproached him in such a way that Mīrzā Qāsim felt offended. The two of them, therefore, became estranged.

---

14. Ḥasan says that the administration of Nowshehr and Bhimber was entrusted to him. See *TḤK*, p. 318.
15. Khwāja Qāsim continued flattering Yūsuf Shāh, at one stage the latter got annoyed with him for flattering him and reprimanded him a number of times. See *TMḤ*, p. 318.

Ya'qūb at Imperial Court

Meanwhile, the aforesaid Rājā despatched one of the trusted officials of his court namely. Tīmūr Beg,[16] as his emissary to Yūsuf Shāh. By combining threats with favours, he expressed the purpose of his mission. Mīrzā Qāsim considered Tīmūr Beg's visit a good opportunity for getting rid of Ya'qūb. He, therefore, impressed upon Yūsuf Shāh that it would be highly desirable to send Ya'qūb to the imperial court along with Tīmūr Beg. Yūsuf Shāh accepted this selfish suggestion and, without caution and consideration, despatched Mīrzā Ya'qūb to the capital city of Lahore[17] along with the emissary.[18]

On arrival at the court of the aforesaid Rājā, Mīrzā Ya'qūb duly observed the decorum and protocol of the

16. Malik Ḥaidar writes that the names of Akbar's emissaries to Yūsuf Shāh were Mīrzā Ṭāhir and Ṣāleh 'Āqil. The contents of the letter they brought him from the Emperor were: "If you are relieved of the anxiety caused by the enemy, and if the domain has been occupied, you should present yourself at the imperial court." See *TMḤ*, MS f. 72^b^. But Ḥasan gives the extract from the letter as follows; Royal patronage and attention were given to you because the signs of sincerity and truthfulness were imprinted on your face since the time of your departure to Kashmir, no report about the affairs of the State has been sent to the concerned at the imperial court. Now that it appears that the insurgents have been subdued, it is desired that the report in question containing the facts be sent without any delay" See *TḤK*, p. 319.
17. Fatehpore in *TḤK*, p. 319.
18. Malik Ḥaidar says that Ḥaidar Khān, the third son of Yūsuf Shāh and not Ya'qūb Khān, the eldest son, was sent to Akbar's court. The cowardly decision caused anguish to Kashmiri nobles and commanders who were reminded of the contents of the letter salvaged from the debris of Parihasapora after it was burnt by Mīr Shamsu'd-Dīn Araki. It said that after a lapse of one thousand and five hundred years, a man from 'Irāq would destroy that idol-house.... During the reign of the Chaks, Kashmir would pass into the hands of the Chaghatāī rulers. See *TMḤ*, MS ff. 73-74.

court, and was then brought to the presence of the Emperor. He had been at the imperial court for only a short time when, as God willed, the news of the: death of Mīrzā Hakīm, the governor of Kabul reached the court. His Majesty, therefore, marched towards the lands of Kābulistān[19] with the intention of conquering it. At each station during this march where His Majesty halted, he asked Mīrzā Ya'qūb to summon his father Yūsuf Shāh. Ya'qūb sent despatches to his father from every halting station stating the course of events in the imperial camp. But on account of the villainy and wickedness of the aforesaid Khwāja, he did not act with farsightedness and paid no attention to the letters of his son. Disappointed this father's failure to appear at the royal court, Mīrzā Ya'qūb felt the overwhelming weight of His Majesty's insistence and also the fear and gravity of the consequences of a defiant attitude. Keeping all these facts in view, he sought permission,[20] and from the village Bahlool (Pore) he marched out post-haste so that within a short time of three days and three nights, he brought himself to the presence of his venerable father.[21] But once again Khwāja Qāsim's inimical attitude towards him got revived:

[*verses*]

Mughal expedition

Before Ya'qūb rejoined his father, two envoys from Akbar, namely, Hakīm 'Alī[22] and Ṣāleh 'Āqil, had been sent to

19. The ancient name of Afghanistan.
20. Whether Ya'qūb got the permission to leave Bahlool Pora is not clear, because subsequent details reveal that he had fled without seeking formal permission. See note 23 infra.
21. Yūsuf Shāh was exceedingly annoyed with the unbecoming behaviour of Ya'qūb, and, in fact, wanted to get him arrested, but the nobles interceded for him. See *TḤK*, pp. 319-20.
22. Mīrzā Ṭāhir in *TMḤ*, MS f. 72^b.

Yūsuf Shāh advising him to present himself at the imperial, court. They were still on their way, when Ya'qūb fled[23] and came to his father. On account of this, the letter drafted by Yūsuf Shāh in the, capital and sent to Akbar, containing expressions of regret, was not entertained by him. In this way, Mīrzā Ya'qūb's[24] detestable behaviour was almost a repetition of the defiant attitude adopted previously by his father; it intensified His Majesty's anger and wrath.[25] Twenty-two nobles of the imperial court, such as Shāhrukh Mīrzā and Shāh Qulī, under the command of Rājā Bhagwān Dās, were entrusted with the task of conquering Kashmir. As the imperial troops were crossing Panbeh [*sic*] Drang,[26] [Yūsuf Shāh] released Muḥammad Bhat, whose mention has already been made in this chronicle, from prison and assigned him the task of guarding the city as well as his household. 'Alam Sher Khān, who too had been put in

---

23. Here is a contradiction. Elsewhere the author says that Ya'qūb left the imperial court after seeking due permission. Regarding Ya'qūb's flight from the imperial court, see also *Akbar-Nāma*, Vol. III, p. 469.
24. There appears to be some confusion about which one of the three sons of Yūsuf Shāh was sent to Akbar's court. Malik Ḥaidar differs from the chronicler by saying that the first delegation was headed by Mīrzā Ḥaidar Khān, the eldest son of Yūsuf Shāh. See *TMḤ*, MS f. 73^b.
25. Yūsuf Shāh received Ḥakīm 'Alī, the emissary of Akbar, with courtesy and was, in fact, inclined to present himself before the Emperor at Lahore. But he was dissuaded from doing so by his nobles. See *TḤK*, p. 320. Elaborating on this, Malik Ḥaidar says that the nobles argued that even after a lapse of few centuries the effect of Zulchu's incursion had not gone off completely. The Mughals could pose a greater threat to them. They added that by succumbing to the incursionists, they would risk the stigma of cowardice. For more details, see *TMḤ*, MS f. 74^b.
26. For *Drang* see *Rajat.*, vii, 14011; Vol. II, 15. 399. Ḥasan thinks that it was Kishanganga river which the Mughal troops had crossed. See *TḤK*, p. 322.

prison at the time of Yūsuf's accession, was released to keep him company:

[*verses*]

At last, accompanied by top-ranking commanders and known fighters,[27] Yūsuf Shāh left the city and, in order to confront the imperial army, adopted a tortuous route and arrived at Gawarmeet. The very next morning of their encamping at the above-mentioned place, some of Yūsuf Shāh's troops got engaged in an encounter with the imperial soldiers, a large number of whom was slain on the battlefield and their severed heads brought to him.[28]

Negotiations begin

Keeping in view the saying, "Have consultations on matters," Yūsuf Shāh held consultations with Mīrzā Qāsim, who held the administrative authority over the domain. Their consultations pertained to the strategy to be adopted in putting an end to the menace of the Mughal incursion. Realizing that conciliation was the best course available under the given circumstances, Mīrzā Qāsim told him in secret that, since sustained resistance to the imperial troops

27. Ḥasan says that Yūsuf Shāh despatched Abu'l-Ma'ālī and Ḥusain Chak via Khohvur route, and Shams Chak, Ya'qūb Khān, Lohar Qūrchī, Bābā Ṭālib Isfahānī, Ḥasan Bhat, Ḥasan Malik Chādūra and the feudal lords of Khakha and Buma clans together with a large force under their command to take up their position at Bulyasa. See *TḤK*, p. 322.
28. The disaster which befell the Mughal army is subtly alluded to in the letter sent by Rājā Bhagwān Dās to Yūsuf Shāh through Shāpur Khān. The extract reproduced from *Akbar Nāma* says: However, even if the imperial troops have met with disaster as a result of the wrath of God Almighty, the great monarch will send back a hundred thousand troops and this land will be trampled under the feet of elephants. You ought to realise the consequences which your attitude will lead to. See *TḤK*, p. 324.

was virtually impossible, the wise course would be to initiate negotiations. He further suggested to him that by making Rājā Bhagwān Dās their patron they could use his good office for gaining access to the imperial court. Acting on the saying that "The affairs of the world progress through means and not through merit," some headway could be made in putting things in order with the help of the aforesaid mediator.

As a result of this thinking, Mīrzā Qāsim proceeded to the court of Rājā Bhagwān Dās and, after impressing upon him his sincerity of purpose, asked him what favours and considerations would be received by them if Yūsuf Shāh was brought to join his service. In order to see that his mission was crowned with success, the aforesaid Rājā agreed to enter into an understanding with Mīrzā Qāsim upon the conditions laid down by him. He (Rājā) assured him of his adhering to his commitments by invoking his qualities of manliness; and, after putting the agreement in black and white, handed it over to him to be delivered to Yūsuf Shāh.[29] It was planned that Yūsuf Shāh would join the Rājā without delay and without consulting his sons:

[*verses*]

Yūsuf's plight

Misled by him [Mīrzā Qāsim], Yūsuf Shāh set out on his horse under the pretext of inspecting the advance columns of his army. Escorted by four to five horsemen, Yūsuf Shāh,

29. Ḥasan says that the Rājā had laid down in the agreement that in case Yūsuf Shāh agreed to proceed to the imperial court along with him, he would be shown special favours and a robe of honour would be presented to him. He would also be assured of the governance of his kingdom and nothing would be reduced from his power and authority. These would remain the same as in the past. See *TḤK*, p. 324. However, Malik Ḥaidar makes no mention of any commitment made by the Rājā.

after arriving at his advance post, bade farewell to his kingdom and regality and turned his horse towards the camp of the above-named Rājā. His counsellors, chiefs and sons tried their utmost to dissuade him from taking this risk, but to no avail.

Ya'qūb enthroned

Thus, without either taking sound counsel from an adviser or giving cool and considerate thought to the matter himself, Yūsuf Shāh took 'the' disastrous decision. Kashmiri nobles and commanders, especially the sons of Mīr Sayyid Mubārak Shāh, found it in the interest of the general public of that land that Mīrzā Ya'qūb should assume the reins of the kingdom in place of his father and resolved to ensure the security of their country. Hence, on the following day, Ya'qūb Shāh was installed on the throne of his father with the consent of Shamsi Chak, 'Alam Sher Khān and Shamsi Dooni. This development led to their hostility and confrontation with the imperial troops.

Mughal invasion

With the purpose of safeguarding Khawora route, Bābā Ṭālib Isfahānī[30] encamped there along with his contingent of troops. The only obstruction between them and the imperial army was the river at Panbeh Drang. The sagacious and mildly-disposed 'master' suggested to the imperial troops that they should construct a strong bridge over the river so that they can cross to the other side and occupy the territories there with considerable ease. Usta Lolo, a person known for his art of flattery in that land, was the 'master' who put forth this suggestion. A strong and functional bridge was built over the river and most of the soldiers in the Mughal garrison, under the command of Shāhrukh Mīrzā

30. Malik Ḥaidar states that Isfahānī was not a Kashmiri. *TMḤ*, MS f. 77[a].

Badakhshi, crossed it one by one and landed on the opposite bank.

Mughals under pressure

With this development the villagers and brave landlords [of Kashmir] were seized, by fear of these brave soldiers; they withdrew but could not decide on any course of action. It so happened that one of the *Zamīndārs* took courage and engaged a Mughal warrior in a fight and, with a single arrow-shot, he put an end to his life. He then snatched the fallen warrior's arms and robes under which he had concealed a scrip full of gold fastened to his loins. His clothes were colourfully rich. The booty whetted the appetite of Kashmiri soldiers for material gains and they fell upon the Mughal soldiers who had crossed the bridge one by one. They slew them on the spot and plundered their belongings.[31] After concluding this operation, they hewed down the bridge, rendering it unserviceable. Thereafter, they effected a total blockade of the imperial garrison which made them face acute scarcity of foodgrains and other provisions. The prices of these commodities soared so high that further increase was almost unimaginable:

[*verses*]

Skirmishes between the two sides continued under such hard conditions. The situation was further, aggravated by natural calamities; rain and snow, in addition to the extremely frightful scarcity of provisions, brought the imperial army to the brink of disaster. It was compelled to despatch 'Alī Akbar Shāh as an emissary to Mīrzā Ya'qūb Shāh,[32] appealing to him for immediate cessation of hostilities. The envoy stated that striking of coins and reading of *khuṭba*

31. The plunderers were Khakhas (Khasas of *Rājat.*), See *TḤK*, p. 325.
32. Ḥasan says that the Mughals initiated this move on the behest of Yūsuf Shāh. See *TḤK*, p. 325.

would continue to, be in the name of His Majesty in exactly the same manner as was done hitherto.[33] The emissary added that Yūsuf Shāh would bring his son Ya'qūb to the presence of His Majesty. Although Mīrzā Qāsim prevented Yūsuf Shāh from standing surety for Ya'qūb, his fatherly affection induced him to make the commitment. A letter of guarantee was drafted and passed on the Rājā Bhagwān Dās.

Bhagwān Dās' discomfiture

From the village of Bolyās, Rājā Bhagwān Dās carried him along to the capital city of Lahore. Marching in triumph and pageantry, Rājā Bhagwān Dās headed towards the court of His Majesty with Yūsuf Shāh.[34] Although Yūsuf Shāh showed utmost sincerity and faithfulness when he was brought to the imperial court, yet luck as well as the promises of Rājā Bhagwān Dās both deserted him; he remained in prison for two years and six months.[35] On noticing that his promise had been broken, Rājā Bhagwān Dās, under the dictates of his sense of honour, which is the distinctive quality of that race, drew his sharp-edged dagger from his belt and thrust it into his belly, which brought out his entrails in a lump. But the hour of death had not yet arrived for the Rājā: he recovered from the wound and was soon up and about.

---

33. Ḥasan writes that Rājā Bhagwān Dās also arranged the marriage of Ya'qūb Shāh with the daughter of Mubārak Khān Khakhar (Ghakkar). See *TḤK*, p. 325.
34. Malik Ḥaidar says that on reaching Pakhli, Yūsuf Shāh was put in chains till the Rājā brought him to the presence of His Majesty. See *TMḤ*, MS f. 77^{b}.
35. From Attock, Yūsuf Shāh was sent to Lahore under the escort of Rām Dās Kachhwaha and then he remained a prisoner of Rājā Todar Mal for two years. Malik Ḥaidar also states that afterwards when Rājā Mān Singh returned from Kabul, he interceded for him and succeeded in seeking his release from prison. See *TḤK*, p. 326, and *TMḤ*, MS f. 77^{b}.

'Alī Dār's rebellion

As already stated, Ya'qūb Shāh ascended the throne of Kashmir in the year A.H. 994 (A.D. 1585/86). This has been found in the chronogram *Zillu'llah*. The office of the Chief Vizir was assumed by 'Alī Dār. He was an amiable man but incapacitated by addiction to narcotics, and was unable to distinguish right from wrong or truth from falsehood, so much so that having conferred a certain *pargana* upon some *jāgīrdār* one morning, he re-allotted the same to another in the evening. When the two allottees staked claims to the same *jāgīr* and the matter was brought to his notice, he, forgetting his earlier orders, observed that the land in question was state-owned and had not been allotted to anybody as a *jāgīr*. This state of maladministration increased chaos and confusion, bickerings and troubles, in the state day by day.

Under these circumstances, Ya'qūb Shāh considered it prudent to assign to Mīrān Sayyid Ḥusain Khān and Shams Dooni the task of ensuring the defence of the city of Kashmir. Himself, he proceeded along with the royal entourage to the village of Halehvaleh [*sic*] for solemnizing the marriage of his adopted son. He returned to the city after the marriage was performed. On reaching the village of Achwal,[36] he came to know that 'Alī Dār had been contemplating rebellion, and had managed to win over to his side some notable leaders like Shamsi Chak, 'Alam Sher Khān, Mīr Ḥasan Chādūra and others to overpower him during his move to the capital. But their attempts were foiled by the outnumbering and powerful troops of the Sulṭān.

The frustrated rebels headed towards Sayyid Ḥusain Khān and Shamsi Dooni to seek their cooperation either by coercion or by persuasion. But Ya'qūb Shāh came to know of this and forthwith set free one Muḥammad Mīr who had been thrown into prison at the time of his accession to the

---

36. Present Achhabal in district Anantnāg.

throne. Together with him, he headed towards the city of Kashmir (Srinagar) and entered into it a little before his opponents could. Minutes later, ʻAlī Dār, along with his accomplices, appeared in the village of Zāldagar after destroying the bridges over the river in the city. On the other side, Yaʻqūb Shāh took position on the Īdgāh maidān.

Battle of Sopor

Yaʻqūb Shāh was greatly fond of ʻAlī Dār and ʻAlī Dār in turn relied whole-heartedly on his friendship. On that basis ʻAlī Dār hastened to see him at Īdgāh, where he made certain suggestions to Yaʻqūb Shāh which he thought suited his purpose. But the counsellors and advisers of Yaʻqūb Shāh did not approve them and ʻAlī Dār returned disappointed and crestfallen. He then sought the assistance of his associates and, in order to strengthen his own position, proceeded towards Sopor. He left ʻAlam Sher Khān on this side of Sopor called Mala Pora and himself encamped in the town proper along with his troops. After seven days and nights, he crossed the river at Mala Pora and was engaged in a fierce battle with ʻAlam Sher Khān. The fighting was so fierce that, but for the timely help and protection given to him by friends and colleagues, ʻAlam Sher would have been killed. With great difficulty they managed to bring him from the battlefield to a safer place and rowed him across the river to join Shamsi Chak at Sopor:

[*verses*]

Sopor captured

After capturing the town of Sopor, the commanders and nobles of Yaʻqūb Shāh entered the bazaar where fierce fighting took place with the soldiers of Shamsi Chak, who were ultimately overpowered. Since the bridge was very narrow in its width, and the number of fleeing troops was large, in the melee that followed some of the soldiers fell into the river and some others managed to cross over in safety.

Maintaining his presence of mind, Shamsi Chak left the town along with his soldiers and headed towards the city, Ya'qūb Shāh sent Abu'l-Ma'ālī, the son of Mīrān Sayyid, in his pursuit and himself, together with Yūsuf Khān, Ibeh Khān and Sayyid Ḥusain Khān made a lightening dash from Sopor and arrived in the city before Shamsi Chak could be there. On learning about this development, he, 'Alam Sher Khān and their allies did not think it advisable to enter the city. Harassed by the enemy's pursuit, 'Alam Sher Khān, in confusion, separated himself from Shamsi Chak and took to Kitchāma mountains. Mīr Ḥasan Chādūra escaped to Shamhāl village and 'Alī Dār sought refuge with the landlords of Bartal.[37]

Deserted by his associates, Shamsi Chak was compelled by circumstances to hide himself in the shrine of Mīr Shamsu'd-Dīn Araki. His associates and soldiers left him in the lurch:

[*verses*]

On being informed about the latest position, Ya'qūb Shāh rode to the shrine, captured Shamsi Chak, and put him in the custody of Ibeh Khān, son of Abdāl Khān.

No doubt Shamsi Chak was a shrewd and resourceful man, but when the pre-ordained misfortune befell him, his innate sagacity was overshadowed by the veil of imprudence and his intelligence deserted him. He abandoned his horse and took refuge in the house of the inmates of the shrine:

[*verses*]

Qāḍī Mūsā executed

After the rebellion was quelled and order was restored in the state, the office of the Chief Vizir was assigned to Muḥammad Bhat. Out of malice and ill-will, some people

37. Nājī Raina was the Zamīndār of Bartal (Barthal). See *TḤK*, p. 420.

had been alleging that it was Qāḍī Mūsā who had caused a rupture in the otherwise cordial relations between Shamsi Chak and Ya'qūb Shāh. It was further alleged that at the time of the Mughal incursion into Kashmir, headed by Rājā Bhagwān Dās, Yūsuf Shāh had requested Kashmiri chiefs to collect arms and equipment [to resist the alien troops], but the Qāḍī had obstructed the supply of these necessary materials. The fact was that the Qāḍī was popular and wielded considerable influence among the people.[38] The reason for his popularity was that he had brought to completion the roofing of the *Jāme'* mosque in Kashmir in one year, which Kashmiri nobles had failed to do. But even in matters of religion and the sect to which he belonged, such malicious things about him were given publicity as were unimaginable in a person of his standing. In this way the malevolent strove every nerve to see the Qāḍī executed, and he was ultimately put to the sword. It goes without saying that had that group of calumniators, with all the power at their disposal, chosen to intercede for him, as the sons of Mīrān Sayyid Mubārak Shāh had done earlier, to save him from the impending fate, their good record would have remained imprinted in the history of the world to the day of the last judgement:[39]

---

38. Qāḍī Mūsā descended from Qāḍī Mīr 'Alī. His house was of the dispensers of justice in Kashmir since the days of Qāḍī Ibrāhīm.
39. Quoting Malik Ḥaidar (*TMḤ*, MS f. 81[a]), and Muḥammad 'Azam (*Wāqaāt-e-Kashmir*, pp. 99-100), Ḥasan writes that the root cause of the tragedy was one Mullā 'Aini who had persuaded Ya'qūb Shāh to get the sentence Alī waliu'llah incorporated in the Muslim call for prayer. But Qāḍī Mūsā, the upholder of Sunni tradition did not oblige him. He was, therefore, accused of collaborating with Shams Chak. He was martyred in the court and his dead body was tied to the tail of an elephant and dragged along the streets. As it reached near the door of his house, his mother covered it with a veil and thanked God for making him a

(*Contd.*)

Repercussions

This event caused considerable unrest and agitation among the nobles and the local people of Kashmir, and almost wrecked the very foundation of Ya'qūb Shāh's regime.[40]

Under the damaging influence of Mullā Ḥasan Aswad and others, he dismissed the wise and sagacious Muḥammad Bhat from the ministry and threw him into prison. This act deepened the crisis within the country. The high post of the Chief Vizir passed into the hands of the incompetent Nāzuk Bhat. He was neither wise nor shrewd and could not resolve the crisis caused by the killing of the Qāḍī. He scarcely had any knowledge of the plight of ordinary people. Eventually the soldiers of several regions got dissatisfied with their patrons and were compelled by circumstances to desert them:

[*verses*]

Qāsim Khān's expedition

Faced with the disorder which prevailed in that land, the nobles and men of consequence in those days reported the

---

martyr. At the end of the day there appeared a dreadful storm which brought hail and torrential rain of such an intensity that many pregnant women aborted and many children were killed by thunder. A thunderbolt which fell on the house of Ya'qūb Khān paralysed the wife of Alī Dār and four women in the household. See *TḤK*, p. 331.

40. Nobles such as Shams Chak, Malik Muḥammad Ḥasan Chādūra, and 'Alīsher Māgray deserted Ya'qūb Shāh and proceeded towards the Indian mountains. However, they, were dissuaded by Malik Muḥammad Ḥasan from going onwards and turned back to Kashmir where, after seven days of sporadic fighting, Bābā Khalīl and Shaykh Ḥasan intervened to step the fighting between the two groups. It was decided that the area beyond Sopor to the right bank of river Jhelum would be ceded to the nobles. However, (*Contd.*)

matter in full detail at the imperial court.[41] His Imperial Majesty honoured a group of warriors by giving them royal robes and gifts and they became a part of the large army raised and despatched for the conquest of Kashmir under the command of Qāsim Khān Mīr Bahr, and also included several high-ranking warriors who were entrusted with responsible jobs. Shaykh Ya'qūb, "the perfect in visage and in method" and Ḥaidar Chak were also given "permission and directed to accompany Qāsim Khān Mīr Bahr as his guides from station to station on his way to Kashmir. They were given directions to show consideration and favour to all people who came across their way so that they were not scared or coerced into abandoning their hearths and homes.

When this news was brought to Ya'qūb Shāh, he placed the city under the command of Nāzuk Bhat's brother and himself came out of it. Sayyid Saif Khān Baihaqī[42] procured robes, horses, and equipment from Nāzuk Bhat's brother[43] and joined 'Alam Sher Khān at the village of Kitchāma.[44] Both of them joined hands and, with the intention of restoring order, turned towards the city.

On reaching Hirpur, Ya'qūb Shāh took the precautionary measure of deploying commanders like Yūsuf Khān, son of Ḥusain Shāh, Ibeh Khān, son of Abdāl Khān, Ibrāhīm Khān, son of Mīrān Sayyid Mubārak Shāh, and others to ensure the

---

the parties did not stick to the agreement, and Ya'qūb marched at the head of a formidable force towards Sopor. His opponents did not feel that they were strong enough to resist him. See *TMḤ*, MS f. 79[b].

41. Among these were Ḥaidar Chak and Shaykh Ya'qūb. See *TMḤ*, MS f. 79[b]. But Ḥasan gives the names Shaykh Ya'qūb Ṣarfī and Bābā Dā'ūd Khākī. See *TḤK*, p. 332.
42. Yūsuf Khān Baihaqī in *TḤK*, p. 332.
43. Ḥasan's revealing statement is that Baihaqī had to employ cunning and guile to get these things. See *TḤK*, p. 333.
44. Present Kitshom, the site of ancient Kṛtyāśrama Vihāra, See *Rājat.*, i, 147n.

safety of Kenchil [*sic*] route, before the expected arrival of imperial troops.

Some of the soldiers of Ya'qūb Shāh found that there was disunity in his camp; therefore, they joined together and, after arresting Fatḥ 'Alī known by the title Nowrang Khān, proceeded towards the imperial army. Bahrām Nāyak, Ismā'īl Nāyak and Shanki Charlu, who had been sent to safeguard the Kenchil [*sic*] route joined the imperial army. The position of the defectors could best be explained by the idiom, "between the devil and the deep sea."

Yūsuf Khān, son of Ḥusain Shāh, Ibeh Khān, son of Abdāl Khān, and Ibrāhīm Khān, son of Mīrān Sayyid, retraced their steps and joined Ya'qūb Shāh. Frustration overwhelmed Ya'qūb Shāh and his troops were in disarray at this critical juncture. At last, Mīrān Sayyid Shāh Abu'l-Ma'ālī thought it expedient to release Shamsi Chak and Muḥammad Bhat from prison.[45] He proposed fresh agreements and understanding with them and also suggested necessary reforms in Ya'qūb Shāh's army by upgrading the ranks of soldiers. The proposal was well received and highly appreciated by Ya'qūb Shāh. Some of his nobles, who had been recently admitted to superior social rank, outwardly endorsed his decision of releasing the two detenues, but, in truth, they were not happy about it. They misled Ya'qūb Shāh by advising him to proceed towards Chitar [*sic*] mountains early next morning without further delay or deliberation:

[*verses*]

Driven by circumstances, the commanders and soldiers of his army got an opportunity to run away in different directions.

45. Ḥasan writes that Ya'qūb Shāh's action to release Shamsi Chak and Muḥammad Bhat encouraged the masses to set on fire the *khānqāh* at Zadibal, desecrate the grave of Shams Araki and plunder the houses of the Shias. The destruction of the Shias continued for three days. See *TḤK*, p. 334.

Ṣarfī's mission

A report stating that utter confusion prevailed in the army of Ya'qūb Shāh was brought to the Emperor. He despatched to that land Shaykh Ya'qūb "the perfect in visage and method,"[46] Mīr Ṣibī and Shanki Jarariyeh (Charareh ?) Kashmiri with a strong force to bring relief and comfort to people in those lands.[47] They were directed to promulgate in the length and breadth of that realm the orders and ordinances of His Majesty's deputies.

On reaching the locality of Hastīwanj,[48] the Mughal contingent was attacked by a large group of local troops, who inflicted a number of casualties on them. Mīr Ṣibī was wounded and both Shaykh Ya'qūb and Shanker Jarariyeh [*sic*] were captured and were not subjected to torture or harsh treatment, for the reason that the former was a man of learning and the latter a blood relation of Ḥasan Chak [*sic*]. They were pardoned and set free:

[*verses*]

Meanwhile Shamsi Chak managed to unite with himself veterans such as Sayyid Ḥasan Khān Baihaqī, Ḥusain Khān, son of Ibeh Shāh 'Alam Sher Khān, Muḥammad Bhat and almost all the soldiers who had left Ya'qūb's service and had been scattered all over the land. They took position atop Kunandehbal[49] hills and soon got engaged in skirmishes with the imperial troops:

[*verses*]

46. *majma'-e sīrat wa sulūk.*
47. These areas refer to Kashmir. It appears that this portion of the chronicle was written by the author when he was outside Kashmir.
48. On Pīr Pāntsāl route. See *Rājat.*, i, 302n.
49. Keterbal/Kenzbal in *TMḤ*, MS ff. 80ᵃ-81ᵃ and Kunehbal in *TḤK*, p. 334.

Muḥammad Chak, son of Nājī [*sic*] Chak, was a renowned warrior of Kashmir. Like a brave soldier, he took the lead and displayed feats of valour on the battlefield. He got locked in a duel with a soldier of the opposing side: they held each other fast by the belt. Then Ghakkar soldier, Jalāl Khān by name, came on galloping to the pit where the two warriors were struggling to overpower each other. This horseman put an end to the life of Muḥammad Chak. The event made Zafar Khān Nāyak's blood boil; he made a lightening move and charged at the adversary of Muḥammad Chak in the manner of a brave and valiant soldier. But he fell a victim to the musket shot of Qanbar 'Alī, the attendant of Mīrzā Hakīm. At that time this Qanbar 'Alī was enlisted in the staff of the imperial artillery. This is how Zafar Khān met with his death. Despite their best efforts, Kashmiri commanders and nobles met with defeat and ran helter-skelter.

Mughal Victory

The triumphant and victorious Mughal troops occupied the Hastīwanj hill. In A.H. 994 (A.D. 1585), Nawwāb Qāsim Khān entered the city at the head of his victorious army. Ḥaidar was suspected of fomenting trouble and, therefore, was thrown into prison. Citizens, soldiers, as well as the general masses of Kashmir assessed the situation, and expressed regret and repentance over their base deeds and acts of perfidy towards earlier (Mughal) officials. Out of fear and dread, they withdrew into obscurity.

The news of Ḥaidar Chak's arrest was brought to Ya'qūb Shāh. Without loss of time, he set out along with his troops from Kashmir in full pageantry and encamped at Tserehwani. He rallied round him all those militant people who had hitherto been in a state of disarray and disunity, and provoked them to rise and fight the Mughals.

When this frightful news reached Qāsim Khān, he deputed Mubārak Khān Ghakkar along with some of his reputed warriors to support him. When this contingent was on its way to Ya'qūb's camp, the counsellors and the advisers of Ya'qūb Shāh's army decided that before the arrival of the enemy on the scene they should launch a night-assault on Qāsim Khān in the city itself. They hoped that this strategy would yield satisfactory results.

Acting on this decision, Ya'qūb's soldiers made a night-assault on Qāsim Khān:

[*verses*]

In the course of the assault, his opponents had taken a firm resolve to see him killed. Therefore they did not appear at their appointed places [during the night-assault]. The reason was that all of them were unhappy with his rule.

After analysing the course of events Ya'qūb Shāh came to a definite conclusion that friendship of the people could not be relied upon; the love of fellow beings was unsteady. In a state of helplessness he sealed his lips and withdrew silently from the locality of Zāldagar to Tsereh-Wudar:

[*verses*]

The bravest of the Baihaqī Sayyids, Mīrān Sayyid Shāh Abu'l-Ma'ālī, fearlessly came to the appointed place and made awe-inspiring assaults on the enemy, setting on fire the gateway of the mansion of Yūsuf Shāh, presently under the occupation of Qāsim Khān and his numerous troops. Some of the factional leaders like Mīr Ḥasan Chārū (Chādūra ?), depending on and confident of the remarkable bravery and indomitable courage of Shāh Abu'l-Ma'ālī, cooperated with one another and launched powerful attacks in the fashion of war veterans and disallowed the opponents any advantage of closing in. Meanwhile Ḥaidar Chak, who had been put into prison by Qāsim Khān's orders was hastily executed.

Abu'l-Ma'ālī attacks

When the dark night turned into a kind of bright day by the leaping flames of fire, crowds of people rushed out from every lane and street and, laying their hands on sticks, stones, brickbats, etc., attacked and wounded the Mughal soldiers. Royal treasure which remained in the custody of 'Abdu'r-Razzāq Māmurī had been deposited in the same place. Kashmiri soldiers assisted by the above-mentioned Mīrān Sayyid rushed forth to plunder it. A fierce and bloody battle took place between the Mughals and the above-mentioned Amīr. Qāsim Khān saw the extraordinary and remarkable valour of Kashmiri warriors and retired temporarily to a more secure place by the lake side, and did not extend help and assistance to Mīr 'Abdu'r-Razzāq Māmuri. He beheld that leader of the redoubtable Sayyids (Shāh Abu'l-Ma'ālī), whose Hashimite descent needs no introduction, as a man of incredible valour, who stood like a solid rock on the battlefield, and led a fierce fight against the Mughal troops. A large number of soldiers on either side was wounded and badly mauled.

Meanwhile the people of this land learnt that Pāyandeh Qazzāq, a warrior of the imperial camp, had raised a contingent of soldiers to reinforce the group guarding the treasury. Learning of their arrival, the Kashmiri soldiers suspended their attack on Mīr 'Abdu'r-Razzāq, and turned to fight the supporting contingent. Pāyandeh Qazzāq was a renowned and experienced warrior, and obviously it was no mean task to face him on the field of action:

[*verses*]

No warrior of this land could muster courage to come out on the pit to challenge him; however, 'Alī Mīr Bilāw [*sic*] took the lead in this. Issuing forth from his ranks he struck a blow with his sword at the Mughal warrior. But that brave man, displaying his manly power and courage, dodged the thrust.

Then on the point of his lance he lifted 'Alī Mīr up from his saddle and hurled him on the ground. People who witnessed the alacrity and bravery of this warrior loudly warned that none should hazard a combat with him, for heroes like Rustam and Sām would be amazed at the sight of his might and skill.

Mīrān Sayyid Shāh Abu'l-Ma'ālī too witnessed his bravery and valour. Without any hesitation and taking it as a challenge to his sense of honour, he began his attack on him. Soldiers and onlookers watched the two warriors in action, Pāyandeh Qazzāq took the lead and struck a terrible blow of his lance at the Sayyid. But with God's help, he successfully dodged the thrust. In return, he dealt him a deadly blow of his sharp-edged sword, which sent him down reeling on the heap of dust, putting an end to his life.

Abu'l-Ma'ālī withdraws

Pāyandeh Qazzāq's warriors witnessed the bravery of the Sayyid and, therefore, avoiding a battle, withdrew to the main body of their troops. [Later on] the imperial troops came out like ants and locusts to attack the Kashmiri soldiers. About seventy to eighty soldiers encircled Sayyid Shāh Abu'l-Ma'ālī and wanted to capture him alive. He brought his horse into quick action and managed to scare them away by shooting arrows at them:

[*verses*]

Had the warriors of this land also come out and engaged the enemy with as much intrepidity as the Baihaqī Sayyids did, God would have certainly rewarded them with victory. But as the saying goes, "the master-key to the treasures of climes lies in God's own coffers; none has ever opened it with the sheer force of arms." Since God's will was not in their favour, they were not rewarded with victory.

Qāsim Khān's plans

After this event, Nawwāb Qāsim Khān assigned Mubārak Khān Ghakkar the duty of dealing with Shamsi Chak, Sayyid Ḥusain Khān Baihaqī and Shamsi Dooni who were in the town of Sopor. Mubārak Khān's troops came out of the city and halted at the village Denwārī, where Shamsi Chak, in cooperation with Sayyid Ḥusain Khān Baihaqī, Shamsi Dooni and others made a night-assault on them. The result was a battle in which many people got killed. But, because they had no divine help, they suffered a defeat and withdrew to the town of Sopor. On account of bitter cold, they chose to retire to Karnāv mountains.

Ya'qūb Shāh, along with his brethren, proceeded to Kāthwār (Kishtwār) ranges and Mīrān Shāh Abu'l-Ma'ālī left for Ludov in the Nāyak ranges. On account of severe cold, the rest of the local soldiers found shelter in the house of the landlords of this country and did not enter the services of the imperial army.

Yūsuf Khān, son of Ḥusain Shāh, and Ḥusain Khān, son of Ibeh Shāh, joined the imperial army after obtaining some firm commitment from Nawwāb Qāsim Khān. After they joined, Nawwāb Qāsim Khān confiscated such of the *jāgīrs* as had been in possession of the Kashmiri soldiers. Consequently, the soldiers of this land felt dispirited; and, taking advantage of winter, they deserted the imperial army and dispersed in different quarters.

After the winter was over, Nawwāb Qāsim Khān considered it expedient to send Mīrān Sayyid Mubārak Shāh, Bābā Khalīlu'llah, and Bābā Mehdī, Ḥusain Shāh, son of Yūsuf Khān, to the imperial capital along with Khanjar Beg. Sayyid Mubārak Shāh had totally renounced worldly affairs and gone into seclusion for meditation and prayers. Bābā Khalīlu'llah and Bābā Mehdī were saintly persons unique in their qualities of celibacy and resignation to the Divine Will, and Ḥusain Shāh held the title *Khān-i-thānī*. The purpose in sending them to the capital was to put an end to disruption and chaos in this land, for all times to come.

Decisive battle

The party escorted by Khanjar Beg appeared in the presence of His Imperial Majesty at a time when the winter also came to an end. The Kashmiri soldiers, who had hitherto been lying low, came out of their hideouts and resumed hostilities against the imperial troops. Ya'qūb Shāh, together with his brother, Mīrzā Ibrāhīm and Ibeh Khān, son of Abdāl Khān, and the *Zamīndārs* of Bring and Chitar [*sic*] issued forth from Katwar and encamped at the village of Dagwan.[50] Mīrān Sayyid Shāh Abu'l-Ma'ālī, Ibrāhīm Khān, Nājī Raina, the *Zamīndār* Bartal, along with his sons, Bahrām Nāyak and Aḥmad Nāyak, *Zamīndārs* of Nāgām(a). Yūsuf Shee, *Zamīndār* of Kother,[51] and others came out of Ludov and in the ranges of Nājī Raina[52] [*sic*], set up their headquarters at Ghāzī Nari. Shamsi Chak, in alliance with Shamsi Dooni, the *Zamīndār* of Kāmarāj, descended from Karnāv mountains and they established their stronghold in the Kāmarāj mountains.

When this frightening news reached Nawwāb Qāsim Khān, he deputed Jalāl Khān Ghakkar and Mubārak Khān Ghakkar to fight Mīrān Sayyid and Shamsi Chak, respectively. Himself he came out of the city and arrayed his troops near the village of Ghasu. In the battle fought between Ya'qūb Shāh and the Mughals, Mīrzāda 'Alī Khān,[53] along with many other soldiers of the imperial army, fell slain in the battlefield.[54]

50. In *pargana* Ular. See *TḤK*, p. 419.
51. Gīr in Ḥasan. The name of its *Zamīndār* was Yūsuf Shee. See *TḤK*, p. 419.
52. The mountain ranges of Nājī Raina: this is not clear. Perhaps the name Nāyak ranges also applies to the same mountain.
53. For more details see *Ma'āṯhiru'l-Umarā*, Vol. III, p. 258.
54. This happened in A.D. 1586. *TḤK*, p. 420n.

Observing the turn of the tide, Nawwāb Qāsim Khān resorted to dilatory tactics and returned to the city. He then recalled Jalāl Khān and Mubārak Khān Ghakkar from their posts to reinforce his troops and strengthen his position.

Ya'qūb Shāh moved from Ghasu[55] [*sic*] and appeared on the Suleymān mountain. He despatched Ibeh Khān, son of Abdāl Khān, to meet and bring Sayyid Shāh Abu'l-Ma'ālī to his presence. Mīrān Sayyid's joining Ya'qūb Shāh added to his prestige and strength and he felt glorified. Shamsi Chak and Shamsi Dooni, both of whom had hitherto declined to show allegiance to Ya'qūb Shāh, were also drawn to make overtures to him when they heard that a compromise had been reached between him and Mīrān Sayyid Abu'l-Ma'ālī. They crossed the river and camped at the village Hanjeek.

Qāsim confronted

When Nawwāb Qāsim saw that Kashmiri troops were gathering in large numbers, he took all necessary measures to ensure the security of the fort[56] [there]. Each day witnessed renewed fighting between the Kashmiri soldiers and the Mughals which continued for two and a half months.[57]

The aforesaid Nawwāb ultimately realized that the signs of slackness and weariness in the imperial army had become fairly visible. He was compelled by circumstances to send through his emissary a message to the imperial court that he was faced with a situation of hardships and shortages of provisions. On receiving this report, His Imperial Majesty sought the counsel of senior government officials for providing relief to his troops in Kashmir. Their unanimous opinion was that suppression of the uprising in Kashmir

55. Gāsū in Ḥasan. *TḤK*, p. 420.
56. For details see *TḤK*, pp. 420-21.
57. For details about Qāsim Khān's defeat by the Kashmiris, see *TMḤ*, MS f. 83[b] and *TḤK*, pp. 422-23.

could be possible only through the instrumentality of Sayyid Mubārak Shāh.

Mubārak dies

His Imperial Majesty extended royal favours to the aforesaid Sayyid and ordered that he should proceed to Kashmir in the company of Mīrzā Yūsuf Khān and others and see to it that the insurgents in Kashmir were subdued. His Imperial Majesty showed extraordinary interest in this mission and insisted on Mīrān Sayyid to undertake it, but he indicated his reluctance to do so on one pretext or the other. This earned him the displeasure of His Majesty who then ordered that he should proceed to Bengal to join Shahbāz Khān Kambū. A year later, when this Shahbāz Khān returned to pay a courtesy call at the Imperial Court and reached Ferozabad, the call from the unknown to return came to Mīrān Sayyid and he had no alternative but to respond. The chronogram containing the date of his death has been recorded in these verses:

[*verses*]

He was survived by three sons, namely, Mīrān Sayyid Ḥusain Khān, Mīrān Sayyid Shāh Abu'l-Ma'ālī and Mīrān Sayyid Ibrāhīm Khān. A mention of them has already been made in the earlier pages and, God willing, more about them shall follow.

Qāsim Khān liquidated

When Mīrān Sayyid refused to accept the assignment of His Majesty, Nawwāb Qāsim Khān became arrogant and high-handed towards Kashmiri commanders. This news was brought to His Majesty, who deputed Mīrzā Yūsuf Khān to govern Kashmir with the help of Bābā Khalīu'llah and Muḥammad Bhat. Muḥammad Bhat was a handsome person who was gifted with a noble disposition and a suave manner. People in those lands considered his appearance on the scene as nothing short of a boon. Through his efforts Lohar Chak, son of Bahrām Chak, and Ismā'īl Nāyak joined Yūsuf Khān while he was still on his way. The imperial troops entered the city without facing any resistance.

Resistance

On learning of this development, Ya'qūb Shāh, accompanied by Mīrān Sayyid Shāh Abu'l-Ma'ālī, Ibeh Khān, son of Abdāl Khān, and others moved to set up his headquarters in Kāthwār mountains, while Shamsi Chak, assisted by Shamsi Dooni and others, encamped in Poonch.

In the year A.H. 995 (A.D. 1586/87, Mīrzā, Yūsuf Khān occupied the seat of authority of this country, and with that Nawwāb Qāsim Khān was forced to proceed towards the imperial court along with some Kashmiri commanders, such as 'Alam Sher Khān.

The sagacious Muḥammad Mīr (?) Bhat soothed and encouraged the rank and tile of the Kashmiri troops by providing each one of them with a *jāgīr* commensurate with his rank. In this way, he brought them under his control and subordination, and induced them to take up arms against Ya'qūb Shāh and Mīrān Sayyid to an unimaginable extent.

Shamsi Chak's insurgence

With the onset of spring, Shamsi Chak and Shamsi Dooni came out of their dwelling places and began to fan the flames of chaos and disorder in Kashmir. Mīrzā Yūsuf Khān, taking notice of these developments, despatched Muḥammad Bhat and Sayyid Bahāu'd-Dīn and Kashmiri troops to deal with them. The aforesaid Sayyid marched his troops to the village of Nasu [*sic*] in Biru *pargana*. But Shamsi Chak and Shamsi Dooni took the initiative and, exhibiting remarkable bravery, made a night-assault on them in which Kashmiri soldiers [of Muḥammad Bhat] suffered severe reverses. On coming close to the tent of Mīr Sayyid Bahāu'd-Dīn, one of the brothers of the Sayyid dashed out of his tent barefooted and with his sword struck a blow on his enemy's horse, but only to slit the reins. The rider was rendered powerless but the horse in a bid to return to its stable, bore him away from that dangerous pit to the contiguous lands of Poonch. In this battle Kashmiri soldiers indulged in a large scale killing of each other. Shamsi Chak's troops withdrew to Poonch.

Muḥammad Bhat becomes vain

Muḥammad Mīr (?) Bhat came to Mīrzā Sayyid Yūsuf Khān along with the imperial troops. [The sentence after this is incomplete in the text and has not been translated.] On his advice, Mīrzā Sayyid Yūsuf Khān honoured each Kashmiri soldier with a befitting reward and induced them to fight against Ya'qūb Shāh.

Finding that the strategy of putting Shamsi Chak's soldiers to rout had worked well, Muḥammad Mīr (?) Bhat lost his head and began to make boastful claims. Ya'qūb Shāh and Mīrān Sayyid Abu'l-Ma'ālī came to know of Muḥammad Mīr (?) Bhat's vain utterances. It challenged their sense of honour and, dashing forth from Kāthwār mountains, they encamped at the village of Panjyārī (Penzyari) in Dachhanpara *pargana*. Mīrzā Yūsuf Khān received the news of their movement. He directed Muḥammad Bhat and Ḥājjī Mīrak, a renowned noble of his army, to lead a strong and well-equipped force to confront the enemy. A large number of horses was placed at their disposal; in addition to this, robes of honour and substantial amounts of cash were also given to them.

Muḥammad Bhat, accompanied by Ḥājjī Mīrak, took to guile and treachery and sent them conciliatory messages, completely disregarding his previous acquaintance with them. He hoped to take them unawares and, using all the means at his disposal, tried to make them his captives:

[*verses*]

Some of the warriors [of Ya'qūb Shāh] were taken in by his soft and conciliatory words and could not decide whether to join him or not. But Mīrān Sayyid Shāh Abu'l-Ma'ālī could read the writing on the wall. However, he responded to his overtures in an equally soft tone, using the sweetest of phrases. At the same time, he held consultations about how the impending serious threat could be warded off. His aids and commanders unanimously agreed to trust his authority, after the true spirit of the verse that "what you deem right is also right for us".[58]

Fighting breaks out

It was Mīrān Sayyid's considered opinion that a night halt was certainly fraught with the danger of their being made prisoners the next morning. He, therefore, resolved to trust in Providence and make a quick assault on the enemy:

[*verses*]

"Should the adventure succeed, our objective will be realized. If it does not, the story of our bravery will get imprinted on the book of the world."

Accepting this advice, Ya'qūb Shāh and his group of soldiers numbering nearly five hundred girded their loins and made a charge on the imperial army. On coming closer, they stopped for a while to assess the enemy's strength. By late afternoon, when about one-fourth of the day was still left. They clashed with the vanguard of the imperial army led by Muḥammad Mīr. In this fighting they displayed feats of extraordinary bravery. Their attack was so fierce that Muḥammad Mīr got unnerved and ran away from the battlefield along with his soldiers and joined the imperial army. In the course of fighting, Mīrān Sayyid Ibrāhīm Khān was wounded and fell from his horse. This incident diverted the attention of some of the commanders away from the

58. *ṣalāh-i mā hameh ānast kān turāst ṣalāh.*

battle for some time. But the sudden appearance of clouds on the sky which brought torrential rains as had never been witnessed before, led to suspension in fighting. Soldiers on either side retired to their camps or lodgings. Muḥammad Bhat levelled accusations against his troops and criticised them, and waited at his camp for two days.

Acting upon the silly advice of some incompetent persons, Ya'qūb Shāh moved away from his present position towards the *pargana* of Ular, with the purpose of raising troops. In the course of this shift in tactics, some of his soldiers, perhaps out of fear of the imperial army, deserted him and defected to Muḥammad Mīr. The remaining soldiers crossed the Lank Nay and arrived in the vicinity of the *pargana* of Ular at the village Nāristān to camp on the heights of the lofty mountain [of Naristan].

Abu'l-Ma'ālī captured

As against this, Muḥammad Bhat, commanding a large number of troops, took position on the slopes of the mountain of Nāristān. Fighting broke out in the early hours of the morning. Since the number of the imperial troops was very large and Ya'qūb Shāh had only a handful of troops at his disposal, it became obvious to him that resistance was futile as well as impossible. Ya'qūb Shāh, Mīrzā Ibrāhīm and Ibeh Khān managed to draw themselves away from that deadly place by their superb feats of archery and proceeded towards the mountains of Kāthwār. Mīrān Sayyid Abu'l-Ma'ālī held on obdurately to his position along with a small number of his men, fighting with their back to the wall.

The imperial troops, on noticing that there were not many soldiers with Mīrān Sayyid Shāh Abu'l-Ma'ālī, issued forth in groups from the top and the slopes of that mountain. Their strategy was to block the pathways. They gave them a hot pursuit up to the village Tsrār and people came out in multitudes and surrounded Mīrān Sayyid. At last he was made a captive and brought before Mīrzā Yūsuf Khān. Although on that day also he was unmistakably valorous and heroic, yet, since fate was not in his favour, he could not escape to a safe place:

[*verses*]

Abul'-Mu'ālī treated well

The aforesaid Mīrān Sayyid held a distinguished place among the warriors of this land because of his remarkable bravery and heroism. Besides, he was gifted with the qualities of honesty and integrity. Consequently, Mīrzā Yūsuf Khān considered the matter of his captivity as one of singular importance. He fully observed the established norms of respect and courtesy and, as a mark of due consideration to his dignity, took off his gorgeous gown – a gift from the Emperor – and put it on the shoulders of Mīrān Sayyid. Mīrzā Yūsuf Khān took care that not even the slightest reference was made to the events Which had occurred before this. A lodge was reserved for his dwelling.

Treatment of Kashmiri Commanders

Shamsi Chak and Shamsi Dooni came to know of these developments. They approached Sayyid Bahāu'd-Dīn for rapprochement and disposal of their cases. The Sayyid, gifted with prudence as he was, assuaged their fears by extending firm promises of his effective intervention in their case. In the course of his talk with Mīrzā Yūsuf Khān, he expressly mentioned to him the well-known principle of diplomacy that a formidable enemy should be won over by stratagem and his enmity neutralized by munificence:

[*verses*]

His clear suggestion to him was that Shamsi Chak and Shamsi Dooni be treated cordially so that they could be assured of their safety and security; it would result in their agreeing to enter the imperial service by presenting themselves before Mīrzā Yūsuf.

Mīrzā Yūsuf took his advice and promised to act in full conformity with it. Consequently, after securing fresh and reaffirmed commitments from him, Sayyid Bahāu'd-Dīn brought them to the presence of Mīrzā Yūsuf. Khān who, in turn, granted them funds, provided them with horses and, in the company of Sayyid Bahāu'd-Dīn, sent them out of their native land to the presence of His Majesty:

[*verses*]

His Majesty was disposed to deal leniently with them and treat them with kindness because they were foreigners. He allowed to each of them a rank (*manṣab*) commensurate with his status. As a result of the insinuations [of some malicious persons] and summons from Prince Salīm, Ibeh Khān, son of Abdāl Khān, a close associate of Ya'qūb Shāh, was made to part company with him. He came to Kashmir for a meeting with Mīrzā Yūsuf Khān and then brought himself to the presence of Prince Salīm.[59]

Subsequent to these events, Mīrzā Yūsuf Khān despatched Sayyid Ḥusain Khān Baihaqī, Alī Dār, Lohar Chak, son of Daulat Chak, Shamsi Chak, son of Lohar Chak, Ismā'īl Dooni, and others to the imperial capital as prisoners under military escort. His Majesty bestowed upon each a rank commensurate with his status. Some of them were granted higher ranks, while others had to rest content with the *aḥādī* rank.

Yūsuf Khān's malice

Soon after, Bahrām Nāyak, along with his sons, was poisoned. Saif Khān Baihaqī, 'Alī Khān of Dachhinpāra, Ibrāhīm

59. Ḥasan says that Ibeh Khān established contact with Prince Salīm. He severed relations with Ya'qūb Khān, and on the instance of Yūsuf Khān proceeded to Dehlī, where he became a courtier of Prince Salīm. *TḤK*, p. 429.

called Ibeh Shetān, the brother of Ḥaidar Chak, were deprived of their eyesight under various pretexts. Lohar Chak Qūrchī was sentenced to death.

Mīrzā Yūsuf Khān was greatly fascinated by the scenic beauty and invigorating climate of Kashmir. As a result, he began to implicate the nobles of that land in false and fabricated cases, and in this way found pretexts to do away with a few of them every day.[60]

When the affairs of the lands of Kashmir came to be shaped in accordance with the predetermined policy of the administration and a report analysing this situation was submitted to the Emperor,[61] the latter decided to make pleasure-trip to Kashmir by way of *tamāshā*. This land was honoured by the royal visit.[62] Ya'qūb Shāh, who was living in peace, pleasure and happiness along with his family at Kāthwār, without being disturbed by malicious persons, desired to enter the service of His Majesty. He was able to do so through the good offices of Mīrzā Yūsuf Khān, after making him agree to certain commitments and conditions and then came to the presence of the Emperor.

---

60. Invariably the chronicler piles up details without providing linkages of any kind. In this case; it seems the possible link between the two sentences is that Yūsuf Khān desired to continue staying on in Kashmir and, therefore, created conditions in which he could make himself look indispensable. That is why under various pretexts he started the policy of liquidating Kashmiri commanders.
61. In fact, Yūsuf Khān had proceeded to the imperial court leaving behind his brother Bāqir Khān in charge of Kashmir. His courtier, Ustā Lolo Najjār made Bāqir Khān apprehend an uprising and insurgency by the Kashmiri nobles. *TḤK*, p. 430.
62. It took place in A.D. 1587. For details regarding the route adopted by the royal entourage, repairs of bridges and hewing of boulders etc., see *Akbar Nāma*, Vol. III, p. 537 *et seq.* Akbar's arrival in Kashmir was an unprecedented pageant for Kashmiris who brought numerous presents to His Majesty.

Mīrzrā Yūsuf's intrigue

After this, the Emperor proceeded to Kabul and ordered Mīrzā Yūsuf Khān to accompany him, leaving behind his brother Shāh Bāqer in his place. Ustā Lolo, who was notorious for his villainy, was prompted by Mīrzā Yūsuf Khān to encourage Shāh Bāqer to place Mīrān Sayyid Shāh Abu'l-Ma'ālī, 'Alam Sher Khān, Lohar Chak and several others under detention till the return of Mīrzā Yūsuf Khān from Kabul, with the purpose of foiling attempts at creating disorder and disruption in the state:

[*verses*]

Acting upon the counsel of that depraved person, he got the above-mentioned persons imprisoned. A despatch was sent to the Emperor stating that Mīrān Sayyid Abu'l-Ma'ālī, 'Alam Sher Khān, Lohar Chak, Bahādur Khān and others were a source of disorder in Kashmir and, in order to deal effectively with the menace, it would be judicious to ask Mīrzā Yūsuf Khān to assume [rather resume] the governing authority of these lands as early as possible, otherwise Kashmir would be lost to the empire. On receiving this report, His Majesty forthwith permitted Mīrzā Yūsuf Khān to leave the imperial headquarters. Yūsuf Khān found development conducive to his larger interests and headed towards Kashmir in great hurry. Shortly after arriving in Kashmir, he released Mīrān Sayyid Shāh Abu'l-Ma'ālī from prison on the security furnished by Muḥammad Mīr, and sent him away to join the service of Rājā Mān Singh. 'Alam Sher Khān, Lohar Chak, Bahādur Khān and others were sent to the Imperial Court.[63]

Ustā Lolo's perfidy

Since most of the Kashmiri commanders were scattered and banished from the land, disorder and insurgence were

63. Yūsuf Khān Rizvī contrived to secure the orders of. His Majesty to return to Kashmir.

eliminated totally. Therefore, Muḥammad Mīr could not enjoy the confidence and respect of Mīrzā Yūsuf as he did earlier. In particular, the garrulous and glib-tongued Ustā Lolo, the prominent businessman of that land, because of his innate wickedness and his habit of fault-finding and selfishness, succeeded in vitiating Mīrzā Yūsuf Khān's impression about him:

[*verses*]

It was through this art of flattery and sycophancy that he made himself known to the Emperor who afterwards summoned him to his presence. His Majesty made detailed enquiries about all the happenings in Kashmir from him. In response to them, Ustā Lolo told him the stories of (Kashmir's) past, present and future[64] (?) kings in the form of a narrative, which made a good impression on the Emperor. Consequently, Ustā Lolo's prestige and stature increased day by day, so much so that the title *Nādirū'l-'Aṣr* meaning "the rarity of the age" was conferred upon him. Out of their innate nobility, Mīrzā Ya'qūb Khān and Muḥammad Mīr had confided in that base and malicious person. Taking him as one of their friends "the veil of duality between them had been lifted." Thinking that his knowledge of their affairs could help him in eliciting special favours from the Emperor, he reported to him about their affairs as well as true and false accounts of Mīrzā'i Yūsuf Khān's excesses in such an effective manner that His Majesty got annoyed with Mīrzā Yūsuf:[65]

[*verses*]

(Keeping company with a base person is like carrying a venomous snake under your arm).

---

64. This is quite an apparent error of logic.

65. *makun tā tawānī ba nājins mel*
chu mastī kih af'ī nihad dar baghal.

Prudence and sagacity demand that we act upon this principle so that we are safe against the treachery of a foe in a friend's garb.

Muḥammad Mīr summoned

In the course of these events, Shāh Mīrzā, the son of Mīr Badla, left for heavenly abode. His miraculous spiritual powers were known to people in these lands. He enjoyed full confidence of Mīrzā Yūsuf Khān and had been very close to him. He did everything possible to gain the friendship and affection of Muḥammad Mīr. His death has been recorded in the chronogram *Shāh Mīrzā maqbūl-i dargāh-i ilāh*.

Bābā Khalīl, who had acted as a surety to Muḥammad Mīr, too abandoned the prison house of this world. The chronogram *Khalīlu'r-Raḥmān* gives the date of his death. These events led to a decline in the prestige of Muḥammad Mīr. Ustā Lolo, the arch sycophant of his day, realized the extent of disintegration which Bābā Khalīl's death was likely to cause to the government of Mīr Muḥammad. He secretly reported to the Emperor that it was Bābā Khalīlu'llah who had exercised a restraining influence over Muḥammad Mīr in his efforts to foment trouble in Kashmir. Now that Bābā Khalīl was dead, Muḥammad Mīr was likely to create disturbances. It would, therefore, be in the fitness of things and in the interests of the state that Muḥammad Mīr was summoned to the imperial court so that the chances of his instigating trouble in the country were eliminated.

In this way Muḥammad Mīr was summoned to the imperial court. Some time later, he worked in league with Mīrzā Yūsuf Khān to incite Ibeh Shāh, Lohar Chak, brother of Shamsi Chak, and Ḥusain Wulu (Dulu ?) to proceed to Kashmir, for the purpose of creating trouble and work towards disruption of law and order and to Spread discord among various sections of people in such a way that they would clash with one another. He thought that such a situation would lead the Emperor to recall Yūsuf Khān and enable himself to assume their earlier positions of administering the realm of Kashmir. This group of foolish people acted upon their promptings and left for Kashmir.

Tables turned

They came to the house of 'Alī Raina, the landlord of Bartal. This 'Alī Raina behaved without any sense of gratitude; acted without generosity, and considerateness; ignored the obligations of kinship and loyalty, and took recourse to wickedness. He handed them over to the agents of Mīrzā Yūsuf Khān. They begged for their release saying that they had come in these lands under the instructions of Mīrzā Yūsuf Khān, but their entreaties were of no avail. On the contrary, their explanation recoiled on them, because the agents took these words to be an attempt at defaming Mīrzā Yūsuf Khān. Thereupon, without the slightest hesitation and without wasting time, [they ordered that] their heads be severed from their bodies:

[*verses*]

On his way to Lahore, 'Alī Raina, as a consequence of this wicked deed, was afflicted with some malignant disease and died an ignoble death so much so that no one undertook to give him a burial:

Muḥammad Mīr's intrigue

Thus Muḥammad Mīr's expectations about the outcome of his intrigue were frustrated. As a result of this, he resumed his activities of creating disruption in Kashmir. He sent Yūsuf Khān Kashmiri to those lands to serve the aforesaid purpose so that the Emperor would be constrained to send them back to govern Kashmir. This was the plan they drew up secretly. Accordingly, Yūsuf Khān set out from the capital city of Lahore towards Kashmir, but the powerful stars of the Emperor forced him to retrace his steps.[66] This news was conveyed to the Emperor but, as he was disposed kindly towards his subjects, he overlooked his crime and did not punish him. Ya'qūb Shāh was also implicated in this matter. But, because His Majesty had entered into some agreement with him and made some commitments, Ya'qūb Shāh continued to be at the imperial court.[67] However, escorted by Ḥasan Beg Turkmān, he was brought to the presence of Rājā Mān Singh to join his father Yūsuf Shāh.

Ḥasan Beg's narrow escape

In this way, instigated by some base and unwise people and with the consent of his brother, Ya'qūb Shāh, Mīrzā Ibrāhīm took advantage of the opportunity and dealt a blow with his sword on the head of Ḥasan Beg Turkmān. Ḥasan Beg was a man of genial disposition and fair in his intentions. With God's protection, not even a hair of his head was touched: his alert soldiers sprang at Mīrzā Ibrāhīm and slew him on the spot:

[*verses*]

This incident made Ya'qūb Shāh immensely dejected. He was overwhelmed by despondency and repented sorely over what had came to pass. Ḥasan Beg took notice of his condition and was moved to compassion. Securing him from any reprisals or hostile action against him on the way. Ḥasan Beg brought him safely to Jonāpūr. But before releasing him from detention, he obtained a surety from Yūsuf Shāh [of his

66. Also see *TḤK*, p. 436.

66. This sentence is rather evasive because as it is the stars of the Emperor could have no effect on him. The chronicler seems to suppress some vital information.

67. It has not been able to find out the terms of agreement between Akbar and Ya'qūb Shāh.

safe conduct]. Later on he was sent to enter the services of Rājā Mān Singh at Rohtās.

Yūsuf Shāh's character

While these things were happening, let us have a look at Yūsuf Shāh. He was gifted with qualities of generosity and charitableness to such an extent that whatever in the shape of cash, kind, gold, robes, ornaments, etc. caught his eye, he gifted it away lavishly and unhesitatingly. Those who were not aware of his innate generosity, attributed it to his mental derangement. After the conquest of Orissa on Tuesday, the sixth of the month of Dhu'l-Ḥijja, he took ill shortly after sunrise and, on Wednesday, on the fourteenth day of the same month in the year A.H. 1000 (A.D. 1591), when about three quarters of night had passed, he surrendered his soul to God:

[*verses*]

The dead body of Yūsuf Shāh was removed by Mīrān Sayyid Shāh Abu'l-Ma'ālī from Jagarnāth – a town abounding in icons and idols – with such elaborate ceremonies as would befit magnificent kings and masters of equipage and large retinues. The entire journey was covered in two months and, on each day, alms and charities, food and *sherbet* were distributed among the poor and the destitute. On Sunday, the 23rd of the month of Rabī'u'l-Awwal, in the late afternoon his mortal remains were buried in the *pargana* of Bisnak[68] in Bihār. A spacious garden was laid out adjoining his grave and a deep well lined with baked bricks was also dug near it. The date of his death has been found in the chronogram *Yūsuf Shāh mord faryād.*

Ya'qūb poisoned

When Yūsuf Shāh left this transient world for the everlasting abode, Rājā Mān Singh bestowed great attention upon his

68. Present-day Biswak in Bihar.

son, Ya'qūb Shāh. He conferred upon him the *jāgīr* and the rank of his late father. This arrangement continued for more than a year, After that His Imperial Majesty summoned Rājā Mān Singh to his august presence. On the eve of his departure to the imperial court – the meeting place of the choicest of men of the day – two persons of criminal disposition who still bore on their foreheads the dark marks of servitude to Yūsuf Shāh, hatched a conspiracy against Ya'qūb Shāh. They made a submission to Rājā Mān Singh that leaving Ya'qūb Shāh in that part of the country with freedom of movement amounted to letting a bird out of the cage or a falcon out of one's clutches. They suggested to him that Ya'qūb Shāh should at least be interned so that he was rendered incapable of returning to his native land and hunt birds there:

[*verses*]

Rājā Mān Singh was alarmed by this possibility and detained Ya'qūb Shāh in the fort of Rohtās. Some time later, Rājā Mān Singh was permitted to leave the imperial court for Rohtās. Meanwhile the afore-mentioned detestable and accursed persons once again conspired to put an end to the lie of Ya'qūb Shāh. They made Qāsim Khān an accomplice in their crime, who had been known as an illegitimate son of Yūsuf Shāh. As a punishment for his hideous deeds in the past, (Qāsim Khān) had served a year's term at imprisonment under the orders of the Emperor. It was Rājā Mān Singh who had interceded for him at that time and secured the orders of his release from prison. The truth is that he was the offspring of a butcher. As he was depraved and inherently wicked. Qāsim Khān took the initiative to realize his objective and waited for a suitable opportunity.

On the eve of Rājā Mān Singh's arrival in the fort of Rohtās, the two malicious persons accompanied his troops in those regions. Ya'qūb Shāh sought the permission of the

Rājā to proceed on a pleasure trip to his *jāgīr* and the town of Bhera. Out of courtesy he dropped at Qāsim Khān's residence to take his leave. The treacherous villain, taking advantage of this opportunity, offered him a few betel leaves, one of which concealed deadly poison. Offering of a betel leaf was in accordance with the custom prevailing among the people in those lands. With his sinful hands, Qāsim Khān selected this very poisonous leaf for him and, simulating affection, kinship and special regard, he made him accept it. After accepting the betel leaf, Yaqūb Shāh took leave of his murderer and returned to his lodging. Soon after he could feel the effect of poison spreading in his body. A few days later, on reaching the town of Bhera, the colour of his face changed to deep blue. On the eighth day of Muharram, A.H. 1001 (A.D. 1592), he breathed his last:

[*verses*]

On learning of this tragic event, Rājā Mān Singh despatched Qāsim Khān to those regions with the purpose of informing and consoling the survivors of the bereaved family. Mān Singh was under the impression that Qāsim Khān, being the next of kin, and one of the members of the bereaved family, would be the proper person to be entrusted with this missions. But this ungodly (*Khudā nā-tars*) fellow joined hands with some abominable wretches to hatch more conspiracies. He subjected Ya'qūb Shāh's offspring to harassment and victimization in many ways. Household effects, property, gold and ornaments, all that was left with his legitimate queen was seized and taken possession of by him. There was none at the court of Rājā Mān Singh who gave any attention to their grievances.

The death of a noble father and his illustrious son was a tragedy of great magnitude for their compatriots. Eventually Mīrān Sayyid Shāh Abu'l-Ma'ālī, who was their kinsman, besides also having affectionate relationship with the household, brought the dead body of Ya'qūb Shāh to the *pargana* of Bisnak to be buried by the side of his father, Let benign God forgive his sins.

Murderer's fate

Subsequent to these events, and after a lapse of about three or four years, that rascal of a man fell a victim to the wrath of the Wrathful (God) and two carbuncles, horrible to look at, appeared in his armpit and in his anus. On account of acute pain he could not move about for nearly a year. Though he applied ointment to the ulcers, it seemed as if some invisible power made the medicine ineffective; and, in fact, made the sores more putrid. Out of repentance he spoke before everybody, high and low, all that he had done and made no attempt to conceal his feelings of regret and sorrow. The disease, finally, proved fatal. At present he remains buried at the village of Tanda in the province of Bengal:

[*verses*]

Ya'qūb's death-scene

It has been said that prior to his death by poisoning, Ya'qūb Shāh once suffered amoebic dysentery because of his excessive use of narcotics like opium. The Indian physicians took no interest in curing him of this disease: They neither touched his body, nor went anywhere near his bed. But, despite that, Ya'qūb Shāh did not let despondency overpower him. He emphatically declared that his departing hour had not come. "It will be the Friday of Muḥarram, the day of martyrdom of Ḥusain, the son of 'Alī. At that time none of my true and affectionate friends should shed tears or lament my death. They should rejoice just as a friend rejoices on meeting his friend, because there goes the saying that "death is the bridge that links a friend with a friend."

After he was poisoned, Ya'qūb Shāh found that the symptoms of death had begun to appear and with that he lost hope of his recovery, which led his friends and dear ones to utter loud cries of distress and agony. But he slightly blinked and held his tongue between his teeth – obviously in alarm and to express his disapproval of the lamenting and sobbing going on around him: he even spoke loudly against it. Then he closed his eyes once again. Mīrān Sayyid Shāh Abu'l-Ma'ālī quickly placed his one hand on his face and the other on his chin and managed to release his tongue from his closed jaw. He poured a few drops of *sherbet* down his throat. With that "the bird of his soul winged away from the cage of his body and made its lasting nest on the branches of the lote-tree (*sadreh*) in Paradise."

[*verses*]

Kashmiri nobility breaks

Briefly speaking, the sagacious Muḥammad Mīr, who bore Ya'qūb Shāh's unlimited affection was subjected to much harassment by the cunning Ustā Lolo and Firāq Kashmiri. Unable to withstand these shocks, he soon followed Ya'qūb Shāh to the other world.

[*verses*]

Thus the nobles of Kashmir were completely wiped out. The aforesaid Ustā Lolo made a submission to His Majesty that Kashmir could provide large revenue to the imperial treasury. If a revenue officer were appointed by His Majesty to make proper assessment, the possibilities of an increase in revenue could be reported to him. This resulted in the deputation of Ḥasan bin Shaykh 'Umarī and Qāḍī 'Alī, the renowned revenue experts in the cadre of the imperial government, to Kashmir. According to the instructions from the imperial court, they came to Kashmir where they formulated their own system of levy and collection of revenue which were in the interests of the governing machine.[69] They harassed and oppressed the people in many ways. Eventually the people were forced to join Mīrzā Yādgār, the brother of Mīrzā Yūsuf Khān, and give a tough fight to Ḥasan Beg Shaykh 'Umarī, who was routed and overpowered, and he suddenly found himself cut off from his friends and supporters. Bare-footed and without a headgear, he wended his way through narrow and tortuous paths till he reached in the presence of Rājā Rājpāl. Qāḍī 'Alī was slain in the vicinity of Kamelna [*sic*] fort and Mīrzā Yādgār was installed in the seat of government of that land.

Yādgār killed

The news of these detestable actions reached the Emperor who, followed by his victorious legions, set out to conquer that country. When. Mīrzā Yādgār came to know of this, he marched out of the city of Kashmir (Srinagar) and after ensuring the security of Konehbal route, took up position in the village Hirpur. But suddenly, under some divine dispensation, as also under the good fortune of the king, Ibrāhīm Khān Ghakkar and. Sāro Beg Turkmān, two employees of Yūsuf Khān and presently in Mīrzā Yādgār's combat forces, found an opportunity, during the hours they were keeping watch, to assassinate Mīrzā Yādgār. On account of the resultant chaos, most of his field commanders like Mīr Muḥammad, Bahādur Malik, son of Idī Raina, and many others ran away in confusion in different directions The army of that land could no longer remain united and the soldiers were reduced to such a state of demoralisation that,

69. Ḥasan writes that two revenue officers registered free lands as state-owned and decided to make cash payment of allowances to soldiers on account of fodder for their horses. This caused dissatisfaction to those who were in the habit of misappropriating state lands because they could not continue their corrupt practices. See *TḤK*, p. 436.

in order to earn their livelihood, they had to approach the *jāgīrdārs* for service.

Mutch Bhavan episode

Muḥibb 'Alī was one of the officials of Yūsuf Khān who had been assigned military duties in the *pargana* of Dachhanpāra and Khovurpāra. He had made solemn promises and commitments to a group of local soldiers who had entered his service; he brought them collectively to *Mutch Bhavan*[70] spring under the pretext of recording their identity, and then put them all to the sword. In this way the blood of Musalmans was shed like the gushing waters of *Mutch Bhavan* spring. This is how he (Muḥibb 'Alī) invited perpetual torture in the world hereafter in return for petty gains of the base material world.

Lohar Chak killed

After this event, Qāsim Khān Namgi [*sic*], on the advice of some local people, extended many promises and pledges of renewed friendship to Lohar Chak and his brothers and sons, and making them forget their sins and faults, brought them to his presence from Drāv [*sic*] and then, ignoring his pledges and promises, had the whole group assassinated in the town of Sopor:

[*verses*]

After this event, Ḥusain Chak, son of Shamsi Chak of Kupwāra, in collusion with some people of the borders of Kashmir, killed Jalīl Beg. But later, through the treachery of Mullā Jamīl Beg who gave him a false sense of security, he was lured into entering the service of Yūsuf Khān; Thus, without apprehending danger, Lohar Chak entered his service. He even forgot what Muḥibb 'Alī did (at *Mutch Bhavan*) and entertained no fears in his mind. At last, Mullā

70. Ancient *Matsya-Bhavan*. See *Akbar Nāma*, Vol. III, p. 1084n.

Jamīl found his opportunity, and in the village of Regipora "levelled his enemies to dust." Prior to it, Ḥusī Chak had died in an accident: he fell from his horse in the course of *shikar* and then never rose again.

Chaks vanquished

Shamsi Chak, son of Daulat Chak, died in the province of the Deccan and his grave is at Burhanpore. His sons, Ḥusain Chak and Zafar Khān, became sorely distressed and were almost out of their mind on account of the circumstances in which their kinsmen perished one after the other. And since they had been pining for the bracing climate of Kashmir, they left Hindustan and came to dwell in the highlands of Kāmarāj and Marāj where they lived by lifting cattle and plundering the crops of local peasants.

Tibetan involvement

After the death of Emperor (Akbar), the crown passed on to Jahāngīr Pādshāh. Ibeh Khān, son of Ḥusain Khān, son of Ibeh Shāh, Ḥusain Chak, Zafar Khān and several others, in collusion with the governor of Tibet, whom they had persuaded to give them military assistance, raised a banner of rebellion against the imperial forces in the *pargana* of Lār, which continued for two months. By then the governor of Tibet found that they were disunited which made him change his mind. Besides he also found them overtaken by sloth, and he retreated to Tibet.[71]

The group involved in the insurrection continued to be defiant at Sherkot,[72] flirting with the idea of carving out an independent province for themselves. They became vain and indulged in rapacious activities, such as looting and

71. For details, see *Ain-i-Akbari*, Vol. III, pp. 823-24.
72. Now Bābā Shakūru'd-Dīn hill-top between Khuihāma and Sopor. In ancient times, Rājā Prāhlād had built the Prateśwara temple here. It was called Bosangari. See *TḤK*, p. 226.

plundering houses, property, cattle and belongings of the peasants, and squandered their ill-gotten wealth in orgies of drink and dissipation. This resulted in a famine and dearness in that part of the land to an unimaginable extent. These people became totally indifferent to the presence of the imperial troops in their neighbourhood. Thus unmindful of the realities of the situation, they perpetrated acts of brigandage to their hearts' content.

'Alī Khān's fate

The imperial troops had been biding time. When the opportunity came their way they rushed out of Sopor and attacked them on a dark night while they lay in deep slumber. Many of them were slain and their severed heads were sent to Kashmir [Srinagar] in a boat where they were piled up like a minaret to serve a warning to other insurgents.

Later on 'Alī Khān, son of Ḥusain Khān, sent Ibeh Shāh and Ḥusain Chak towards the borders of Kāmarāj on the principle that "two swords cannot be accommodated in one scabbard." Ḥusain Chak thought it expedient to adapt a conciliatory attitude towards 'Alī Khān for he could read the writing on the wall. Proud of his bravery, 'Alī Khān, along with a body of ـٮـٮـ (illeg.) called on Ḥusain Chak to bid him farewell. But Ḥusain Chak seized the opportunity and slew the whole group of soldiers accompanying him. 'Alī Khān was taken prisoner and handed over to the imperial troops. But as he was being carried there, the Imāghāts[73] came to know of the incident and put an end to his life in the village of Denwārī. In order to chastise the Imāghāts, Zafar Khān sent a contingent of foot soldiers and horsemen there and made a night-assault on them in the *pargana* of Aedwan, leading to fighting and killing between them in the village of

73. Imaghan in *pargana* Aedwan. This *pargana* was rehabilitated by Rājā Swarna (1245 *Loukika*) in which he ordered the digging of a canal called *Sonehman*. See *TḤK*, p. 72 and 447.

Door. A large number of Kashmiri soldiers on the side of Zafar Khān perished and he himself sustained wounds which forced him to abandon fighting and flee towards the jungle in the *pargana* of Bīrū.

Jahāngīr's governors

This event was followed by the death of Muḥammad Qulī, the Governor of Kashmir, who had endeared himself to the people of that land. He was succeeded by 'Alī Akbar Shāhī[74] whose appointment was made under the orders of Jahāngīr Pādshāh. In the beginning, he took recourse to flattery, deception, and cunning and, through the instrumentality of Qāḍī Ṣāleh, extended many promises and pledges to Zafar Khān, but with no sincere intentions. He told him that Muḥammad Qulī and his former officials had committed acts of maltreatment and rascality on the basis of religion. "But since I am a staunch Sunni and you too are one, God forbid that even the slightest act of ill-will prejudicial to your interests should occur from my side," he said. In confirmation of this statement he swore by the name of venerable Four Friends[75] as well as the Companions of the Prophet of Islam.

Thus, through deception and perfidy, he brought that group of people to his presence, and got them arrested with the connivance of Mullā Jamīl Beg. This was followed by a policy of mass punishment in the city. All those people who came across their way – soldiers, landowners, artisans, weavers, and others – from dawn to noon were butchered. Ten days later, Zafar Khān and seventeen young nobles were released from prison and handed over to Ḥātem Khān the landlord, who, in turn, despatched them to the other

74. For details see *TḤK*, p, 450n, and Ma'āthiru'l-Umarā, Vol. III, pp. 355-57.

75. Four chosen companions of Prophet Muḥammad, viz. Abū Bakar, 'Umar, 'Uthmān and 'Alī.

world. At the time of his death, Zafar Khān repeated the content of the verses:

[*verses*]

Ḥabīb Khān, son of Ḥusain Khān, was killed by Ḥusain Nāyak. Yūsuf Chak was placed in the custody of Ya'qūb Shāh only to perish after suffering a number of privations and tortures. Alī Khān, son of Yūsuf Khān, got Nowroz Chak killed by the son of Ḥātem Khān.

Chaks liquidated

In short, all those seven budding youngsters who had yet to taste the fruits of life in the garden of this treacherous world, were totally uprooted by its pestilential gusts. They [the kinsfolk of Chaks] were humiliated and deprived of their name and identity, and forced to live a vagrant life in the streets and lanes of the locality of Raināwarī. No one was even permitted to bury them [when dead]. However, the inhabitants of the locality, in order to avoid the stench of their putrid corpses, removed them to a potter's kiln in the neighbourhood, and concealed them under mud and dust. The spheres mourned the tragic end of those people by shedding tears in the shape of torrential rain and by giving out loud laments of lashing thunderbolts, so-much-so that it appeared like the clarion sound of Isrāfīl calling the dead to rise:

Sher Afghan[76]

Ibeh Khān, son of Abdāl Khān, was one of the warriors of that land. On the eve of Jahāngīr Pādshāh's accession to the throne, he proceeded to his *jāgīr* at Burdwan under orders of the Emperor. A brave man, Sher Afghan by name, was a former *jāgīrdār* now living in comfort at that place.

---

76. For more details about the story of Sher Afghan's killing see *Tuzak-i-Jahāngīrī*, p. 55, *TMḤ*, MS f. 95 and *TḤK*, pp. 462 *et seq.*

Quṭbu'd-Dīn Khān, the Governor of the province of Bengal, had, as a sequel to his disagreement with and jealously towards that gallant man, reported to the Emperor that all the people in Bengal except Sher Afghan have submitted to the authority of His Majesty. Whatever orders there were from His Majesty about him [Sher Afghan] would be carried out by him unhesitatingly. Forthwith orders were issued by the Emperor that Sher Afghan's head be severed from his body and sent to the imperial court. On receiving these orders, Quṭbu'd-Dīn proceeded to confront that brave man along with a contingent of two thousand soldiers. In spite of suspecting danger to his life, he [Sher Afghan] came out of his fort along with seventy or eighty horsemen to receive the governor formally. He had hardly come close to them when he understood the suspicious movement of Quṭbu'd-Dīn's troops and was convinced that their only intention was to kill him. Meanwhile the mahaut of Quṭbu'd-Dīn manoeuvred his exasperated elephant in such a manner that Sher Afghan's horse took fright and got out of control. Consequently, Sher Afghan was forced to be on guard. He addressed Quṭbu'd-Dīn in these words: "You commander of the Khāns, what do you mean by this move?" The aforesaid evaded a direct reply. Thereupon Sher Afghan's companions spoke to him reproachfully in the Turkish language: "If there is anything of manliness and bravery left in you, what other occasion would you seek to put these to test?" On hearing these words, the brave man mustered heroic strength and made an assault on Sher Afghan. But with the first stroke of his sword, Sher Afghan chopped off his arm from his shoulder. The next stroke pierced his belly letting his entrails drop down in a lump. Thus ended the life of Quṭbu'd-Dīn.

The next man who advanced to cross swords with him was Ḥaidar Malik Chādūra. He too sustained a wound in that battle and looked round to run for his life. Ibeh Khān, son of Abdāl Khān, saw what was happening; he summoned his manliness and spurred his horse towards the pit. The two warriors came close to one another. On account of the presence of elephants on the battlefield, the horses of both the warriors found it rather difficult to stick to their positions. They were compelled to dismount and began fighting each other. Ibeh Khān, son of Abdāl, took the lead and inflicted a blow on Sher Afghan's face, cutting open half of his skull. But that valiant warrior, mustering whatever life and strength was left in him, made a counter-attack in which he embedded his sword like a spike in the belly of Ibeh Khān resulting in his instantaneous death. But Sher Afghan too died at the same time. The grave of Ibeh Khān is to be found beside the tomb of Bahrām Saqqā in the village of Burdwān.

Yūsuf Khān's fate

Five to six months later, Yūsuf Khān, son of Ḥusain Shāh, once mounted a she-elephant and proceeded on a stag hunt in Salīm Ābād area. But as God willed it, all of a sudden a wild and detestable buffalo appeared almost from nowhere on that hunting ground and made a violent charge on the elephant which, while fleeing, hurtled down its rider in the dense forest. He became a game for the brute and was killed.

In short, the nobles of this land could not be rescued either by friends or by luck from the whirlpool of death in India, and the sun of their career went down westward, faraway in the horizon of oblivion:

[*verses*]

A few incidents pertaining to the commanders of that land, such as Ḥusain Khān, son of Yūsuf Shāh, and others have not been recorded for being unwieldy for this brief account.

Aspersions on Governors

In short, such odious deeds resulted from Mīrzā 'Alī Akbar Shāhī's ill-advised statesmanship in this land that a group of supplicants, seeking redress of their grievances, were forced to recount these to the courtiers of Jahāngīr. The Emperor became displeased and objected [to his misdeeds]. Mīrzā ‘Alī Akbar Shāhī was dismissed as Governor of that land and the office passed on to Nawwāb Qalīj Khān. The administration of the State of Kashmir was entrusted to Ḥaidar Malik Chādūra and he was given freedom to run its affairs as he desired fit, so that people in Kashmir were meted out justice and equity under imperial rule. They were thus liberated from the onslaughts of their oppressors.

Ḥaidar Malik eulogised

Ḥaidar Malik took special care for the development and progress of these lands. He turned his attention to the economy of the country in a way that eatables like foodgrains, pulses, etc., were made available to the rich and the poor in plenty. The title of *Chaghatāī* was conferred on him. He undertook the onerous task of ensuring public welfare and providing efficient administration to common people as well as the nobles of the land:

[*verses*]

In the course of these events, Rājā Mān Singh died on the seventh of Jumāda al-Ukhrā in the year [*sic*]. The chronogram commemorating the event of his death runs as this [illegible].

Abu’l-Ma‘ālī’s assignment

Mīrān Sayyid Abu’l-Ma‘ālī was in the service of Rājā Mān Singh for twenty-four years during the reign of Akbar. During this period he exhibited extraordinary feats of bravery, which is an inherent trait in the noble clan of Hāshimites. He took active part in numerous battles fought against the enemies of His Imperial Majesty, from which he always emerged victorious with the grace of God. He lived his days in comfort and pleasure enjoying trust and respect [of the Emperor] to a remarkable extent. After the death of Akbar, he, along with Ḥaidar Malik, came to present himself before Emperor Jahāngīr.

Through his perceptive genius, Jahāngīr Pādshāh found in Mīrān Sayyid Shāh Abu'l-Ma'ālī merit and ability, bravery and dauntlessness and, therefore, extended to him special royal favours by conferring a high rank on him. He was allowed a *jāgīr* along with Sayyid Ibrāhīm Khān in the *sirkār* of Sindh and was permitted to proceed thither.[77]

Mīrān Sayyid, himself a man of parts, conducted himself towards the learned men of Thatta in such a commendable way that they loved him more than their own selves. They considered his arrival in that land as nothing short of a providential boon and a blessing. The date of his arrival in the *sirkār* of Thatta has been found in the chronogram *abr-i raḥmat āmad nāgehān*.

[*verses*]

The chronogram recording the date of completion of this chronicle is *Nāmeh-e Shāhan-i Kashmir*.

77. After the death of Rājā Mān Singh, Mīrān Sayyid came to Kashmir and was approached by many members of Chak clan. But 'Etiqād Khān, the Mughal governor, sent him to His Majesty who ordered him to go to Sindh where he was provided a *jāgīr* of twenty-five thousand rupees. *TḤK*, p. 481. This seems to be another example of Mughal diplomacy.

Afterword

I am happy to write this Afterword for a new edition of Kashi Pandit's translation of *Bahāristān-i-Shahī*. It takes me back to those good old days when Pandit and I spent months at his place in the Bal Garden locality of Srinagar on readying the manuscript of *Bahāristān* for its first printing. It is a valuable work for understanding the chequered history of Kashmir, especially the advent of the Muslim rule there. Pandit's "Translation Methodology" testifies to his meticulous attention to the art of translation and the "Introduction" confirms his sound grip over the period covered in it.

Before Kashi Pandit's translation was published for the first time from Calcutta in 1990, students of history could access *Bahāristān* only as a manuscript, and that too if they knew the Persian language. Because of this, accounts of the Muslim intrusion into Kashmir, particularly about the manner in which the Muslim faith was propagated there, which claimed reliability on the basis of their grounding in *Bahāristān* were accepted by most of their readers without demur. The excellently annotated English translation of *Bahāristān* provides readers the opportunity to examine the reliability of such accounts.

A brief example from a history related to the subject by Ishaq Khan will clarify this. Khan's main thesis is that the conversions of Hindus to the new faith were the result of the good work done by the Sufis, which did not necessitate any use of force. Since *Bahāristān* is one of the key texts that provide vital information regarding the issue, Khan makes several references to it but overlooks the details related to the spread of the Muslim faith in Kashmir.

Bahāristān records the visit of Sayyid Ali Hamadani to Kashmir during the reign of Sultan Qutbu'd-Din. When Hamadani found that the king had two wives, who were uterine sisters, he told him to divorce one of them and enter into a proper marriage contract with the other. He also advised him to wear a proper Muslim dress, to set an example for his subjects. The king accepted his advice and built a *khanqah* (hospice) for him for offering prayers. *Bahāristān* also mentions that "at the site where the *khanqah* was built, there existed a small temple that was demolished and converted into an estrade on which he offered *namaz* (prayer) five times a day and recited portions of the Quran morning and evening." Destroying a temple to raise a *khanqah* (hospice) for offering prayer is an act of vandalism that does not fit Khan's thesis of *rishi* culture.

Khan builds his thesis by making a selective use of details from *Bahāristān.* He uses information from it to show that Sayyid Muhammad was given a warm welcome by Sultan Sikandar and how grand and dignified he looked. The sentence that follows this is ignored by him, because it does not suit his purpose. It reads: "To him [Sayyid Muhammad] goes the credit of wiping out the vestiges of infidelity and heresy from the mirror of the conscience of the dwellers of these lands." And, further, the Sultan "proved his loyalty to him by translating his words into deeds. He eradicated aberrant practices and infidelity." *Bahāristān* also mentions "how Sultan Sikandar and Saifu'd-Din [the converted name of Suha Bhat], God bless them both, joined hands to gear their full efforts towards the eradication of infidelity and other aberrant practices... They were rewarded with victories wherever they led their armies, confirming the saying that "God helps those who help Muhammad's religion." *Bahāristān* describes the Sultan as "idol-breaker," which clearly suggests what he must have done to earn that epithet.

Because of the overwhelming evidence of what Sikandar did to please his mentor, Khan admits at one place that one cannot deny that some temples were destroyed during his reign, but softens it up with two qualifiers, which only show how weak his thesis is. He bails out the king by stating that his actions were "more as a result of the abetment on the part of the zealous, high-ranking convert to Islam," for which *Bahāristān* does not provide any evidence. When he states that "the evidence regarding the construction of a Shiva temple with a golden *linga* by the Sultan's wife Shobha Devi, should not be lost sight of," Khan fails to see the difference between the demands of a state policy and conjugal tact. That the king allowed his wife to have a temple of her choice hardly means that the responsibility that the Sayyid had put on him would in any way be lessened.

In his introduction, Pandit states that *Bahāristān* contains several references to another Persian history *Toḥfatu'l-Aḥbāb.* Since he found that it provided a detailed account of the manner in which Muslim faith was firmly planted in the Valley, he translated that manuscript too, which is now available in English as *A Muslim Missionary in Medieval Kashmir.*

The two translations have proved invaluable for the students of medieval history, for they clarify vital issues regarding the spread of Islam in Kashmir. In his scholarly Introduction to *Toḥfatu'l-Aḥbāb*, Kashi Pandit also explains how many people in Kashmir, and even outside Kashmir, have a wrong impression about Sufis, that they are pious people who use only persuasive and peaceful methods for meeting their religious obligations. Pandit has shown that they are also ruthless and brutal in their drive for propagating Islamic faith.

I am sure this new printing of *Bahāristān* will stimulate students of medieval history to rethink what has already been written about the time that it deals with. Perhaps because of that Pandit has dedicated the English translation of *Tohfatu'l Ahbab* to the historians who specialize in writing on Medieval India.

Tej N. Dhar

Bibliography

A Gazetteer of Kashmir, Bates, C.E., Calcutta, 1873.

A Literary History of Persia, Browne, E.G., 4 vols. London, 1902-1924.

Āin-i-Akbari, Abu'l-Faḍl, vol. I, tr. Blochmann, Calcutta, 1927. Vol. II & III tr. Jarett, Calcutta, 1948-49.

Akbar-Nāma, Abu'l-Faḍl, tr. Beveridge, H., 3 vols. Calcutta, 1897-1939.

Bahāristāhī-i-Shāhī, Anon. MS.

(a) I.O. 509.

(b) Br. Museum Add 16, 706.

(c) Transcript copy RPD. Acc. No. 691.

Bühler's Report (*Tour in search of Sanskrit MSS*), Bühler G., R.A.S.B., Bombay, 1877, RPD Acc. No. 2080.

Central Asiatic journal, No. II (3), London, 1956.

Dāiratu'l-Ma'ārif-i-lslāmī, vol. X, Lahore, 1973.

J.B.R.A.S., London, 1861.

Kings of Kashmir, Dutt, J.C., 3 vols., Calcutta, 1879-98.

Kashmir, Sufi, G.M.D., Lahore, 1942.

Kashmir under the Sulṭāns, Moḥibbu'l-Ḥasan, Calcutta, 1959.

Kashmir Polity, Drabu, V.N., New Delhi, 1986.

J.A.S.B., 1854, xxiii.

Muntakhabu't-Tawārīkh, 'Abdu'l-Qādir Badāuni, 3 vols., tr. Ranking, Low and Haig, Calcutta, 1884-1925.

Muntakhabu'l-Tawārikh, Narayan Koul 'Ājiz, MS, RPD Acc. No. 934, 11931.

Majmu'-at-Tawārikh, Birbal Kāchroo, MS, RPD. Acc. No. 130.

Rājataraṅgiṇī, Kalhan Pandit, 2 vols. tr. Stein, M.A., London, 1900.

Tabaqāt-i-Akbari, Niẓāmu'd-Dīn Badakhshi, 3 Vols., tr. Dey, B., Calcutta, 1927-35.

Tārīkh-i-Firishta, 4 vols., tr. Briggs, J., Calcutta, 1808-10.

Tārīkh-i-Ḥasan, Pir Ghulam Ḥasan, 2 vols., Srinagar, 1954.

Tārīkh-i-Malik Ḥaidar, Malik Ḥaidar Chādūra, MS RPD Acc. No. 39.

Tārīkh-i-Rashīdī, Mīrzā Ḥaidar Dughlat, tr. Ross, E.D. and Elias No., London, 1895.

Tārīkh-i-Sayyid, 'Alī, Sayyid 'Alī, MS RPD Acc. No. 739.

The Cambridge History of India, vol. III, ed. Haig. Wolseley, New Delhi, 1958.

The Rājataraṅgiṇi of Jonarāja, ed. Śrikanth Koul, Hoshiarpur, 1967.

The Rājataraṅgiṇī of Śrivara and Śuka, ed. Śrikanth Koul, Hoshiarpur, 1966.

The Rājataraṅgiṇī of Jonarāja, tr. Dutt, J.C., New Delhi, 1986.

Toḥfatu'l-Aḥbab, Anon, transcript copy RPD Acc. No. 1155.

Waqa'āt-i-Kashmir, Dedamari, Muḥammad Āzafn, MS RPD Acc. No. 2067.

Index